16 95
✓

✔ KU-514-343

77141

the complete guide to

JAVA

ANDREW COBLEY

COMPUTER
STEP

Computer Step
Southfield Road . Southam
Warwickshire CV33 OFB . England
http://www.computerstep.com

Tel: 01926 817999 Fax: 01926 817005

First published 1997
Copyright © 1997 Computer Step

All rights reserved. No part of this book may be reproduced or
transmitted in any form or by any means, electronic or
mechanical, including photocopying, recording, or by any
information storage or retrieval system, without prior written
permission from the publisher.

Notice of Liability
Every effort has been made to ensure that this book contains
accurate and current information. However, the publishers and
the author shall not be liable for any loss or damage suffered
by readers as a result of any information contained herein.

Trademarks
Java and all Java-related trademarks and logos inluding the
Coffee Cup and Duke are trademarks or registered trademarks
of Sun Microsystems Inc. All other trademarks are
acknowledged as belonging to their respective companies.

ST. HELENS
COLLEGE

005 133
        COB

89014

5 JAN 1998

LIBRARY

Printed and bound in the United Kingdom

ISBN 1 874029 48 2

ACKNOWLEDGEMENTS

Personal

I would like to express thanks to my Mother and Father, to Tracey for putting up with the clacking of keys and to Karen for no particular reason. I would also like to thank Bob Rickard of the "Fortean Times" for getting me kicked off on this whole writing thing.

Technical

Thanks to Harshad, the publisher, for his endless patience, and to Leon for laying out this book. I would also give a big hand to all the members of the Internet community who have helped with my silly questions. Thanks also to the staff and students of the Applied Computer Studies Division here at the University of Dundee, in particular to Dr Glen Rowe for his technical assistance. Of course, a big thank you has to go to the developers of the Java language, without whom this book would be but the flapping of a butterfly's wings.

> "We were born to go, as far as we can fly
> Turn electric dreams into reality..."
> Hawkwind
> *"The Space Ritual"*

CONTENTS AT A GLANCE

PART A

PART B

PART C

PART D

PART E

TABLE OF CONTENTS

■ ■

INTRODUCTION

Who is this book for?

This book is aimed at anyone who wants to learn the Java programming language. In particular, it is aimed at web developers who have no experience of programming but would like to join in the coming revolution. The book assumes that you have never programmed a computer before, but you should have some experience of web page construction. If you have used a programming language before (such as Basic, C or Pascal) then the early parts will be familiar material. In particular, if you are familiar with Object Oriented Programming (OOP) then you should be able to fly through Parts A and C, picking up only the differences between Java and the language you are familiar with.

What will you learn?

This book is divided into five parts, each with a different aim and each taking you further into the world of Java programming. Each section is full of code examples with complete explanations and often screen output of the results you can expect.

In Part A

The aim of this section is to introduce the Java compiler and the concept of a Java Applet. All the necessary techniques and library routines will be introduced to allow a beginner to construct their first applet and include it on their HTML page. The graphics libraries will be covered in some detail, and techniques for animation will be introduced. The use of sound in an applet will be detailed, including repeating sounds and stopping them from playing.

After completing Part A you will be able to create simple applets that include graphics, images, animations and sound.

In Part B

This part will describe in detail the use of the AWT (Abstract Windows Toolkit). The AWT allows the programmer to add interface components to the Java applet, such as buttons, text-entry fields, check boxes and labels. The section describes how to arrange components within the applet by using layouts, including the very versatile Gridbag layout. The section finishes with a description of how to handle mouse events for interactive applets.

After reading Part B you will be able to include interface components in Java code, making your applets more interactive than ever before.

In Part C

This part introduces Object Oriented Programming (OOP) and how to use it in Java programming. The basic ideas of OOP are described, along with the strengths of OOP. It then goes on to explain how to use OOP techniques to "extend" the capabilities of the AWT, and finally introduces the concept of security in OOP, explaining how to make code more reliable and reusable.

After reading Part C you will have a good grounding in OOP techniques and will be able to use them to create complicated Java programs by extending the AWT.

In Part D

This part will detail the simple use of networking within Java. The important security implications will be demonstrated, along with some simple methods of transferring data between your Java applet and your information provider's server.

After reading Part D the reader will be able to use Java to display web pages on a browser, communicate with the server using a POST command and be able to retrieve information from the server.

In Part E

This section introduces more advanced topics for developers and tackles techniques needed for Java in a large project. Advanced security techniques are described, along with methods for creating libraries of Java classes. The error-handling techniques are described, and their applications to libraries for publication are demonstrated.

Finally, the method for turning an applet into a stand-alone application is shown.

The Java Virtual CD

This book has a companion Web site, at **http://www.computerstep.com/ 1874029482.htm**, which includes a number of useful items that complement the information provided in this book, e.g:

Download   Follow our up-to-date link to download the latest version of the Java Development Kit.

Code Lists   Most chapters in this book include examples of Java code which you can enter into a word-processor and then compile to create Java applets. If you're in a hurry or don't really feel like entering a lot of code, you can quickly download the complete code listings, organised by chapter, from the companion web site.

Examples   Links are provided to several Internet sites making interesting use of Java applets. Use these for inspiration when deciding what to include in your own applets.

Resources   A wealth of resources for Java developers is already available on the Internet. Web sites offer information on the latest developments in the world of Java, and provide examples of applets using the latest techniques; while newsgroups and mailing lists provide a range of forums where you can chat about Java, or ask technical questions of other Java developers and experts.

Job Links   When you're ready to take your knowledge out in the field and pursue the high-paying, high-tech jobs, check out the job links.

PART
A

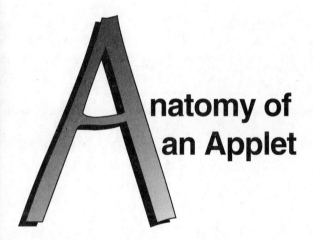

Anatomy of
an Applet

CHAPTER 1

What is Java and Where Did it Come From?

A lot has been written about Java over the past months, but I believe many Internet commentators are missing the point. Java has been described as a way to bring sound and animation to your web pages; while it certainly can do this, it is capable of much more. Quite simply, I believe that Java is the programming language to take computers into the next millennium. Just as "C" was the programming language of the 70s and early 80s and "C++" came into its own in the 1990s, Java will take computing towards the year 2000 and beyond. It's not that these other languages will die out; they all have advantages of their own. Each language has its own strengths and weaknesses, but Java has been designed for the challenges that the Internet brings. With the growth of the Internet and the emerging Intranet idea a whole new language is needed.

Java is based on the earlier languages of "C" and "C++". If you are familiar with these languages then much of Java will be familiar. Java has dropped some of the language features of "C++" that caused problems for software developers, such as operator overloading and multiple inheritance, but it stays true to the founding ideas of Object Oriented programming.

Let's look at some of the features that make Java the language of the future:

Distribution

A Java program can be included on a World Wide Web page and can communicate with other programs on the page. It can also communicate back to the server where your page lives. This means that Java brings program execution to the World Wide Web and the distribution of data throughout the Web can be programmed into your web page. In Java terms, a program that lives on a WWW page is called an applet. Applets are normal programs with a few minor restrictions and a couple of changes to the source code.

Portability

Java is portable in that a program written on one platform will perform exactly the same on any other platform that supports Java. At present you can use just about any variant of UNIX, Microsoft's Windows NT or Windows 95 and the current range of Apple platforms to develop Java programs. Once the program has been developed it does not need to be recompiled to run on another platform. If your program is present on a World Wide Web page, you do not need multiple versions to support the platform your visitors might be using.

Robustness

If a Java program is badly written and falls over, it does not affect the operation of the computer running the application. Java has advanced features to manage unexpected results: if a Java program is properly written it can deal with the unexpected in a reasonably safe way, perhaps continuing execution after correcting the problem. Whilst loading it is verified that the byte codes of the applet are syntactically correct to help ensure that it won't cause problems when it is run.

Simplicity

Because Java has inherited the experience that language designers have gained from other Object Oriented programming languages such as C++, it has been designed to be easy to learn. Some of the features that made C++ very powerful also made it difficult to learn and even more difficult to maintain the code. Java has removed some of these features but without removing too much of the functionality they added. In some cases the functionality has been kept by adding a simpler way of doing things.

Security

Java has been written for the needs of the Internet. Because the Internet is a relatively insecure environment, Java has been written to remove the possibility of creating insecure applications. A Java applet on a web page can not attack the computer it is running on. The applet only has access to the screen and the input devices; it can not write to the local disk, or talk to the local operating system. Of course, a particularly nasty programmer could write an applet that eats all the computer's resources. The applet would spawn copies of itself, forcing the computer to stop. However if someone did this it wouldn't be long before that programmer's area on the web became a no-go area. When an applet is loaded off the server into your browser, it is given a complete security check to ensure it hasn't been tampered with, or hasn't been created with malicious intent.

Extendibility

In common with other Object Oriented languages, Java is easily extendible; that is, it is easy to add new features to the language and have them available for others to use. Some of these extensions will be available free over the Internet, whilst others will be available only from commercial software providers. Already Borland and Symantec are providing their own class libraries for purchase.

All these features and more make Java the language for the Internet, bringing animation, sound and interaction to the World Wide Web. Before we launch into how to get hold of Java and how to use it for yourself, let's look at the things other people have been using it for.

Animation and sound

Animation is something that Java can do rather well. There are other packages available that can animate pictures, but only Java can create the picture from scratch and then move it around. For instance, you can create a line of text and move it about your applet; you can create a scrolling line similar to the marquee tag in Microsoft's Internet Explorer. You can load images and move them about, or scroll through a set of images in an advertising feature. These techniques have been put to good use by a newspaper, the "Nando Times". Their current page has displays with scrolling text and headlines with rolling pictures. You can view their great web page at "http://www2.nando.net/nt/?java".

Java is fast enough to go further than simple animation. One company has taken animation to its extreme and produced a video viewer in Java. This viewer displays a window on the web page showing a space shuttle launch. The user of the page can control the video, stopping/starting it, fast forwarding/rewinding and pausing it. Their video viewer can be seen at "http://polaris.net/~lss/java/JavaMovie.html".

A number of pages have used Java to add background music to their site, including my own. Sound can be played continuously, or as a result of some action by the user. You can check out the music on my own page at "http://alpha.mic.dundee.ac.uk/ft/ft.cgi?-1,ft". Be sure to have the volume control handy if you're in a busy room!

Interaction

Interaction with Java means everything from simple forms to full-scale arcade type games. Graphics images can be manipulated by the user as simply as text entities. Because handling the interaction is taking place completely within the user's computer, there is no delay caused by client-server communications. One really hot applet for interaction is Dave Danny's Java piano at "http://www.best.com/~danny/piano.html". This applet draws a piano keyboard and allows the user to play it either with the keyboard or with the mouse. The piano lets you play more than one note at a time using the keyboard and does a passable imitation of a real piano.

FIGURE 1-1

Automatic information from the Internet

Because Java has networking built in, it can deal with network entities as easily as any other sort of entities. The Press Association has created an applet that connects up to a live news wire that constantly keeps the news coming to your browser. Interaction over the network allows a host of applications including multi-user games, chat applications, and all sorts of information-gathering systems. You can try the Press Association's vidiprinter at "http://www.pa.press.net/news/vidi/".

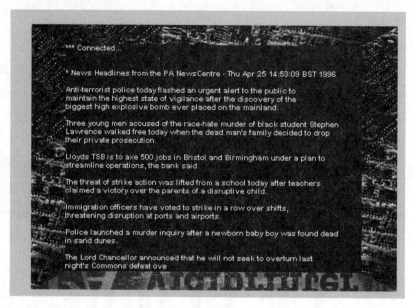

FIGURE 1-2

Java's short history

Java really isn't a very old language; its origins can be traced back to August 1991 and a language called OAK. This language was created to allow people to interface to a virtual world to control consumer products such as cable TV receivers and video recorders. The virtual world was accessed through a small control pad running an OAK application that allowed the user to wander round a virtual house controlling the virtual objects in the house. That application didn't see the light of day, but with the appearance of the World Wide Web, OAK was given a new life and renamed JAVA in January 1995. At that point only one browser could view Java applets, Sun's HotJava. It was not until Netscape bought a licence from Sun to include Java in its popular browser that Java really took off.

The initial release of Java was called the alpha release, and only the HotJava browser from Sun could view the applets that it created. The second release was called the beta release; HotJava could not view the applets that this release produced, but Netscape's Navigator version 2.0 could. The first proper release of Java (version 1.0) came in early 1996. It was still limited to the Netscape browser but it could run on a large number of platforms. Late spring 1996 saw the release of early versions of a new HotJava from Sun and

FIGURE 1-3: NETSCAPE

PowerBrowser from Oracle, both of which were fully compliant (Figures 1-3 to 1-5).

Microsoft have started to release early versions of their Internet Explorer which have the capability of viewing Java-enriched pages, and it seems companies all over the world are signing up for the Java experience!

FIGURE 1-4: HOTJAVA

In the late spring of 1996 several large companies, amongst them Novell, Microsoft, IBM and Apple, committed themselves to including Java into their operating systems. This will bring the power of Java to just about anybody with a personal computer on their desk or at home. It is not entirely clear what type of

FIGURE 1-5: POWERBROWSER

applications this innovation will bring, but you can imagine that computers' file systems will be extended to include web directories and applications from anywhere in the world. It will be possible to include shortcuts to applets directly on the desktop of the computer. Double-clicking on the shortcut will fetch it from a remote server or from the cache on the local machine. In the long run it may be possible that the use of applets will be charged for. The cost of using an applet will be directly related to the length of time the applet is in use.

In the summer of 1996 Microsoft started to ship a beta version of their own Java programming environment. The package is called Visual J++ and will only run on computers with Windows 95 or Windows NT (version 4.0). The package has many features for the professional programmer (Graphical User Interface editor, real-time debugger etc.), and costs a professional amount to purchase. You don't absolutely need tools like Visual J++, but if you have access to them then you will definitely feel the benefit.

Most recently, in 1997, Java version 1.1 was released.

The ins and outs of Java

When we write an HTML document we do not normally have to do anything special apart from place it on a web server in order to make it available to the World Wide Web. An HTML document is plain text with some embedded commands that tell a web browser how to display the document. Thus, for instance, "" tells the browser that the next section will be in bold, whilst "" tells the browser to turn the bold off. A Java program is completely different. The code we write is not understandable by a web browser. Our code (known as the source code) must be converted by a Java compiler into code that the web browser understands. We can then place a pointer to the special code (known as a class file) into a normal HTML document.

The source code is a complete set of instructions that tell the Java applet how to behave. These instructions are entered into a normal text file by using any suitable text editor. Although the instructions are easily readable by us, they are not in plain English: they use a set of keywords that are understood by the Java compiler. When we learn to program in Java we are learning how to use these keywords and what effect on the Java applet these words will have. The process of creating a Java applet can best be summed up in four steps.

1) Using pen and paper (or a word processor), generate a design for your applet
2) Create a text file with the source code using a text editor
3) Compile the source code using programs from the Java Development Kit
4) Place the class files on a web server and create links to the files from an HTML document.

This book is designed to help you to learn about steps 2 through 4, although we do touch on step 1 in Part C. Designing an applet can be a major step in the process; a poor design will generally lead to a poor applet. If the applet you are writing is likely to be small then the design can generally be small as well. If the applet is going to be large, and you expect to have a large number of people working on it then the design will have to be very carefully worked out. For the most part, the applets in this book are very small – the designs were created usually in less than a page of text. It's important to note, however, that although designing an applet is an important part of the process, the design only influences the text you create for the source file.

Chapters 3 and 4 of Part A explain exactly how to carry out steps 3 and 4 of the process. Remember, the source code of a Java program is just a plain text file and can be edited by any simple editor, such as "Notepad" under Microsoft Windows, "emacs" or "Vi" under Unix, or "Simpletext" on an Apple. However, if you decide to use something more complicated such as a word processor (for example "Word") then you will have to remember to save the file as plain text.

Figure 1-6 shows how the elements of a Java applet fit together and where the elements need to be located in order for the applet to work on a web page.

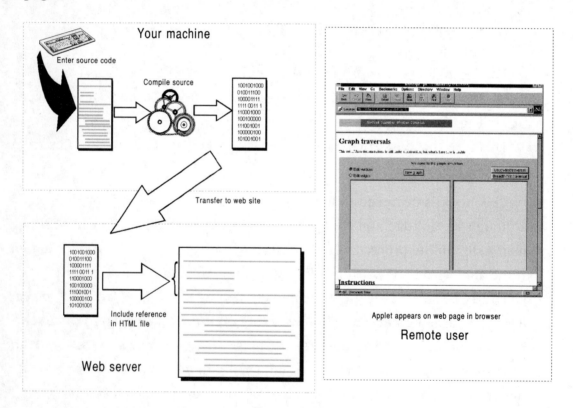

FIGURE 1-6

How to Get a
Java Compiler

Currently one of the most convenient ways to access the latest
version of Java is to download it over the Internet. Within the UK and
Europe the closest site is "SunSite Europe" at Imperial College, London.
Depending on which platform you are interested in, the Java compiler file is
currently 3-5 megabytes long, so be prepared for a long wait if you're
downloading over a modem. The following instructions are for version 1.1.1;
there may be a later version available when you visit – the file names will be
similar but the numbers within the name may have changed. Before you begin
it is a good idea to make sure your network or Internet connection is
working correctly by connecting your web browser to this book's web page.
Whilst you are there you should check the latest version that is available.

Under Windows NT

Open File Manager and select "Disk", followed by "Network connections".
(This assumes you are already connected to a network. If you use a modem,
you should connect to your ISP first.) In the "Connect to" box enter
\\sn.doc.ic.ac.uk\Archive and click on the Connect button: this should create
a drive window pointing at SunSite Europe. Open the directory "0-most-
packages" and look for the Java directory. Open this directory and then open
the pub directory. Find the file JDK-1_1_1-win32-x86.exe and copy it onto

your hard disk. The file is in the form of a self-extracting zip file that will unpack itself when executed. To do this, either double-click on your local copy or use the "File-Run" menu from File Manager. Figure 2-1 shows a File Manager connected to SunSite and ready to copy the file.

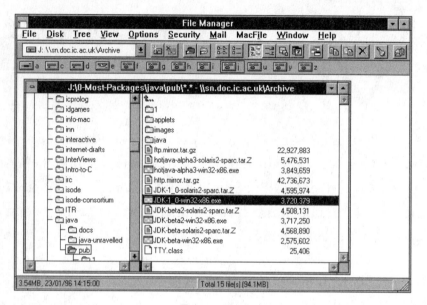

FIGURE 2-1

Under Windows 95

From the desktop, double-click on the "My Computer" item and then click on the Map Network drive button to connect a drive to \\sn.doc.ic.ac.uk\Archive. Open the "0-most-packages" folder and look for the Java folder. Open the folder and then open the pub folder. Find the file JDK-1_1_1-win32-x86.exe and copy it onto your hard disk by dragging the file to the C: drive in "My Computer". The file is in the form of a self-extracting zip file that will unpack itself when executed. Double-click on the file's icon; it will start a DOS box and start to extract itself.

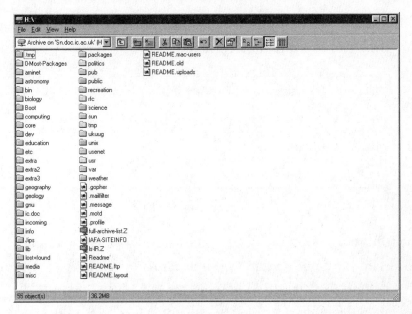

FIGURE 2-2

On a Macintosh

You can either retrieve the files using FTP as shown below, or you can use a web browser to connect to http://www.javasoft.com/ and access the file archive. The release is available either as a .bin format file or an .hqx format file. If you use Netscape to access the web site, the .hqx file will be automatically decompressed ready to run once it is downloaded, provided you have the appropriate tool ready on your Macintosh.

Using FTP

Open your FTP tool and connect to src.doc.ic.ac.uk as an anonymous user. Make sure your tool is in binary mode and change directory to pub/java/pub. Get the file appropriate to your machine (see Table 2-1) and unpack it.

If you are on a Sun machine, use the Uncompress command to unpack it and then use the Tar command to extract the files. The Windows 95 and Windows NT files will self-extract when the file is executed. The Macintosh file will need to be decompressed using either "Stuffit" for the .bin format file or "BinHex4" for the .hqx format.

JDK-1_1_1-solaris-sparc.tar.Z	Kit for Suns running Solaris
JDK-1_1_1-win32-x86.exe	Kit for Windows NT or Windows 95
JDK-1_1_1-MacOS.sea.hqx	Apple Mac OS 7.5
or JDK-1_1_1-MacOS.sea.bin	

TABLE 2-1

The following is a typical session on a Solaris Sun machine. First we open an ftp session to SunSite and log in as an anonymous user. Before we get the Java Development Kit file, it is important to ensure that the session is in binary mode by using the "bin" command. The file is then transferred using the Get command. Once the transfer is complete, end the ftp session, uncompress the file and finally extract the separate files using the Tar command.

```
kappa% ftp sunsite.doc.ic.ac.uk
Connected to phoenix.doc.ic.ac.uk.
220 sunsite.doc.ic.ac.uk FTP server (Version wu-2.4(24) Fri May 30 17:39:31
GMT 1997) ready.
Name (sn.doc.ic.ac.uk:acobley): anonymous
331 Guest login ok, send your complete e-mail address as password.
Password:
230-                    The Archive  —  SunSITE Northern Europe
230-                    =========================================
230-
230-    SunSITE Northern Europe is located at the Department of Computing,
230-    Imperial College, London and is running on a SPARCserver 1000 (with
230-    8 CPUs and 61 GB of RAID5 disk space) kindly donated by Sun
Microsystems.
230-
230-:::::::  PLEASE use hostname sunsite.doc.ic.ac.uk to access here.
230-:::::::  If you cannot then use the IP address: 193.63.255.1
230 Guest login ok, access restrictions apply.
ftp> cd 0-Most-Packages
250 CWD command successful.
ftp> cd java
250 CWD command successful.
ftp> cd pub
250 CWD command successful.
```

```
ftp> bin
200 Type set to I.
ftp> get JDK-1_1_1-solaris2-sparc.tar.Z
200 PORT command successful.
150 Opening BINARY mode data connection for JDK-1_1_1-solaris2-sparc.tar.Z
(459597
 4 bytes).
226 Transfer complete.
local: JDK-1_1_1-solaris2-sparc.tar.Z remote: JDK-1_1_1-solaris2-sparc.tar.Z
4595974 bytes received in 5.4e+02 seconds (8.3 Kbytes/s)
ftp> quit
421 Timeout (900 seconds): closing control connection.
0.1u 4.6s 18:56:43 0% 0+236k 0+564io 25pf+0w
kappa% ls *.Z
JDK-1_1_1-solaris2-sparc.tar.Z     mbox.Z
kappa% uncompress JDK-1_1_1-solaris2-sparc.tar.Z
26.0u 6.4s 0:42 75% 0+416k 564+987io 564pf+0w
kappa% tar xvf JDK-1_1_1-solaris2-sparc.tar
x java/include/solaris/oobj_md.h, 1035 bytes, 3 tape blocks
x java/include/solaris/typedefs_md.h, 2525 bytes, 5 tape blocks
x java/include/solaris/timeval_md.h, 987 bytes, 2 tape blocks
x java/include/StubPreamble.h, 1089 bytes, 3 tape blocks
x java/include/bool.h, 968 bytes, 2 tape blocks
x java/include/byteorder.h, 935 bytes, 2 tape blocks
x java/include/common_exceptions.h, 1260 bytes, 3 tape blocks
x java/include/config.h, 958 bytes, 2 tape b
```

What should have been unpacked

The directories created by the unpacking process are shown in the following table:

bin	The Java-executable files including Javac and appletviewer
demo	Example source code and applets for you to view.
include	Files for the compiler.
lib	The library files used when compiling a Java program

You will also find a number of files in the root directory (where the original file was stored), including a zipped version (for Windows) of the source code for Java. You will also find some text files concerning copyright issues of using the Java Development Kit.

Setting the execution path

Now that you have installed the package, you need to tell your machine where the Java package is stored. The following table gives instructions for each of the platforms described above.

Windows NT	Windows 95
Open the Control Panel from the main group and click on the System applet. Use the dialog to add the path to the "bin" directory of the Java Development Kit as shown in Figure 2-3.	You will need to update your path statement in your autoexec.bat file. Open a DOS box and change to the root directory. *CD c:* Edit the autoexec.bat file: *EDIT autoexec.bat* Add a line at the end of the file: *PATH=%PATH%;c:\\java\\bin* (the exact path depends where you have put the bin directory). You will need to restart your machine. (See Figure 2-4.)
SUN	**Apple**
Use your usual editor to change the PATH environment variable, usually set in your .login or .cshrc scripts.	After the file has been downloaded and unpacked, you need to install a folder for the Java Development Kit. If you used Netscape then this should have been done automatically for you. Once the folder has been created the tools are available for use, as shown in figure Fig 2-5.

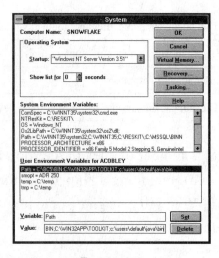

FIGURE 2-3

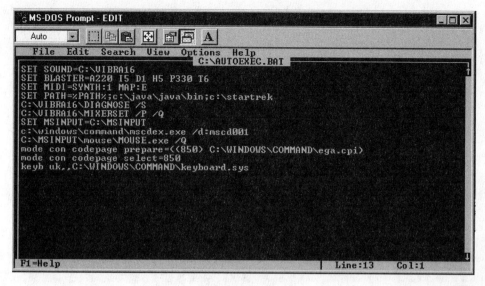

F IGURE 2-4

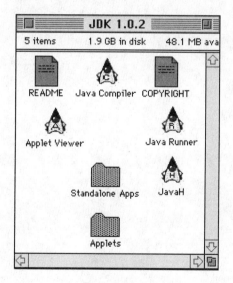

F IGURE 2-5

CHAPTER 3

Including an Applet on a Web Page

Before we move on to writing and compiling your own Java applets we will examine in some detail how to include an applet on a web page. When we compile a Java program a file is produced that contains the instructions for that program to run. This file always ends with the extension ".class". To include an applet on a web page an HTML tag is needed that points to the ".class" file. This is the <applet> tag that is closed by the </applet> tag. The <applet> tag must include details of the size of the applet – that is, the width and the height of the applet's appearance. The general form of the <applet> tag is as follows:

```
<applet code="myApplet.class" height=hhh width=www></applet>
```

This assumes that the applet's ".class" file is stored in the same location as the HTML file that is going to point to the applet. You can display as many applets as you want on the page. However, you should be aware that the more applets that are running, the more strain you will put on the browser that is trying to display them.

The width and height variables tell the browser how much space should be left for the applet to be displayed. Some applets manage to work with both of these set to zero, effectively hiding the applet on the page. You may see some web sites with scrolling text in the bottom of the Netscape window –

this can be achieved with a Java applet whose width and height are to zero. (Although you could do this using Java, currently the fashion is to use Netscape's JavaScript to obtain this effect.) The width and height should be just big enough for your applet. If the area is too small then some of your applet's drawing surface will be missing. If the area is too big then an ugly grey border will be displayed to the right of and below the applet.

If you want to store your applets in a different location to the HTML file that contains them then you need to add the "codebase" keyword to the <applet> tag. The "codebase" keyword needs to point to the directory on your home Internet site that stores your applets. For instance, suppose my home page is "http://www.netaccess.com/~acobley" and I decide to store all my applets in a directory "classes" below the top directory of my home page: then the codebase variable will be "http://www.netaccess.com/~acobley/classes/".

I have created a test applet for you to experiment with on "http://snowflake.mcs.dundee.ac.uk/java", called java.class. You can create your own web pages by pointing your <applet> tag to this class. If you prefer, you can download the Java ".class" file from the anonymous ftp server at snowflake.mcs.dundee.ac.uk. The applet is a fairly simple affair but does allow you to play around with all the aspects of the <applet> tag without having to compile your own applet.

You need to consider how your page will appear on non-Javatized browsers: you can either display text or a picture (even a simple animated gif) within the </applet> code.

```
<applet codebase="URL" code="myApplet.class" height=hhh width=www>
<img src="myPicture.gif">
</applet>
```

You can align an applet on your web page either to the left or to the right using an "ALIGN" statement in the applet tag. Text on the web page will flow around the applet. The applet can be aligned vertically to the text on the web page as shown in this table.

ALIGN=LEFT		Applet is displayed on the left with the text wrapping around it
ALIGN=RIGHT		Applet is displayed on the right with the text wrapping around it
ALIGN=TEXTTOP	This is the Test Applet	Aligns the top of the tallest character in the text with the top of the image
ALIGN=TOP	This is the Test Applet	Aligns the top of the text with the image; some of the taller characters will have portions above the image. (Don't worry if you can't tell the difference between the two, neither can I.)
ALIGN=ABSMIDDLE	This is the Test Applet	Aligns the middle of the text with the middle of the applet
ALIGN=MIDDLE	This is the Test Applet	Aligns the bottom of the text with the middle of the applet
ALIGN=BOTTOM	This is the Test Applet	Aligns the baseline of the text with the bottom of the applet. Parts of some characters will be below the applet
ALIGN=ABSBOTTOM	This is the Test Applet	Aligns the absolute bottom of the text with the applet. No part of any character will be below the applet

FIGURES 3-1–3-8

The diagrams in the table on the previous page (Figures 3-1 to 3-8) were obtained from a variety of web browsers, giving each a slightly different appearance. As you can see, some browsers do a better job of rendering the location of the text than others, which is a good thing to remember when creating your web pages. You should also note that unless the width of the browser can accommodate both the text and the applet, the text will not appear next to the applet. The text will be popped either above the applet or below it depending on the location of the text in the .HTML file.

As we have seen, an applet should fill the window provided for it by the <applet> tag, but you may want to vary the amount of space between the applet and the surrounding text. You can use the HSPACE and VSPACE statements to produce a gap around the applet. HSPACE sets the amount of space to the left and to the right of the applet, while VSPACE sets the space below your applet. If your web page has a picture for the background then the space surrounding the applet will be filled with your background image. The following <applet> statement displays the applet aligned to the left with a horizontal and vertical spacing of 10. The result of this statement is shown in Figure 3-9.

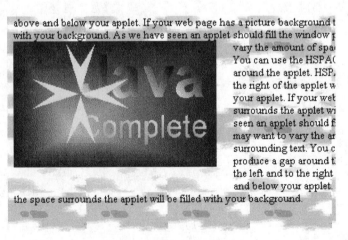

FIGURE 3-9

```
<APPLET code="java.class" codebase ="http://snowflake.mcs.dundee.ac.uk/ftp/
java/"
  width="250"
  height="150"
  align=left
  vspace=10
  hspace=10
  >
  </applet>
```

Many applets (including the sample mentioned earlier) can vary their behaviour by having parameters passed to them from the applet tag. Parameters have two components, the name of the parameter and its value. The value is always included between a pair of quotation marks. The test Java program java.class takes two parameters, the colour of the rotating cross and the speed that the star moves. When specifying the applet tag, you can specify a value for either of the parameters, or both, or neither. The parameter tag sits between the <applet> and </applet> tags.

```
<applet codebase="http://snowflake.mcs.dundee.ac.uk/java" code="java.class"
height=150 width=250>
  <param name=Colour value="Red">
  <param name=Speed value ="100">
  </applet>
```

For the example program, the speed value can be any integer from 0 upwards (but values in the range 20-200 are best). The Colour parameter can be any one of Red, Green, Blue, Black or Orange. The default colour is yellow (but you can't use Yellow as a parameter). It is very important that the spelling of any parameter name is correct, including the case of letters.

CHAPTER 4

Compiling an Applet

Providing your path variable is set correctly (see Chapter 2), compiling an applet is very simple. Just to get the hang of it, we will compile one of the sample applets that are provided with the Toolkit. Under Windows 95 or Windows NT, fire up a DOS box and change to the directory that contains the Toolkit. On any system except an Apple, change to the directory "demo". At the command prompt type:

```
javac Animator.java
```

On the Apple, open the Java Development Kit folder and run the compiler. From the File menu, select "Compile file". Use the interface to navigate to the "demo/Animator" directory and select "Animator.java".

Depending on the system you are using, the case of the file name may be important. The "javac" command invokes the Java compiler, reads the source code files (stored as text files with the extension .java) and creates the actual runtime code in files with the extension ".class". This runtime code is not readable by people and consists of a stream of bytes that tell the web browser how the applet will behave. Every time you write a Java applet you will start with the source code, compile it using the "javac" command and create a link to the ".class" files using the applet tag.

You can view the applet either by firing up your web browser and pointing to the example1.html file, or by using the Toolkit's applet viewer. For Microsoft Windows systems or UNIX-based systems, type the "appletviewer" command at the prompt.

```
appletviewer example1.html
```

Again, the Apple system is slightly different. The appletviewer can be found in the Development Kit folder; just click on it to start it running. From the File menu choose "open local" and navigate to the "demo/Animator" directory. Click on the file "example1.html" to start the Animator applet.

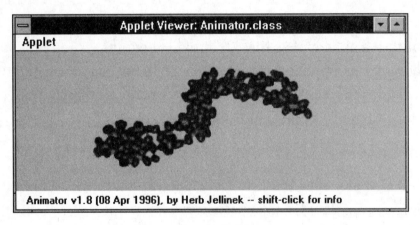

FIGURE 4-1

The applet should fire up in its own window, as shown in Figure 4-1. The appletviewer is a great little tool for testing applets – it allows you to look at applets on your file server or applets from remote locations on the Internet. Try viewing the sample applet on my server using the appletviewer.

```
appletviewer http://snowflake.mcs.dundee.ac.uk/ftp/java/java.html
```

Remember, the appletviewer is not loading the source code, but the byte stream from the ".class" file. If you want to distribute your applet to other users, you need only send the ".class" file, keeping the source code to yourself.

The appletviewer lets you restart and reload applets as well as making copies of itself on the screen. The appletviewer can be set up to use a security firewall or proxies and allows full control of the security aspects of applet loading. Although the security features will be dealt with later in the book, you can take a look at the parameters by looking at the Properties menu of the viewer.

Note – for Windows NT and 95 users

Although Windows NT and Windows 95 allow you to save files using upper-case and lower-case characters, many applications ignore the case. The Java compiler does not! You have to be careful when typing the compile command (Javac) that you include the case of characters in the name of the source code.

CHAPTER
5

The Hello World Applet

Using your favourite editor (Notepad will do in Windows or Simpletext on the Apple), enter the following text:

```
public class hello1 extends java.applet.Applet {
  public void init(){
    System.out.println("Hello world");
  }
}
```

Save the file as "hello1.java" and create an HTML file to contain the applet. You can now compile the program by opening a DOS box (under Windows) and typing:

```
javac hello1.java
```

The compiler will not generate any output unless you have made mistakes in typing the source code. If the compiler does complain, check your work carefully with the code above. If you see an error similar to this:

```
hello1.java:1: Warning: Public class helo1 must be defined in a file called
"helo1.java".
  public class helo1 extends java.applet.Applet {
              ^
  1 error
```

then you have either saved the file with the wrong name or typed the "hello1" after the class statement incorrectly. Once the compiler has run correctly, you should be able to see a file called "hello1.class" in the same directory as your source code. If you try and type this file you will see some funny symbols appear and the computer will possibly beep at you. You can view the applet by creating an HTML file with the following content:

```
<title>Hello World</title>
<hr>
<applet code="hello1.class"
  width=200
  height =200
>
</applet>
```

If you have named the file "hello1.html", you can then view the applet using the appletviewer:

```
appletviewer hello1.html
```

FIGURE 5-1

FIGURE 5-2

With luck, a window similar to the one shown in Figure 5-1 will appear on your screen – not very exciting to say the least. You will notice that there appears to be no sign of the text "Hello World" – what happened to it? If you look in the DOS box you will notice after the appletviewer has loaded your class it has printed "Hello World". This is the output of your applet! Because Java is very heavily based in graphics, a simple println is not enough to create output to the Java window. The applet needs to make use of predefined methods from the graphics library and needs to be told when to use those methods. Enter the text below and save it as "hello2.java". You should compile it in the same way as before and create an HTML file to point to it. Once compiled, you can view it using the appletviewer: a window similar to that in Figure 5-2 should appear.

```
import java.awt.Graphics;
//This is our first Java Applet !
public class hello2 extends java.applet.Applet {
  public void init(){
    System.out.println("Hello world");
  }
  public void paint(Graphics g){
    g.drawString("Hello world",20,20);
  }
}
```

At last! The "Hello world" appears where it is supposed to be in the applet window. You can try viewing this applet from Netscape or Internet Explorer if you prefer. Now we have the outline of an applet, we need to look in detail at the major sections in the source code. All Java applets will have at least the following sections:

- an Import section (if it is going to do anything useful);
- a Class definition section;
- some methods definitions.

Optionally the source code may well include comments as well, and any definitions of variables. Figure 5-3 shows an outline of a typical Java applet.

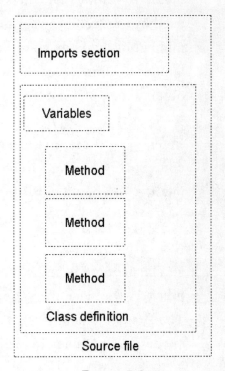

FIGURE 5-3

Classes and methods

Java is an object-oriented programming language, which means that when we program with Java we are creating and manipulating program objects. In Java an object is called a class. In our example above we have created a class called "hello2". In order for an object to be able to do things, we need to create methods for the object. Our example has two methods, "init" and "paint". If you are used to programming in C or Pascal, you can think of methods as being similar to (but not quite the same as) functions and procedures.

A method contains the source code statements that determine the behaviour of the class whilst it is executing that method. Methods can have any name you like, but for an applet there are a set of predefined method names that may be needed by the applet. Our example above defines two methods, "init()" and "paint()". In the case of applets, these two methods are used by the web browser to run and display the applet. You may define any number of methods you like, each defining a particular behaviour for the applet. In some cases the web browser will execute the method, whilst in others the applet itself will start a method executing.

All methods begin with a name which is followed by a pair of brackets. Later we will see that these brackets can contain other statements. The contents of a method are contained within a pair of "{}". So, the most basic method you could construct would look like:

```
Method_Name(){
}
```

This method is empty and would not do anything at all. Within the "{}" brackets we place the statements that define the behaviour of the method. The first statement to execute is directly after the first "{". Statement execution continues in order unless one of the statements redirects the execution order. The statements are made up of the special code words that define the Java language.

For the moment, you can think of a class as simply bringing together a collection of methods into a single object.

As you will find out later, you can have multiple classes within a single file, or you can spread the classes into different files. However, a class must be completely defined within a single source file.

For the simple applets we will be working on to begin with, we will only have one class that will have a number of methods within it. In Part C we will explore the ideas of Object Oriented Programming (OOP) in detail.

The import section

At the very top of any Java code is the import section. This section explains to the Java compiler what pre-defined libraries of classes will be used by the applet. In our example we import java.awt.Graphics, letting the compiler know we intend to use graphics methods in our program. These external methods are included in the distribution of the Java Development Kit and in the distribution of any Java-aware browser. You do not need to be aware of how these libraries work, only that they contain many useful methods to make your applets more interesting. Indeed, without these library methods applets would be limited to very simple functions.

Comments

Comments are statements in your source code that are ignored by the compiler. However, comments are very important to include in your code. They let other readers know what your code is going to do. In fact, when you come back to an applet's code at a later date you will be glad of the comments as well. It is remarkably easy to forget of what you were thinking of at the time of writing your code. You can (and should) include comments at any point of your source code.

There are three methods to include comments. If the comment is to be a single line then two "/" characters will start the comment. That is how we included a comment in the code above. If the comment is to cover more than one line, start the comment with /* and end it with */ as shown in the example below.

```
public void init(){
   /* This is a multi line comment in the init method.
    This simple example method doesn't do very much
   */
   System.out.println("Hello world");
}
```

There is a special form of comment that can be used along with the automatic documentation-generating program, javadoc. If the comment is started with /** then javadoc will use it for creating your documentation.

Like the programming language 'C', comments can not be nested, so the following will generate a host of errors if you try and compile it.

```
public void init(){
  /* I've commented this out for a while
  System.out.println("Hello world");  /* Do a print line */
  */
}
```

You can use comments to:

- Include any copyright statements (generally placed at the top of your source code)
- Explain to the reader the general purpose of your code
- Explain the purpose of your methods. (Place these comments just before a method is defined.)
- Explain the purpose of particular command statements
- Explain any tricky algorithms that your code implements

Remember, comments are your friend. They will help you to maintain your code at a later date, and if for some reason you have to pass the code to someone else, they will help that person to understand the code. Do not be afraid to add comments to your code as you are writing it. It will be a lot easier to take out unhelpful comments at a later date than it will be to try and add comments. Try to avoid leaving the comments until the code is finished and working – if you are like me you won't get round to it!

The class and extends statements

The second line of our example applet tells the compiler that we are creating a new "class" called hello2, and this class will extend the standard applet class. Notice that this line also defines the class as "public" to allow other classes access to it. If the class was not public then the browser would not be allowed to look at it and so could not run your applet.

It is the standard applet class (java.applet.Applet) that allows your applet to be displayed by a web browser. You can think of that class doing all the hard work of putting the applet on the page whilst your applet code is free to do what you want it to. Because we extend the standard java.applet.Applet class, there are methods that must be defined in our code for the applet to work. We have defined two methods, init() and paint().

Note – About the class name

Java insists that the name of the applet and the name of the file in which the source code is stored are exactly the same. This includes whether any characters in the class are upper case. Thus, if an applet is called "MyFirstApplet" in the class statement then it must be stored in a file called "MyFirstApplet.java". You will get an error when you try to compile the applet if the file name is in any way different to the class name.

The init method

As might be imagined, "init" is short for "initialise", and you would be right to guess that it is the first method that is called when an applet starts. More often than not, you will put all your initialisations in here, such as setting variables to known values. Our init method shown here has only one call to a library method (System.out.println), which writes text to the system console or the Java console in your browser. Spreading System.out.println statements liberally thoughout your source code can be a useful method of tracking. When your code is executing, the println statements allow you to follow the progress of execution. Remember to remove them before the code is released, though, as they do slow your code down marginally.

The paint method

The "paint" method is called whenever the applet needs to be redrawn, for example when the web browser is resized or is uncovered from behind another window. You should try to make sure that only the paint method (or a method called by paint) does any drawing to the screen. As you will see in Chapter 11, by causing a repaint to occur at regular intervals you can create animations.

A worked example

Before we go on and talk about the basics of Java, including some fundamental programming ideas, it would be fun to put together an applet that actually does something. Many of the statements in the source code for this applet will be unfamiliar and you may not understand exactly what is going on. However, it will be worthwhile following the example and trying it out on your own computer.

The example applet we will create will take 5 lines of text and scroll them from the bottom of the applet to the top. You can think of the applet as being used to display the credits for your web page. To write the applet, open a text editor (such as Notepad or Simpletext) and enter the text in the order it appears here. We will present each line of text and explain briefly what it means. You might not understand the full meaning or implications of the text just now, but all will be revealed later on in this book.

```
import java.awt.*;
```

This first line tells the compiler that we are going to use the graphics library. These libraries are part of the Java Development Kit, but you need to tell the compiler each time you are going to use one.

```
public class Credits extends java.applet.Applet implements Runnable{
```

This is the start of our applet. In this line we define the name of our applet along with some other important information for the compiler. The line looks complicated but can be broken down into three parts:

public class Credits	Defines the name of our applet: "Credits"
extends java.applet.Applet	Tells the compiler that it is an applet we are writing. If we missed this text out, the compiler would assume we were writing an application. Applications can not be run from a web page; they need to be run from the hard disk of your machine.
Implements Runnable	Tells the compiler that our applet is going to be multi-tasking. That is, the applet will be capable of doing more than one thing at a time. We need to make our applet multi-tasking in order to make the text scroll up the screen.

Notice also that this line ends with the "{" symbol. This tells the compiler that everything after that symbol is part of this applet. At the very end of our applet we will use the "}" symbol to tell the compiler that the applet source code has ended.

```
String titles[] ={ "My application",
    "Written by",
    "Me and the Complete guide to Java",
    "Compiled using the JDK",
    "On a Pentium P120" };
```

These five lines define a variable called "titles". This variable is an array of strings, five of them in all. Each string of text is contained within a pair of quotation marks: these are the lines of text we are going to scroll up the applet. You can change any of the text within the quotation marks to reflect your particular situation. Each of the strings is separated by a "," and the whole definition is contained within a "{}" pair. We tell the compiler that the definition is finished using the ";" character.

```
int CurrentY;
```

This line tells the compiler we are going to use a variable called "CurrentY".

```
Thread myThread;
```

This line tells the compiler we are going to use a variable called "myThread".

```
public void init(){
  CurrentY=this.size().height+15;
}
```

These three lines define the "init" method for our applet. The only thing we want to do when our applet first starts is give an initial value to the "CurrentY" . Our "init" method sets the initial value of "CurrentY" to be slightly bigger than the height of the applet. We use the "size()" method to retrieve the height of the applet and add a little bit more to make sure the text is not visible when the applet starts. Notice that the definition of the "init" method is contained within a "{}" pair. All methods in our applet will be contained in that pair of symbols.

```
public void start(){
  if (myThread ==null){
    myThread=new Thread(this,"MainThread");
    myThread.start();
  }
  Thread.yield();
}
```

These lines define a new method in our applet named "start". These lines are executed after the "init" method but before any of the other code in our applet. We only need to define the start method if we included the "Implements runnable" text in the class definition. This code creates a new thread: you can think of this as starting the multitasking in the applet.

```
public void stop(){
  if (myThread !=null){
    myThread.stop();
    myThread=null;
  }
}
```

Again, we define a new method, this one called "stop". This method will be called when the applet stops, and makes sure that the thread we started in the "start" method ends properly.

```
public void run(){
  if (Thread.currentThread()==myThread){
    while(true){
      try{
        Thread.sleep(100);
      }catch(InterruptedException ignored){
        return;
      }
      CurrentY-;
      repaint();
    }
  }
}
```

When a thread is started it will immediately try and execute a method called "run". Here we define exactly what the run method will do. We will leave the details of this method until later in the book. For now it is enough to know that this method decreases the value of "CurrentY" by one every tenth of a second. After the value is decreased, we tell the applet to redraw itself.

```
public void paint(Graphics G){
  for (int i=0;i<4;i++)
    G.drawString(titles[i],0,CurrentY+15*i);
  if (CurrentY<-50)
  CurrentY=this.size().height+15;
}
```

The code here defines a method that will be called whenever the applet is told to redraw itself. Again we leave the details except to note that each of the strings will be drawn on the applet's surface. The first line will be drawn at the "CurrentY" value, with the other lines underneath. Once the "CurrentY" value is below a a certain value we set it back to the original value.

```
}
```

Finally we close the applet with a "}". You have to be careful with the number and locations of the "{" and "}" symbols. There needs to exactly the same number of each in the source file. Once you have entered all the source code into your editor, save the file as "Credits.java". You now need to compile the source code to create the ".class" file. Use the javac command you learned about in the previous chapter to compile the applet. As we learned earlier, you will need to create an HTML file to display the applet. Open your text editor and enter the following text:

```
<title>Test</title>
<hr>
<applet code="Credits.class"
  width=300
```

```
  height =40
>
</applet>
```

Save this file as "Credits.html". You can now use the "appletviewer" command you learned about earlier to view the new applet, or you can include the applet on your web pages with text of your choice.

Note – Source code layout

You will notice that the source code we have presented in this worked example is indented in a curious fashion. This is common practice with modern programming languages. Although it makes no difference to the compiler, it does tend to make the code easier to read. As a simple rule, the source code is indented every time a "{" character is encountered. The source code is unindented every time the "}" character is met. The number of spaces that are added to the indent each time is a matter of personal taste. I like to use 3 spaces but some people prefer to add an entire tab character.

If you're lucky enough to be using an editor designed for programming, or even an Integrated Development Environment, then you may find the editing tool indents your code for you. Either way, you should develop a style of source code that is easy to read and easy to navigate through.

CHAPTER 6

Variables and Assignments

In this chapter we will explore the look and feel of Java programming. Most of the material presented here is similar to most modern programming languages (such as C or Pascal), so if you're familiar with one of these languages this chapter should be a breeze! If you haven't done any programming before then you will need to pay careful attention, since the material presented represents the building blocks of Java. If you like, this material is the taste of Java!

Variables can be defined anywhere within a class definition. You can define variables just after the class identifier or within any methods in the class. You should however be aware that the visibility of variables depends on where they are defined. This visibility is known as the scope of variables and is discussed in some detail in Chapter 8.

A variable is defined in the source code using the following form:

```
type variable_name= initial_value.
```

The type identifier defines what kinds of values the variable can hold. The variable name is a handle which we can use to refer to the variable in the source code. If you want, you can assign an initial value to the variable, which must match the type of the variable. Java has a number of built-in variable types: Boolean, Integer, Floating Point and Strings. This chapter will explain these built-in types and other types you can use.

Variables

Variables are a means of storing data: you can think of a variable as being a pigeon-hole that can contain only one piece of paper with a value written on it. Each variable has to have a name that is unique – this is the name that is written above the pigeon-hole. As we will see, we can take the paper out of the pigeon-hole to look at the value written upon it, or we can change the value written on the paper.

However, not all pigeon-holes are the same shape or size. Larger holes can hold bigger pieces of paper, and so the paper can hold a bigger value. Thus we can have a pigeon-hole that can only contain integers (whole numbers) up to a certain size, or a larger hole that takes numbers up to a much larger size. If the hole is a different shape then integer pieces of paper will not fit in. Differently shaped pieces of paper are used for different types of numbers or even different types of information altogether.

So one shape of hole may take floating-point numbers, another may take strings (a collection of characters). Although you can not fit a piece of paper (a variable) from one type of hole into another, Java provides a mechanism to copy the value of one type of variable to a variable of another type. This technique is called casting.

Over the next few pages the types of variables that Java can handle will be defined and the values that those variables can take will be explained. It is always a good idea to use a variable type that is best fitted to its use. So although integers are a sub-set of floating-point numbers, if you are dealing with an integer-type quantity (such as the number of items shipped from a warehouse), use an integer. If you use a floating-point number in the wrong circumstance then you may find the results your program produces are strange to say the least. For instance, if your program generates invoices for computers shipped from a warehouse, using a floating-point number in the wrong place could end up with invoices for 10.3 computers shipped!

Variable names

It is important when you create variables that you give them meaningful names. Calling a variable "foo" or "bar" doesn't mean very much and leaves the reader wondering what information the variable is going to contain. More meaningful names such as MaximumNumberOfSquaresToDraw or TelephoneNumber are much more useful and worth the effort of the extra typing.

Variable names can be as long as you like but must start with a letter, underscore character or $ sign. For the sake of simplicity, although Java implements the Unicode system, all our examples will use characters from the ASCII code. The use of Unicode means that you could, if need be, have all your variable names written in Greek.

Integers

Integers are whole numbers that can be either positive or negative. The maximum value for an integer is 2,147,483,647 and the minimum is -2,147,483,648. If you find that range too limiting you can create a "long" integer whose range is -9,223,372,036,854,775,808 to 9,223,372,036,854,775,807 ! To create an integer you must declare it, at which point you can set it to an initial value.

```
int myVariable;
int NumberOfBoxsToDraw= 25;
int WidthOfBox =200;
int HeightOfBox=300;
long myBigInteger= 2233720368547;
```

There is also a small integer known as "byte" whose value ranges from 0 to 255. This is analogous to the "char" type of C and can in some circumstances be used to replace it. However, Java also includes its own "char" class which is not stored as a single byte (remember Java supports Unicode which gives a lot more characters than the ASCII set).

Floating-point numbers

Floating-point numbers are any number that is not a whole number. The largest possible value is 3.40282346638528860e+38 and the smallest is 1.40129846432481707e-45. If these are too small you can use the larger 64-bit floating-point representation, "double". This has a range 4.94065645841246544e-324 to 1.79769313486231570e+308. Both float and double can have negative values such as -32323.28271 or -7.4545e-2.

```
float myVariable;
float Tolerance= 25.003;
float  myNegativeFloat=-200.524;
double myBigNumber= 2.233720368547e+75;
```

Boolean

Boolean variables in Java are true Booleans and are not implemented as short integers as in 'C'. A Boolean can therefore only have the value true or false.

```
boolean LastPage=false;
boolean ReachedTheEnd;
boolean FirstPage=true;
```

Characters

Character variables are single characters selected from the Java character set. Remember that Java supports the Unicode character set. To define a simple character, include it in a pair of single quotes.

```
char aCharacter ='a';
char bCharacter= 'b';
```

You can include a Unicode character by using a special escape sequence followed by the character number you want. The escape sequence consists of a "\" followed by a "u" character. So to use the Tibetan zero digit (whose Unicode value is 1040), use '\u1040'.

```
Char TibetanZero= '\u1040';
```

To find out more about Unicode, see *The Unicode standard: Worldwide Character Encoding,* ISBN 0-201-56788-1. Be warned, although you can include Unicode characters in your applet, it may not be shown by the applet. The support for Unicode will depend on your operating system and on the browser you are using.

Strings

Strings can be created either by defining their initial contents or by using the "new" method that will create an empty string. You can create long strings by breaking them up over several lines and joining them with the "+" operator. Note however that the final LongString example below does not produce a string with line breaks but a single line: "We were born to goAs far as we can flyTurn electric dreamsInto reality".

```
String myString="This is a test";
String mySecondString =new String();
String LongString "We were born to go" +
                  "As far as we can fly" +
                  "Turn electric dreams" +
                  "Into reality";
```

The "+" operator has a special meaning when applied to string types – it joins the two strings together to make one larger string. Thus, the result of:

```
String myString = "This is the first, "+ "and this is the second";
```

is a string myString whose content is "This is the first, and this is the second". If the second operand is not a string but one of the primitive types (integer, floating point or Boolean) then the result is the first string followed by a string representation of the second operand. For example,

```
int A=5043;
String myString = "Result is "+A;
```

results in a string "Result is 5043";

Arrays

Arrays are lists of objects of the same type. When an array is declared you either have to specify the contents of the array or specify how many objects there will be in the list. Since Java does not implement pointers (as 'C' and 'C++' do), creating arrays of strings is greatly simplified.

```
int IntArray[]= {1,2,3,4,5};
int IntArray2[] = {6,7,8,9,10};
int myArray[] = new int[10];
double DoubleArray[] = {5.67, 3434.2323, 9123.23173 -198723.872};
String StringArray[] = {"String 1 ", "String 2 "};
```

In the first two examples above, we declare two integer arrays each with five elements, and define the contents of the array. In the third example, the array is declared as having 10 elements, but we have not defined the contents of the array. The fourth example declares an array of four double-precision floating-point numbers. The final example defines a string array with two elements. To declare an array of single-precision numbers we can either use the new operator as before, or initialise the array directly. Note however that we have to *cast* the array elements from double-precision to float type. Casting is a powerful way of converting from one data type to another, and will be covered in more detail later in this chapter.

```
float myFloat[] = new float [10];
float myFloat2[]= {(float)10.3543, (float) 2398.934};
```

Each element in the array is accessed by using a number within the square brackets to refer to it. Because of the historical ties to 'C' and 'C++' the first element in the array is number 0 and the last is one less than the total number of elements. If you try to access an array element outside of this range then an error will be generated at run time and the applet will stop.

```
myVariable = IntArray[3];
myArray[5]= 6*3;
```

You can access elements in an array by using another variable as a counter, though you should be careful not to try and access outside the dimensions of the array. In the example below, the first access in the println is acceptable but the second will generate an error.

```
int myArray[]= {1,2,3,4,5,6,7,8,9,10};
int Counter;

Counter =0;
System.out.println("Element 0 is "+myArray[Counter]);
Counter=20;
System.out.println("Element 20 does not exist "+myArray[counter]);
```

The worked example we presented in the last chapter used an array of strings to store the text to be scrolled. Each element in the array represented one of the lines in the text. We initialised the five elements of the string array when we defined the string.

```
String titles[] ={ "My application",
            "Written by",
            "Me and the Complete guide to Java",
            "Compiled using the JDK",
            "On a Pentium P120" };
```

Later, in the paint method of the applet we accessed each of the elements of the string array and painted it to the applet's surface using the "drawString" method. We used the index of the array element to calculate the location of the top of the string.

```
public void paint(Graphics G){
  for (int i=0;i<4;i++)
    G.drawString(titles[i],0,CurrentY+15*i);
  if (CurrentY<-50)
    CurrentY=this.size().height+15;
}
```

Multi-dimensional arrays

We saw in the last chapter how to create a list of objects of a fixed size.
However, each object in the list can itself be a list of objects, providing all
the sub-lists are the same size. At its simplest, this allows us to create a two-
dimensional array that can be thought of as a grid of objects.

```
int SquareArray[][] = new int [10][10];
```

This creates an area of ten elements by ten elements. You can imagine this
two-dimensional array to be similar to a piece of graph paper, with each
element able to hold a single value. The table below shows where each
element is located in the array.

Array [0][0]	Array [0][1]	Array [0][2]	Array [0][3]	Array [0][4]	Array [0][5]	Array [0][6]	Array [0][7]	Array [0][8]	Array [0][9]
Array [1][0]	Array [1][1]	Array [1][2]	Array [1][3]	Array [1][4]	Array [1][5]	Array [1][6]	Array [1][7]	Array [1][8]	Array [1][0]
Array [2][0]	Array [2][1]	Array [2][2]	Array [2][3]	Array [2][4]	Array [2][5]	Array [2][6]	Array [2][7]	Array [2][8]	Array [2][9]
Array [3][0]	Array [3][1]	Array [3][2]	Array [3][3]	Array [3][4]	Array [3][5]	Array [3][6]	Array [3][7]	Array [3][8]	Array [3][9]
Array [4][0]	Array [4][1]	Array [4][2]	Array [4][3]	Array [4][4]	Array [4][5]	Array [4][6]	Array [4][7]	Array [4][8]	Array [4][9]
Array [5][0]	Array [5][1]	Array [5][2]	Array [5][3]	Array [5][4]	Array [5][5]	Array [5][6]	Array [5][7]	Array [5][8]	Array [5][9]
Array [6][0]	Array [6][1]	Array [6][2]	Array [6][3]	Array [6][4]	Array [6][5]	Array [6][6]	Array [6][7]	Array [6][8]	Array [6][9]
Array [7][0]	Array [7][1]	Array [7][2]	Array [7][3]	Array [7][4]	Array [7][5]	Array [7][6]	Array [7][7]	Array [7][8]	Array [7][9]
Array [8][0]	Array [8][1]	Array [8][2]	Array [8][3]	Array [8][4]	Array [8][5]	Array [8][6]	Array [8][7]	Array [8][8]	Array [8][9]
Array [9][0]	Array [9][1]	Array [9][2]	Array [9][0]	Array [9][4]	Array [9][5]	Array [9][6]	Array [9][7]	Array [9][8]	Array [9][9]

The dimensions of each of the "sides" of the array do not have to be the same: you can create rectangular arrays by making the number of elements in each dimension different.

```
int RectangularArray[][] = new int[50][10];
```

However, remember that when working with arrays that do not have the same number of elements in each dimension, you will create an error if you try to access an element that does not exist. In our example we created an array that is fifty elements by ten. Thus we can refer to element [25][5], but an error will be generated if we try to refer to element [5][25]. This error will not be picked up until the applet is executed, and will cause the applet to stop. However, you can create an array with as many dimensions as you require. This example creates a 4-dimensional array:

```
int RectangularArray[][][][] = new int[50][10][10][20];
```

Point and Polygon

The variable types "point" and "polygon" are normally used in conjunction with the graphics library methods. A point is created by using the "new" operator, but you must import the AWT library.

```
import java.awt.*;

public class PointTest extends java.applet.Applet {
  Point myPoint2 =new Point(20,20);
  public void init(){
    System.out.println(myPoint);
  }
}
```

Polygons can be constructed from two arrays of integers or by adding points through the addPoint method.

```
Polygon myPoly= new Polygon();
int Xs = {10,20,30,40};
int Ys = {20,30,40,50};
```

```
Polygon myPoly2 = new Polygon(Xs, Ys,4);

myPoly.addPoint(21,10);
myPoly.addPoint(20,30);
myPoly.addPoint(24,45);
myPoly.addPoint(33,21);
```

Objects

Objects are a different class of variable to the others we have seen so far. Integer, float, double and binary are referred to as the built-in variable types. Objects are the real building blocks of Java programs – you will be using them in the graphics chapters later in Part A. In Part C you will learn how to create your own objects and how to use them in your programs. For now it is enough to know that an object is created using the "new" operator, and that objects can contain variables and methods within themselves.

We have already seen objects in action when we looked at the point and polygon variable types. We created a point using the "new" operator and accessed its internal variables using the "." operator. The point operator separates the object name from the variables and methods within the object.

```
point myPoint = new Point(20,20);
int X = myPoint.x;
```

If you could look into the point object you would see that it has two integer variables, x and y. You would also see that it has a bunch of methods associated with the point type object.

Don't worry if this doesn't make any sense right now. All you need to know is that an object is created using the "new" operator and that you can obtain access to the internals of the object using the "." operator.

The assignment operator and other basic operations

As we have seen, once a variable has been defined, a value can be assigned to it. This is done by using the "=" character. The variable name is placed on the left of the "=" character and the value that it is to take appears on the right. This is slightly different to the "=" character in mathematics: it is not read as "is equal to" but as "becomes equal to the value of". Thus "i=5" is read as "The value of i becomes equal to the value of 5".

This allows statements that are nonsense in traditional mathematics to make sense under Java (and other languages). The statement "i=i+1" is meaningless in traditional mathematics. However, if you read it as "The value of i becomes equal to the value of i +1", it becomes clear that the intention is to increase the value of i by 1.

The right-hand side of the assignment operator can contain any of the traditional mathematics operators. Notice also that each assignment operation ends in the ";" character – this tells the Java compiler that it has come to the end of a statement. All statements (except program blocks, which we will meet later) must end in the ";" character.

+	Addition	i=a+1;	i becomes equal to the value of a +1
-	Subtraction	i=a-1;	i becomes equal to the value of a -1
*	Multiplication	i=a*5;	i becomes equal to the value of a multiplied by 5
/	Division	i= a/5;	i becomes equal to the value of a divided by 5
%	Remainder	i=a%5;	i becomes equal to the value left over after a is divided by 5. So 11%5 gives a result of 1 while 10%5 gives a result of 0

For multiplication, it is possible that the result may be too large or too small to be represented by the variable that is to hold the result. For multiplication of two integers, the result will be an integer: if the result is too large (Overflow) then the result will be unpredictable – even the sign of the result may be wrong. For floating-point multiplication, if the result is too large to represent then the result is said to be infinity of the appropriate sign. If the result is too small to represent then the result will be zero of the appropriate sign, that is +0.0 or -0.0.

For integer division, it is a run-time error for the divisor to be zero – an error condition (known as an exception) will be generated. Note also that integer division rounds towards zero. Thus the result of 7 divided by 3 is 2, and 7 divided by -3 is -2. There are a number of rules for the result of floating-point division, most of which apply in special cases only, such as the result of dividing infinity by infinity. These rules are defined by an international standard known as IEEE 754. So the result of infinity divided by infinity is defined as not being a valid number. Likewise, zero divided by zero is also not a valid number. The following table shows the results in these special cases.

Dividend	Divisor	Result
Either not a Number		Not a number
Infinity	Infinity	Not a number
Zero	Zero	Not a number
Infinity	Any Number	Infinity with the sign defined by normal division
Any number	Infinity	Zero with the sign defined by normal division
Any number other than zero	Zero	Infinity with the sign defined by normal division

For integer remainder operations an error will be generated if the divisor is zero, and the result of a remainder operation will always be less than the divisor.

The unary operators

There are two simple unary operators that can be used for increased efficiency. The first operator can be used to increase the value of a variable, and the second is used to decrease a variable. The double plus (++) operator is used to increase a variable, whilst the double minus (--) operator is used to decrease its value. The table below shows how to use these operators on integer variables.

I++;	Increase the value of I by one
I-- ;	Decrease the value of I by one
I++5;	Increase the value I by five
I--10;	Decrease the value of I by ten

The shift operators

Shift operators directly manipulate the bits that go to make up a number representation in Java. They can be used as handy shortcuts for multiplication and division of integers (they can't be used on floating-point numbers). A single shift of the bits to the left will result in a doubling of the value; a single shift to the right will result in the value halving. The results of shifting by more than one bit are shown in Tables 6-1 and 6-2:

Shift left	Result
1 bit	Multiply by 2
2 bits	Multiply by 4
3 bits	Multiply by 8
4 bits	Multiply by 16
5 bits	Multiply by 32
6 bits	Multiply by 64

Shift right	Result
1 bit	Divide by 2
2 bits	Divide by 4
3 bits	Divide by 8
4 bits	Divide by 16
5 bits	Divide by 32
6 bits	Divide by 64

TABLE 6-1   TABLE 6-2

The syntax for shift operations is shown in Table 6-3:

>>	Shift right	i=a>>1;	Shift the bits of a one place to the right, and store the result in variable i
		i=a>>3;	Shift the bits of a three places to the right and store the result in variable i
<<	Shift left	i=a<<1;	Shift the bits of a one place to the left and store the result in variable i
		i=a<<3;	Shift the bits of a three places to the left and store the result in variable i

TABLE 6-3

Casting

As we have seen, we have a number of basic variable types in Java: integers, floating-point numbers and strings. There are many occasions when we need to convert from one type of variable to another. Suppose we had a source code line similar to:

```
int myInt = 45.668;
```

The compiler would complain:

```
CastTest.java:3: Incompatible type for declaration. Explicit cast needed to
convert double to int.
```

We can fix this using a technique known as "casting". To cast a variable from one type to another you simply place the type name you want the variable to look like in brackets before the variable. So the correct source to convert from a floating-point number to an integer is shown below. The integer will have a value of 45.

```
int myInteger =(int)45.668;
```

We normally only need to cast if the receiving variable type can contain less information than the original type. Table 6-4 shows some of the instances where a cast is needed and where it is not.

	Integer on the right	Long on the right	Float on the right	Double on the right
Integer on the left	N/A	cast needed	cast needed	cast needed
Long on the left	no cast needed	N/A	cast needed	cast needed
Float on the left	no cast needed	no cast needed	N/A	cast needed
Double on the left	no cast needed	no cast needed	no cast needed	N/A

TABLE 6-4

When you create a floating-point constant in Java source code, it is automatically of type "double". If you want to use a constant with a float-type variable you will need to cast it.

```
float myFloat =(float)3.1415;
```

Note

You can not cast a Boolean to another type: if you try you will receive an error.

```
int myOther = (int)true;
```

You will get the error "Invalid cast from boolean to int".

CHAPTER 7

Control Structures

Control structures allow us to control the flow of execution of our Java applet. Normally execution occurs in a linear manner, with each successive line being executed in turn. Using control structures the programmer can alter the flow of execution, missing out some statements, or repeating statements as necessary. This chapter will present each of the control structures in turn and give examples of their usage. The following table gives a brief outline of the control structures and what they can be used for.

If statements	Allow the programmer to execute source code if a certain condition is true
Case statements	Allow only one selection of source code from a number of selections of code to be executed
For loops	Allow a section of code to be executed a number of times in succession
Do loops	Allow a section of source code to be executed repeatedly until a certain condition is true
While loops	Similar to the Do loop, but will always execute the code at least once

The If expression

Suppose in our applet we want a particular section of code to be executed only if certain conditions are met. We can do this using the "if" statement:

```
if (Some Condition)
    Execute a line of code
```

The condition can be any expression that evaluates to either true or false: that is, it could be a comparison of two variables, a test of some string, or a condition returned by some method. The table below lists the conditional test you can apply to numerical types.

<	Less than	e.g. A<B	True if the value of A is less than the value of B
<=	Less than or equal to	e.g. A<=B	True if the value of A is less than or equal to the value of B
==	Equal to	e.g. A==B	True if the value of A is equal to the value of B
!=	Not equal to	e.g. A!=B	True if the value of A is not equal to the value of B
>	Greater than	e.g. A>B	True if the value of A is greater than the value of B
>=	Greater than or equal to	e.g. A>=B	True if the value of A is greater than or equal to the value of B

So our "if" statement might look like:

```
if (A>=B)
    C=A*B;
```

This will make the value of "C" to be equal to the result of multiplying "A" and "B" if, and only if, the value of the variable "A" is greater than the value of "B".

It is possible to create compound conditional statements; that is, you can test for multiple conditions in one "if" statement. You can join conditional statements with either an "and" or an "or" operator. The and condition is represented by "&&", while the or operator is represented by "||".

```
if ((A > B) && (B > C))
    //DO THIS
```

In this example the "DO THIS" statement will only be executed if the value of "A" is greater than the value of "B" AND the value of "B" is greater than the value of "C". Using an and operator means the second conditional test is not always evaluated: the second test is only done if the first test is evaluated to be true.

```
if ((A > B) || (B > C))
    //DO THIS
```

In this second example the "DO THIS" statement will be evaluated if either A is greater than B or B is greater than C. For the conditional if statement, all tests are evaluated regardless of the result of any one test.

We might want to execute more than one line of code if the condition is evaluated to be true. We could use multiple if statements for each line of code we want to evaluate, but that would not be efficient. We can define a block of code to execute by using the "{" and "}" symbols. Any code between these two symbols will be treated as if it is one statement and all the statement will be executed if need be. So if we place a section of code contained by the "{}" symbols after the if statement, then if the test is true, all of the code in the block will be executed.

```
if (A>B){
  A=B;
  B=C*D;
  int E=A*B;
}
```

In our worked example in Chapter 5 we used a program block in the start and stop methods:

```
public void start(){
  if (myThread==null){
    myThread=new Thread(this,"MainThread");
    myThread.start();
  }
  Thread.yield();
}
```

The lines that create a new thread and start it are executed if the value of "myThread" is equal to null. Of course, you can place an "if" statement within a program block that is controlled by another "if" statement. This is called "nesting" the "if" statements.

```
if (A==B){
  if (A!=C){
    //Do This
  }
  //Do That
}
```

In this example the "Do This" statement will only be executed if A equals B but does not equal C. The "Do That" statement will be executed if A equals B.

When we nest "if" statements it is particularly important to pay attention to the layout. In Chapter 5 we mentioned that we indent code whenever we meet a "{" character; we can now expand that to say we indent code whenever a new block of code is met. This helps us to understand which pieces of code are controlled by which control statement. Take the following example:

```
if (A>B){            if (A>B){
C=D*E                  C=D*E
if (C>B){              if (C>B){
B=A                      B=A
D=A                      D=A
}                        }
A=B                    A=B
}                      }
```

A quick glance at the layout on the right shows that the statement at the bottom of the example ("A=B") "belongs" to the first if statement and not the second. The layout of the code on the left does not make this relationship as clear. This example is rather contrived, but in real code the layout really can help to make the code easier to understand. It is generally considered good programming style not to nest too many if statements, as it quickly becomes hard to understand the code.

There may be occasions when you want to execute one block of code if the test is true and a different block if the expression is false. The if statement can add an else statement after the body to allow this.

```
if (A==B)
  B=C;
else
    A=C;
```

In the previous example, if the value of "A" is equal to the value of "B" then the first statement will be executed. That is, "B" will become equal to the value of "C". If the value of "A" is not equal to the value of "B" then the second statement will be executed. That is, "A" will become equal to the value of "C". Of course, the else statement could have been followed by a long block of code contained within the "{}" pair or even by another "if" statement.

There is a potential ambiguity if an else statement is used within a nested if statement – does the "else" refer to the inner or outer "if"? Java defines the resolution of the ambiguity by saying that the "else" statement matches up with the first "if" statement that does not have an "else" statement associated with it.

The Switch statement

The "switch" statement allows the programmer to control which block of code, from a selection of blocks of code, will be executed. The general form of the case statement is:

```
switch (ControllingVariable){
  case Value: Programme statement;
  case Value: Programme statement;
  default: Programme statement;
}
```

In the "switch" statement the value of the "ControllingVariable" is compared to each of the "Values" in turn. If a match is found then that program statement is executed. If no match is found then the program statement following the default tag is executed. Usually the controlling variable is an integer type and each "Value" is an integer. Consider the following example:

```
public class SwitchTest extends java.applet.Applet {

public void init(){
  int test=1;
  switch (test){
    case 0:System.out.println("Case 0");
    case 1:System.out.println("Case 1");
  }
}
}
```

With test having a value of 1, the applet will print "Case 1" to the console. But what happens if the "test" has a value of 0? You would expect that the message "Case 0" would be printed to the console. But this is not the case. The message "Case 0" is printed to the console, but it is then followed by the message "Case 1". What has happened is that once a match has been found, all subsequent tests are deemed to be true and the program statements associated with them are executed. Even the default program statements will be executed. This is known as fall-through behaviour. We need some method to stop the execution after the correct program statement has been executed. We can do this using a "break" statement. The "break" statement stops the current switch statement and continues with the next statement after the closing "}".

```
public class SwitchTest extends java.applet.Applet {

public void init(){
  int test =1;
  switch (test){
    case 0:System.out.println("Case 0");
          break;
    case 1:System.out.println("Case 1");
          break;
    default: System.out.println("Default used");
  }
  System.out.println("Out of the Switch statement");
  }
}
```

This example code will now stop after the correct line has executed. So, if "test" has a value of 0, only "Case 0" will be printed to the console. With a value of 1, only "Case 1" will be printed; any other value will cause "Default used" to be printed.

You can use characters for switch statements if you need to:

```
public class SwitchTest extends java.applet.Applet {

public void init(){
  char test ='A';
  switch (test){
    case 'A':System.out.println("Case A");
            break;
    case 'B':System.out.println("Case B");
            break;
    default: System.out.println("Default used");
    }
  System.out.println("Out of the Switch statement");
  }
}
```

You can use the fall-through behaviour to group choices together. Suppose you had a calculator application that needed to handle keystrokes.

You could group the strokes into three classes: numerals, operators and errors. The switch statement to handle these three cases is shown below.

```
Switch (keystroke){
  case '0':
  case '1':
  case '2':
  case '3':
  case '4':
  case '5':
  case '6':
  case '7':
  case '8':
  case '9':   //Handle the Numeric keystrokes
          break;
  case '+':
  case '-':
  case '/':
  case '*': //Handle the operator keys
          break;
  default: System.out.printn("There is an anomalous key stroke");
}
```

Whenever "keystroke" takes the value of a numeric digit it will match one of the numeric case statements and then fall through until it reaches the break statement. If the "keystroke" is an operator it will match the operator case statements and again fall through until it reaches the break statement for the operator. Any other keystroke will be handled by the default statement.

The For loop

To all intents and purposes, the for loop is a mechanism for executing a section of code a predictable number of times. However, it can be used in other ways. The loop is controlled by a variable that is incremented (or decremented) each time round the loop. The amount the controlling variable is changed is under the control of the programmer. Usually (but not always) the controlling variable is an integer and the increment is also usually an integer. The statements that are to be executed are contained within the usual "{ }" pair delimiting the body of the for statement.

Note

The for loop in Java is very similar to the for loop in both 'C' and 'C++'; anyone experienced in either of those languages should be able to use them in exactly the same way. The only main difference is that a variable can be declared within the for loop definition in Java:

```
for (int i=0; .....etc
```

A simple for loop is shown below which will execute its statements exactly 10 times, first with i=0 then i=1, i=2 and so on until i=9.

```
for (int i=0; i<10; i++){
    //some code
}
```

Let's take the for statement apart. In the first statement (int i=0) we define a new integer (i) and initialise it to 0. In the second statement we test to see if i is less than some constant (10). In the third statement we increase the value of i by 1 using the unary operator (++). When the loop is executed the value of i is initialised, the test is then made, any statements in the body are executed and finally the value of i is incremented. Thus for each iteration of the loop the value of i within the body is the same as at the beginning of the iteration. For the loop in our example i will have a value of 10 after the loop has finished.

The variable for controlling the loop can be a floating-point number, but the test and the changing statements will have to deal with floating-point numbers as shown below. Here the body will be executed with f having the values 0.0, 0.3, 0.6 and 0.9, and will have the value 0.12 after the loop has finished:

```
for (float f=0.0; f<1.0; f=f+0.3){
    //Some code dealing with floating point numbers
}
```

The for statement (like all iteration statements) can be nested. That is, a for statement can have other for statements within its body. We can use this loop nesting to access all the elements of a multi-dimensional array. Remember from the previous chapter that all arrays start with the element 0 and that the last element is one less than the number of elements in the array. In the example below we access each element and set it to an initial value of zero:

```
int myArray[]=new int[10][10];
for (int I=0;I<10;I++){
  for (in j=0; j<10;j++){
    myArray[I][j]=0;
  }
}
```

Just to complicate matters, it is possible to have a for loop with only one line in the body, in which case the "{ }" are not needed to contain the statement:

```
for (int i=10;i<150;i++)
  System.out.println("Statement is "+i);
```

However, it is not a good idea to do this – it makes no difference to how fast the code will execute but can lead to problems later when you make changes to the source code. If you decide to add a second statement to the body of the for loop, you will need to add containing "{}". If you forget, you will get unexpected results that can be hard to spot in your source code.

You can alter the value of the controlling variable within the body of the for loop, but again it's not a good idea. If you alter the value of the controlling variable you will make the code harder to understand: use one of the other loop constructions if you want to do this.

The While loop and the Do loop

A "while" loop allows the program to execute a block of code either no times or multiple times. It consists of a test statement followed by the body of code to be executed. If the test is false then the body is not executed.

```
float i=2.5
while (i<=10.0){
  //Do something
    i=i*i;
}
```

In this example we initialise the controlling variable to a start value and within the body of the loop change the value of the controlling variable. This looks a little like the "for" loop we encountered before, but we are free to change the controlling variable in any way we want. If the value of i is greater than 10.0 before the while loop is encountered then the body of the loop will not be executed.

If you want to make sure the body of the loop is executed at least once, then use the "do {} while" construct. In this example, because the test comes after the body of the do loop, it doesn't matter that the value of i would fail the test even before the body of the loop is entered.

```
i=20;
do {
  //Do something
  i=i+30;
} while ( i<10);
```

Breaking out of loop statements

There may be occasions when you need to leave a loop before all the iterations are complete. Usually you would do this in unusual circumstances such as an error condition that demands immediate attention. Earlier, we used the "break" statement with the switch statement to stop the fall-through effect; we can now use the "break" statement to jump out of the loop to the statement after the loop.

```
for (int i=0; i<10;i++){
  if (i==5){
    break;
  } //Do Some statements
}
//Breaks to here
```

In this example, when i reaches 5 the break statement is executed and execution "jumps" to the line following the body of the for statement. You can put a break statement in the body of a "for" loop, a "while" loop or a "do" loop.

You can cause the execution of a program to "jump over" statements in the body of the loop and continue at the test point of the loop. This is done using a "continue" statement:

```
for (int i=0;i<10;i++){
  if (i==5)
    continue;
  System.out.println("Value is "+i);
}
```

In this example the lines in the body after the "continue" are not executed when i is equal to 5, but are for all other values of i. The output from the code will be:

```
Value is 0
Value is 1
Value is 2
Value is 3
Value is 4
Value is 6
Value is 7
Value is 8
Value is 9
```

CHAPTER 8

Using Methods

When we looked at our first applet back in Chapter 5 we mentioned that the applet contained two methods, the init method and the paint method. Methods are much more than the way to start an applet and to do the painting. You can use methods to break down the job your program is trying to do, making it more manageable. Using methods can also reduce the amount of code you need to write by reusing some of your code over and over again.

Note

If you're a "C++" programmer then methods should be very familiar to you: all you need to know is that the built-in variables' types are passed by value whilst objects are passed by reference.

The "C" programmer can think of methods as being functionally similar to procedures and functions. They consist of a return type, a method name and a set of parameters. Unlike C, parameters are only passed by reference (except the built-in types, integer, Boolean, float and string), and there is no concept of pointers in Java. To be honest, this can make things a little awkward, but in the long run the demise of pointers should be a good thing: no more core dumps from accessing the incorrect memory location!

Suppose we want to create a program that calculates the area of circles for all the values of radius from 1 to 10. We could use a for loop with the formula pi*r*r where r is the radius float Area;

```
for(int r=1;r<=10;r++){
  Area=3.1415*r*r;
  System.out.println("Area is "+Area+" for Radius "+r);
}
```

However, we may want to repeat the process later in the program, displaying the areas for radii from 5 to 15. We could repeat the same code but with different values for r in the "for" loop. This would be inefficient and would make the code much longer than it needs to be. The size of code is especially important in the network environment that Java was created for. We can define a method to do the calculations in one place for any values of radius. This method would be placed in the main body of the applet after the paint method but before the final closing "}":

```
void CalculateAreas(int First, int Last){
  float Area ;
  for(int r=First;r<=Last;r++){
    Area =3.1415*r*r;
    System.out.println("Area is "+Area+" for Radius "+r);
  }
}
```

We could use this method in our "init" class:

```
public void init(){
  CalculateAreas(1,10);
  CalculateAreas(5,12);
}
```

The parameters passed to the method must be of the same type as the parameter in the definition – the javac compiler will complain if it isn't.

As well as doing useful tasks, methods can return values to the code that uses them. Suppose we have a piece of code that performs a complex calculation that we need to do a number of times. We can use a method to encapsulate the calculation and return the final value. The following method will take an array of any size and return the average of all the numbers.

```
public class MethodTest3 extends java.applet.Applet{
  public void init(){
    float MyArray[]={(float)1.0,(float)2.3,(float)5.4,(float) 2.4,(float) 6.7};
    float Result;
    Result=Average(MyArray);
    System.out.println("Average is "+Result);
  }

  float Average(float AnArray[]){
    float sum=(float)0.0;
    int number;

    number=AnArray.length;
    for (int i=0; i<number; i++){
      sum=sum+AnArray[i];
    }
    return (sum/number);
  }

}
```

Although our array in the example has five elements, the "Average" method can take arrays with any number of elements. In fact, it is a compiler error if you try and specify the number of elements the array argument should have.

What happens to variables passed to methods?

When a built-in variable type is passed to a method, only a copy of the value is sent. Any changes made to the argument variable are not reflected in the variable outside the method. This is called passing a variable by value. Consider the following example:

```
public class MethodTest extends java.applet.Applet{
  public void init(){
    int myInt=1;
    Changer(myInt);
    System.out.println("My In now "+myInt);
  }

  void Changer(int PassedValue){
    PassedValue=2;
  }
}
```

When "myInt" is passed to the "Changer" method, a copy of its value is made into the variable "PassedValue". Within the "Changer" method we change the value of "PassedValue" to 2. However, because "PassedValue" was a copy of "myInt", "myInt" does not change value and the println shows that it still has a value of 1. This will be true for any of the so-called built-in variable types, Boolean, integer and float, but does not hold for any objects and arrays. In the following example an array is passed to a method that changes the first element, and this change is visible in the init method that calls the changing method. The println will show that "myArray[0]" has a value of 2.

```
public class MethodTest2 extends java.applet.Applet{
  public void init(){
    int myArray[]={1,2,3};
    Changer(myArray);
    System.out.println("My Array now "+myArray[0]+" "+myArray[1]+"
"+myArray[2]+" ");
  }

  void Changer(int PassedArray[]){
    PassedArray[0]=2;
  }
}
```

The scope of variables

We have seen that it is possible to create variables within methods and indeed within blocks of code anywhere in the Java program. However, we have not explained how this affects the use of variable names. For instance, what will happen if there is a variable named "i" in the class definition and a method has its own variable called "i". Take this example:

```
public class MethodTest4 extends java.applet.Applet{
  int i=0;
  public void init(){
    int i=2;
    AMethod();
    System.out.println("In init i is "+i);
  }
  void AMethod(){
```

```
    System.out.println("In AMethod i is "+i);
  }
}
```

When this applet is executed it shows that the value of "i" is 0 within the "AMethod" method and 2 within the "init" method. Variables within methods override variables of the same name defined within the class definition. This includes variables that are defined within the parameter list of the method definition. Thus the variable "i" in the init method is actually a different variable to the variable "i" defined in the class.

Earlier in Part A we saw that variables can be defined within program blocks such as a "for" loop. Variables defined within a program block are different again to any other variable of the same name defined in the enclosing method or class. Notice also that variables within program blocks only "exist" within the program block. The following example will produce a compiler error because it attempts to access the variable "i" from outside the block in which it is defined.

```
void AMethod(){
    for (int j=1;j<10;j++){
       System.out.println("In AMethod j is "+j);
    }
    System.out.println("In AMethod j is "+j);
}
```

The first "println" is fine but the second will generate an undefined variable error. Remember, variables only exist within the program block that defined them, and a variable within a program block will override any variables of the same name outside that block.

The Graphics Library

Now that we have covered the basics of the Java language, we will launch into the standard graphics library that the Java Development Kit provides. This is a library of simple routines that allow you to draw on your applet's surface to create pictures. All the common drawing methods are here – lines, polygons and circles – plus methods for handling and creating colours. The library also contains routines to load and display images, but these will be covered in the next chapter.

The Graphics library is part of a package known as the Abstract Windows Toolkit (AWT) which contains all the user interface components that you will need for your applet. The AWT user interface components are the subject of the next section. Before you can use the graphics methods and classes you will need to import either the whole of the AWT package or just the graphics class. It is probably a good idea to import the whole thing, since only the bits you need will actually be loaded.

The co-ordinate system

In common with most graphics packages, Java represents a point on the applet's drawing system as a co-ordinate pair, an x co-ordinate and a y co-ordinate. In Java the graphics co-ordinate system starts at the top-left corner of the applet represented by the co-ordinates (0,0). The x co-ordinate increases towards the right of the applet until it reaches the applet's width. The y co-ordinate increases in value towards the bottom of the applet until it reaches a value equal to the height of the applet. This is shown in Figure 9-1.

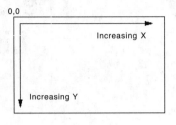

FIGURE 9-1

Because the top-left of our applet is (0,0) the "drawString" method we used in the "hello world" applet that we looked at in Chapter 5 had to paint to (20,20). The "drawString" method's arguments represent the bottom-left of the text – it simply wouldn't have shown up had we tried to paint to (0,0). We will look at "drawString" in more detail later in this chapter.

Our skeleton drawing program

For all our examples you can use the skeleton program shown below and replace the "myDrawingMethod" with the code given in each sub-section. The skeleton program imports only the graphics methods of the AWT into the applet. Notice that the paint method receives a graphics context from the web browser in order to give it a surface to draw upon. An applet always has a default drawing surface and hence a default drawing context. Later in this section we will discover how to create our own drawing surfaces which will have their own drawing contexts.

```
import java.awt.Graphics;
public class graphics extends java.applet.Applet {

public void init(){
}

public void paint(Graphics g){
```

```
    myDrawingMethod(g);
  }

  public void myDrawingMethod(Graphics g){
  }
}
```

CODE 9-1

Although the skeleton program will compile, it will not actually show anything if displayed on a web page. If you try to display the skeleton applet, it will show a grey box where the applet is to appear. The size of the box will depend upon the height and width statements in the <applet> tag. Now we have an outline for a graphics applet, let us look at the graphics methods available to the Java programmer.

drawLine

The "drawLine" method quite simply draws a line from one point to another. The "drawLine" method accepts four integers as its parameters, representing the start and stop locations of the line. The method in the example below will draw a line from x1=10, y1=20 to x2=50, y2=60. The result of this method is shown in Figure 9-2.

```
void myDrawingMethod (Graphics g){
  g.drawLine(10,20,50,60);
}
```

CODE 9-2

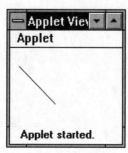

FIGURE 9-2

Java won't complain if you try to draw to negative co-ordinates, nor will it complain if you try to draw a line too far to the right or off the bottom of the applet. If you do go outside the bounds of the applet you simply won't see the result of the "drawLine".

Drawing a simple line is all very well and good, but what if we want to draw a series of lines, say vertically, at regular intervals. We could just make repeated calls to the drawLine method as shown below. That's not very efficient, especially if our drawing starts to get complicated. We need some method of repeating our drawLine with different values. We can use the "for loop" that we met earlier in the section to repeat the line-drawing a number of times. The code shown below (Code 9-4) will draw 40 vertical lines across the applet. Notice the use of '{' and '}' to create a program block for the "drawLine". We declare a variable "i" within the definition of the for loop, which as we explained earlier means that the variable exists only within the loop.

```
void myDrawingMethod (Graphics g){
  g.drawLine(0,0,0,200);
  g.drawLine(10,0,10,200);
  g.drawLine(20,0,20,200);
  g.drawLine(30,0,30,200);
  g.drawLine(40,0,40,200);
  g.drawLine(50,0,50,200);
}
```

CODE 9-3

```
void myDrawingMethod(Graphics g){
  int x=0;
  for (int i=0; i<400; i++){
    x=i*10;
    g.drawLine(x,0,x,200);
  }
}
```

CODE 9-4

However, what happens if the size of the applet as defined in your HTML file is less than 400 pixels wide, or – worse – greater than 400 pixels? In the first case your applet will do unnecessary work, drawing lines that will never be seen: in the second case the lines will not fill the applet. We can find the width of an applet by using the size() method as shown in the code below.

```
void myDrawingMethod(Graphics g){
  int x=0;
  for (int i=0 ; i < this.size().width; i++){
    x=i*10;
    g.drawLine(x,0,x,this.size().height);
  }
}
```

CODE 9-5

Notice that the size() method is prefixed by "this.". The word "this" has a special meaning in Java: it refers to the current object, or in our case, the current applet. Thus "this.size().width" gets the width of the current applet and "this.size().height" gets the height of the current applet.

drawRect and fillRect

It would of course be a relatively simple job to write a method to draw a rectangle using "drawLine", but fortunately the class library defines a method for you. The method takes as its arguments the start location followed by the width and the height of the rectangle.

```
void myDrawingMethod(Graphics g){
  g.drawRect(10,20,40,50);
}
```

CODE 9-6

This method will draw a rectangle from x=10, y=20 of width 40 and height 50, as shown in Figure 9-3.

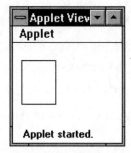

FIGURE 9-3

Suppose we wanted to draw a series of rectangles to fill the applet's window as shown in Figure 9-4. We could use a "for" loop similar to the example shown in Code 9-5 that will stop when the width of the rectangle is greater than the width of the applet.

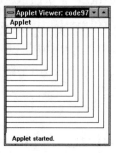

FIGURE 9-4

```
void myDrawingMethod(Graphics g){
  int x=0;
  for (int i=0 ; i < this.size().width; i++){
    x=i*10;
    g.drawRect(0,0,x,x);
  }
}
```

CODE 9-7

However, if the applet's height is greater than the width, then the applet will stop drawing rectangles before the applet is filled. We can fix this using the "while" method as shown in Code 9-8, which will continue drawing rectangles until the applet is full of rectangles. The while loop tests the value of x and will continue as long as x is less than the width of the applet or x is less than the height of the applet.

```
void myDrawingMethod(Graphics g){
  int x=0;
  while ( (x <this.size().width) || (x < this.size().height)){
    g.drawRect(0,0,x,x);
    x=x+10;
  }
}
```

CODE 9-8

FIGURE 9-5

If you want to draw a solid rectangle, replace the drawRect method with the fillRect method – the arguments are exactly the same. Alternatively you can use the clearRect() method to draw a "hole" on your applet. Code 9-9 uses fillRect and clearRect to create a series of parallel rectangles 5 pixels wide.

```
import java.awt.Graphics;

public class code99 extends java.applet.Applet {

  public void init(){

  }

  public void paint(Graphics g){
    myDrawingMethod(g);
  }
```

```
void myDrawingMethod(Graphics g){
  int Start=0;
  int Width=this.size().width;
  int AppletWidth=Width;
  while (Width >20){
    g.fillRect(Start,Start,Width,Width);
    Start=Start+5;
    Width=Width-10;

    g.clearRect(Start,Start,Width,Width);
    Start=Start+5;
    Width=Width-10;
  }
 }
}
```

CODE 9-9

drawRoundRect and fillRoundRect

You can use this function to draw a rectangle with rounded edges. The
arguments to the function allow you to define how "round" the corners are,
as shown in Figure 9-6. The example in Code 9-10 shows how to use the
drawRoundRect method.

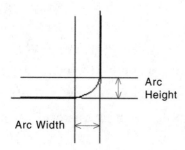

FIGURE 9-6

```
public void  myDrawingMethod(Graphics g){
  int ArcWidth=50;
  int ArcHeight=30;
  int Width =150;
  int Height=175;
  g.drawRoundRect(20,20,Width,Height,ArcWidth,ArcHeight);
}
```

CODE 9-10

By making the arc height and arc width half the width and height of the rectangle respectively, the rectangle "collapses" into a circle! Of course, there is a companion method, "fillRoundRect", which can be used to draw a rounded rectangle that is filled in with the current colour.

draw3DRect and fill3DRect

The idea behind draw3DRect is to create a rectangular area with a "raised" effect, as shown in Figure 9-7. The code should be quite simple, but unfortunately in early versions of Java (version 1.0 and its early updates) it doesn't work very well. Code 9-11 should create a raised rectangle starting at x=20, y=30 of width 150 and height 175. The width of the border should be about 5 pixels, but under early versions of Java it is drawn as only 1 pixel wide, making the effect difficult to see. The example shown in Figure 9-7 was drawn using the method shown in Code 9-12.

```
void myDrawingMethod (Graphics g){
  int Width =150;
  int Height=175;

  g.draw3DRect(20,20,Width,Height,true);
}
```

CODE 9-11

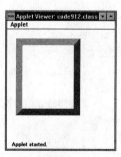

FIGURE 9-7

We can use a for loop to draw multiple raised rectangles within each other to fix this problem. Code 9-12 draws 15 rectangles inside each other, giving the very wide border shown in Figure 9-7. Notice also that we have had to change the colour to grey in order for the effect to be visible. If you try to use the "draw3DRect" method with the colour set to black then the effect is invisible. Using colour will be discussed later in this chapter.

```
void myDrawingMethod (Graphics g){
  g.setColor(Color.gray);
  int Width=150;
  int Height=175;
  for (int i=1;i<=15;i++)
    g.draw3DRect(20+i,20+i,Width-(2*i),Height-(2*i),true);
}
```

CODE 9-12

You can change the final argument from true to false to make the rectangle appear to be depressed instead of raised.

The method "fill3DRect" fills the rectangle with the current colour, but adds a border to give a raised or depressed look. This suffers from the same problems as "draw3DRect": the default border is only one pixel wide and it doesn't work if the current colour is black. Code 9-13 uses the same method as Code 9-12 to give a better-looking effect. The result is shown in Figure 9-8.

```
void myDrawingMethod (Graphics g){
  g.setColor(Color.gray);
  int Width =150;
  int Height=175;
  for (int i=1;i<=15;i++)
    g.fill3DRect(20+i,20+i,Width-(2*i),Height-(2*i),true);
}
```

CODE 9-13

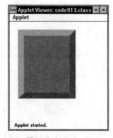

FIGURE 9-8

drawOval and fillOval

Java doesn't have a simple method for drawing a circle: instead, it implements a slightly more generic method, drawing an Oval. The method takes as its arguments the centre co-ordinates together with the width and the height of the oval. The example shown in Code 9-13 draws an oval at x=50, y=50, width 150, height 100, as shown in Figure 9-9.

```
void myDrawingMethod (Graphics g){
  g.drawOval(50,50,150,100);
}
```

CODE 9-14

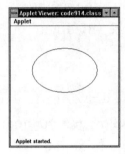

FIGURE 9-9

Of course, setting the height and width to the same value gives a circle. Not surprisingly, the method fillOval takes the same arguments as drawOval, and fills the oval with the current colour.

There is a related method in the graphics AWT that allows you to draw only a section of the arc, the "drawArc" method. Figure 9-10 shows the parameters the method takes, showing how flexible the method is. Notice that the method uses degrees to measure the angle distances, not radians as is often the case when dealing with angles in programming languages. The method takes its arguments in this order:

1) The x and y locations of the top-left corner of the box bordering the arc
2) The height and the width of the box bounding the arc

3) The start angle of the arc (measured from the traditional X axis as shown in 9-10)

4) The width angle of the arc, (measured from the start angle line)

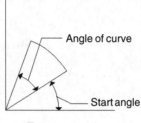

Angle of curve

Start angle

FIGURE 9-10

As usual, there is a companion method, "fillArc" which accepts the same arguments and draws the arc filled with the current colour.

drawPolygon

Although you could use the drawLine function to draw complex shapes, it is a lot easier to use the drawPolygon method. Using this method, you create either two arrays of integers to hold a list of points, or one polygon-type variable. Although using the polygon variable is slightly more complex, it's worth getting the hang of since it is more flexible. If the size of your polygon changes whilst the applet is running, then it is easier to add and remove points with the polygon variable. To use the method with arrays, you will need two, with each element of the array pair representing a point on the polygon. The final parameter passed to the method is the number of elements in the array. The polygon method will not close the shape for you, so you will need to formally include the first point again at the end of the list.

```
void myDrawingMethod (Graphics g){
    int Xs[]={5,100,80, 6,5};
    int Ys[]={10,5,120,160,10};
    g.drawPolygon(Xs,Ys,5);
}
```

CODE 9-15

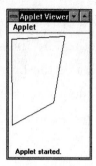

FIGURE 9-11

Instead of using the two arrays, you can use a polygon type to hold the corner points of the polygon. Declare a new polygon and add the points using the addPoint() method from the polygon class. You will also need to import the polygon class at the start of your applet. Code 9-16 shows how to use the polygon type, including the import statement. As with the array method, you will need to include the first point in the polygon in order to close the shape.

```
import java.awt.Graphics;
import java.awt.Polygon;

public class code916 extends java.applet.Applet {
    public void init(){
    }
    public void paint(Graphics g){
        myDrawingMethod(g);
    }
    void myDrawingMethod (Graphics g){
        Polygon myPoly = new Polygon();
        myPoly.addPoint(5,10);
        myPoly.addPoint(100,5);
        myPoly.addPoint(80,120);
        myPoly.addPoint(6,160);
        myPoly.addPoint(5,10);
        g.drawPolygon(myPoly);
    }
}
```

CODE 9-16

The "drawPolygon" method draws a line from each of the points in its parameters regardless of whether the lines will cross. If the points are not in the correct order then the lines of the polygon will cross. In Code 9-16, changing the order in which the points are added will create "figure of eight" patterns. If you want a solid polygon, replace the "drawPolygon" in our examples with "fillPolygon". However, with the "fillPolygon" method you do need to include the first point at the end – the method assumes that it is there.

drawString and drawChars

As we have seen in the "helloworld" applet, you can not simply print to the surface of an applet – you need to use a method known as "drawString". The method takes a string argument along with the x and y locations of the bottom-left of the string. The example in Code 9-17 will draw the string at location x=20 and y=30, as shown in Figure 9-12.

```
void myDrawingMethod (Graphics g){
    g.drawString("This is a string",20,30);
}
```

CODE 9-17

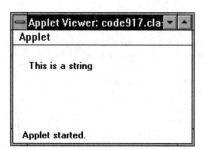

FIGURE 9-12

A related method, "drawChars", takes an array of characters and draws them onto the painting surface as if the array were a string. The method takes the array as a parameter along with a start point in that array and the number of characters to be drawn. Remember that for arrays the first item in the array is number zero. The method shown in Code 9-18 will paint "string" on the applet since "string " starts at location 10 (the 'T' of "this" is location 0) and is 6 characters long.

```
void myDrawingMethod (Graphics g){
    char myChars[]={'T','h','i','s',' ', 'i', 's',' ','a',' ','s','t','r',
'i','n','g'};
    g.drawChars(myChars,10,6,20,20);
}
```

CODE 9-18

Using colour

Up until now, all our applets have been in boring grey and white, but it's not surprising that Java supports full-colour graphics. You can set the background colour of your applet by using the "setBackground" method, and the current drawing colour using "setForeground". Both of these methods affect the overall appearance of your applet, and are usually used in the init method of the applet. You should only use these methods once in your applet, as only the latest setting is used to determine the applet's appearance The Color class library defines 13 standard colours for you to use:

black	blue	cyan	darkGray	gray	green	lightGray
magenta	orange	pink	red	white	yellow	

The init method in Code 9-19 makes the foreground orange and the background yellow, which, although fun, is not a very useful combination of colours. In fact, on some platforms the text may be invisible. Notice also that to use the standard colours defined above we need to import the "Color" class into our applet.

```
import java.awt.Graphics;
import java.awt.Color;
public class code919 extends java.applet.Applet {

  public void init(){
    setBackground(Color.yellow);
    setForeground(Color.orange);
  }

  public void paint(Graphics g){
    myDrawingMethod(g);
  }
  void myDrawingMethod (Graphics g){
    g.drawString("This is a string",20,30);
  }

}
```

CODE 9-19

Note

This is an American language and "colour" is spelt "color"!

Things become a little more complicated if you want to draw in multiple colours on your applet. To do this you will need to use the setColor method within your paint method. This method changes the next colour to be drawn on the drawing surface, and can be used as many times as you like.

Here is a sample applet that draws a representation of the solar system using different colours to represent the orbits of the planets. The output is shown in Figure 9-13, or can be viewed at "http://snowflake.mcs.ac.uk/ftp/Java/planets.html" for a more colourful exhibition.

```
import java.awt.Graphics;
import java.awt.Color;


public class Planets extends java.applet.Applet{

  int PlanetSize[]={10,20,20,15,50,40,30,20,5};
  Color PlanetColour[]={Color.lightGray,    //Mercury
                        Color.orange,       //Venus
                        Color.blue,         //Earth
                        Color.red,          //Mars
```

```
                        Color.yellow,        //Jupiter
                        Color.cyan,          //Saturn
                        Color.magenta,       //Uranus
                        Color.blue,          //Neptune
                        Color.darkGray};        //Pluto
    int  PlanetDistance[]={35,40,50,60,100,190,250,270,295};

      public void init (){
      setBackground(Color.black);
    }

    public void paint(Graphics g){
      int WhichSide=-1;
      g.setColor(Color.yellow);
      g.fillOval(290,290,20,20); //draw the sun
      for (int i=0; i<9;i++){
        g.setColor(PlanetColour[i]);
        g.drawOval((300-PlanetDistance[i]),(300-
PlanetDistance[i]),2*PlanetDistance[i],2*PlanetDistance[i]);   //draw the
orbit
        g.fillOval(300-WhichSide*PlanetDistance[i]-(int)(PlanetSize[i]/2),300-
(int)(PlanetSize[i]/2),PlanetSize[i],PlanetSize[i]);
        WhichSide=-1*WhichSide;
      }
    }
  }
```

CODE 9-20

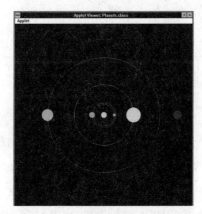

FIGURE 9-13

Creating your own colours

The Java colour class library has three methods for creating your own
colour, the most useful taking three values, each representing the amount of

red, green and blue you want in your new colour. These variables must be in the range of 0 to 255, with 0 representing no component of that colour and 255 representing as much of that colour as possible. This gives a total of 16,777,215 different colours plus pure black. Of course, not everyone's computer is going to be able to display that many colours, but their browser should be able to display an approximate colour. Remember this when designing your applet; don't rely on too many subtle colour changes, since the applet may be being viewed by someone with as few as 256 colours on their computer.

We use the "new" operator to create our colour. The following init() method creates two new colours and uses them for the applet's foreground and background. (The colours I have used here are not really suitable for an applet but do show the idea!)

```
public void init (){
  int red=255;
  int blue=255;
  int green=64;
  Color myBackgroundColour = new Color(red,green,blue);
  red=64;
  green =64;
  blue=255;
  Color myForegroundColour = new Color(red,green,blue);
  setForeground(myForegroundColour);
  setBackground(myBackgroundColour);
}
```

CODE 9-21

Two other methods exist for creating colours using the red, green and blue concept. The first takes floating-point values in the range 0 to 1, the second combines the 3 values into a single integer. It's possible that with the floating-point method the designers were "future-proofing" Java to allow displays with greater than 16 million colours to be accommodated. To use the "single value" method you need to combine the red, green and blue values into a single integer. The red component is placed into bits 16-23, the blue value into bits 8-15 and the green value into bits 0-7. The following "init()" method uses these methods to create new foreground and background colours. Notice how we use the shift operators to combine the colour components together to create the integer for the "Color" method.

```
public void init (){
  int red=255;
  int blue=255;
  int green=64;
  Color myBackgroundColour=new Color(0.5,0.67,0,333);
  Color myForegroundColour=new Color((red<<16+green<<8+blue);
  setForeground(myForegroundColour);
  setBackground(myBackgroundColour);
}
```

CODE 9-22

You can get hold of the red, green and blue components of a colour using the getRed(), getGreen() and getBlue() methods, or you can get the integer representation of the colour using the getRGB method.

```
int red=myColour.getRed();
int blue=myColour.getBlue();
int green=myColour.getGreen();
int rgb=myColour.getRGB();
```

CODE 9-23

The Java colour class provides two useful methods to create brighter and darker versions of a colour: myColour.brighter() will return a brighter version of the colour, whilst myColour.darker() will return a darker version. Code 9-24 uses the "darker()" method to create a set of colour strips across the applet. If you use "darker()" repeatedly, the colour will fade to black.

```
import java.awt.Color;

public class code924 extends java.applet.Applet {
  Color myForegroundColour;
  public void init (){
    int red=255;
    int blue=254;
    int green=128;
    myForegroundColour = new Color(red,green,blue);
    setBackground(Color.black);
  }

  public void paint(Graphics g){
    myDrawingMethod(g);
  }

  void myDrawingMethod (Graphics g){
    int Steps=10;
    for (int i=0; i<Steps; i++){
      g.setColor(myForegroundColour);
      g.fillRect(i*(int)(this.size().width/Steps),0,(int)(this.size().width/
Steps),this.size().height);
      myForegroundColour=myForegroundColour.darker();

    }
  }
}
```

CODE 9-24

The Hue, Saturation and Brightness model of colour

As an alternative to the RGB model, the Java colour class provides methods
to work in the Hue, Saturation and Brightness (HSB) domain. The HSB (or
HSV – the V here simply stands for Value) colour model is believed to be
more intuitive to work in, especially for those more used to physical paints
than the Cathode Ray Tube. The model is a hexagonal colour cone with the
brightness axis running up the middle. The saturation is the distance from the
middle of the cone to the edge of the cone and the hue is the angle of
rotation around the cone. Figure 9-14 gives a representation of the colour
model. Note that when the brightness is zero the saturation and hue are of
no consequence. If the saturation is zero the hue does not matter and the line
up the centre of the cone is a grey scale from black to white. The HSB

colour model does have the advantage that you can pick a hue and saturation and change the brightness by altering only one value. Similarly, you can pick a brightness and saturation and alter the colour by changing only the hue parameter. Under the RGB model this is much harder, due to a number of factors including the eye's response to various colours.

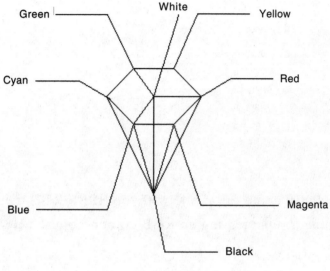

FIGURE 9-14

You can create an HSB colour using the "getHSBColor()" method, or convert from an RGB colour to HSB values using the "RGBtoHSB()" method. You can of course go the other way and convert from the HSB model to the RGB model using the "HSBtoRGB()" method. The "RGBtoHSB()" takes three integer values for red, green and blue and returns an array of three floating-point numbers representing the hue, the saturation and the brightness.

```
int red=127;
int blue=134;
int green=128;
float HSBValues[]=   Color.RGBtoHSB(red,green,blue,null);
```

CODE 9-25

The final argument to the method (null in Code 9-25) can be an existing array that will contain the HSB values when the method finishes. Once you have the HSB values you create a colour using the getHSBColor method.

```
import java.awt.*;

public class HSBColour extends java.applet.Applet {
  float HSBValues[] = new float[3];
  public void init(){
    Color myHSBColour;
    Color.RGBtoHSB(34,56,253,HSBValues);
    myHSBColour = Color.getHSBColor(HSBValues[0],HSBValues[1],HSBValues[2]);
    setForeground(myHSBColour);
  }

  public void  paint (Graphics g){
    g.drawString("This is in a HSB Colour",20,20);
  }
}
```

CODE 9-26

Finally we have come full circle with the HSBtoRGB method, which returns an integer representing an RGB colour from the HSB co-ordinates.

```
int myRGB= HSBtoRGB(HSBValues[0],HSBValues[1],HSBValues[2]);
```

setPaintMode and setXORMode

These two methods work as a pair, each reversing the effect of the other. The default mode is setPaintMode causing any painting to over-write anything that may already be on the applet's painting surface. When the mode is set to XOR mode the situation is completely different. The effect is that any point on the applet that is in the current colour gets changed to the colour in the XOR mode statement. Any colour that is the colour of the XOR mode statement gets changed to the current drawing colour. Other colours on the applet get changed in a predictable but surprising manner. In a complex colour drawing this can cause weird and bizarre effects.

Let's start with black and white. The following table gives the result of an XOR draw at one point on the applet's surface:

Current Surface Colour	Painting Colour	New Surface Colour
Black	Black	Black
Black	White	White
White	Black	White
White	White	Black

Code 9-27 illustrates the effect using black and white colours. First the background is set to black and a white rectangle is drawn along the top. According to the table above, a white rectangle appears. A second rectangle is then drawn along the left-hand side of the applet, the bottom appears in white, whilst the top turns to black (since, according to our table, two whites make a black!). The result is shown in Figure 9-15.

```
import java.awt.Graphics;
import java.awt.Color;

public class code927 extends java.applet.Applet {
  public void init (){
    setBackground(Color.black);
  }

  public void paint(Graphics g){
    myDrawingMethod(g);
  }

  void myDrawingMethod (Graphics g){
    g.setXORMode(Color.white);
    g.fillRect(0,0,this.size().width,(int)this.size().height/2);
    g.fillRect(0,0,(int)this.size().width/2,this.size().height);
  }

}
```

CODE 9-27

FIGURE 9-15

If colour is used, the effect is far more dramatic and difficult to predict. The exact algorithm that is used is difficult to work out – there is no real need to know it anyway. Code 9-28 draws a selection of colours and then uses the XOR mode to change the top half to different colours.

```
import java.awt.Graphics;
import java.awt.Color;

public class code928 extends java.applet.Applet {
  Color myForegroundColour;
  public void init (){
    setBackground(Color.black);
  }

  public void paint(Graphics g){
    myDrawingMethod(g);
  }

  void myDrawingMethod (Graphics g){
    g.setColor(Color.red);
    g.fillRect(0,0,this.size().width/3,(int)this.size().height);
    g.setColor(Color.green);
    g.fillRect(this.size().width/3,0,this.size().width/
3,(int)this.size().height);
    g.setColor(Color.blue);
    g.fillRect(2*this.size().width/3,0,this.size().width/
3,(int)this.size().height);
    g.setXORMode(Color.yellow);
    g.fillRect(0,0,this.size().width,(int)this.size().height/2);

  }

}
```

CODE 9-28

Fonts

Until this point, all our sample applets have used the standard font the applet viewer provides. Java provides support for displaying your text in different fonts, sizes and styles. However, before you consider using different fonts, remember that if you are programming for the Internet you cannot predict the platform, operating system or viewer that will be used to display your applet. This means you can have no idea of the fonts loaded into your target audience's machine. Remember also the adage that using too many fonts on a page can be very distracting, and could cause you to end up with an applet looking like a circus poster (which is fine in some cases!).

However, Java does provide a method to retrieve a list of fonts the current browser does support, the getFontList method. This method returns a string array of the font names. You should select a font from one of these names and use it to create a font using the new operator. The Font constructor takes the name of a font, a style (BOLD, ITALIC or PLAIN) and an integer point size. The example in Code 9-29 gets a list of all the fonts the browser supports and writes a line of text in that font to the applet. The output is shown in Figure 9-16.

```
import java.awt.*;
import java.awt.Font;

public class FontList extends java.applet.Applet {
  String FontList[];
  public void init(){
    FontList =Toolkit.getDefaultToolkit().getFontList();
  }

  public void paint (Graphics g){
    for (int   i=0;i< FontList.length;i++){
      Font myFont = new Font(FontList[i],Font.PLAIN,12);
      g.setFont(myFont);
      g.drawString("This is in new Font "+FontList[i],20,20+i*20);
    }
  }
}
```

CODE 9-29

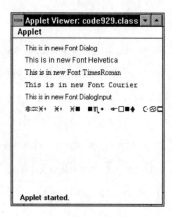

FIGURE 9-16

Because you may be drawing with your font on an unknown canvas size, you will need to grab details of the font's appearance. The following table shows the font metrics you can obtain from the FontMetrics class:

myFontMetric.getAscent()	Get an integer representing the distance from the font's baseline to the top of the characters
myFontMetric.getDescent()	Get an integer representing the distance between the font's baseline and the bottom of the font
myFontMetric.getMaxAscent()	No character in the font will go further above the baseline than this number
myFontMetric.getMaxDescent()	No character in this font will go further below the baseline than this number
myFontMetric.getHeight()	Get the height of this font including the vertical space between characters
myFontMetric.getLeading()	Get the number amount of vertical space between characters for this font
myFontMetric.getWidth(char)	Get the width of the specified character

In order to get these measurements you need to create a fontmetrics class for the font and then get the required measurements using one of the methods from the FontMetrics class library. In Code 9-30 we first check that the "Courier" font is available and create a bold Courier font. In the paint method we get the applet's size and the size of a string in the Courier font and use that to centre the string on the applet.

```
import java.awt.*;

public class CenterText extends java.applet.Applet {
  String FontList[];
  Font myFont;
  FontMetrics myFontMetric;

  public void init(){
    FontList =Toolkit.getDefaultToolkit().getFontList();
    for (int   i=0;i< FontList.length;i++){
      System.out.println("'"+FontList[i]+"'");
      if (FontList[i].equals("Courier")){
        System.out.println(FontList[i]);
          myFont = new Font(FontList[i],Font.BOLD,12);
          break;
      }
    }
    if (myFont ==null){
      myFont = new Font(FontList[0],Font.PLAIN,12);
    }
    myFontMetric= getFontMetrics(myFont);

  }

  public void paint (Graphics g){
      int StringWidth= myFontMetric.stringWidth("This is in Centred
"+myFont.getName());
      int StringHeight = myFontMetric.getHeight();
      int AppletCentreX = this.size().width/2;
      int AppletCentreY = this.size().height/2;
      int StringXCentre = AppletCentreX-(int)(StringWidth /2);
      int StringYCentre = AppletCentreY-(int)(StringHeight/2);

      g.setFont(myFont);

      g.drawString("This is in Centred "+myFont.getName(),StringXCentre,
StringYCentre);
    }
  }
```

CODE 9-30

CHAPTER 10

Loading and Viewing Images

At present Java can load and display any picture file in .gif or .jpg format. The picture can be drawn anywhere on the applet's drawing surface and can be resized by the drawing tool. Although Java could take your image from anywhere on the Internet, for now we will limit ourselves to taking the image from your server; that is in the same place your HTML file is stored.

To load an image you need to create a base URL pointing to the location of the picture. If the picture is stored in the same location as the web page loading the applet, the URL can be obtained by a call to "getDocumentBase()". However, if the <applet> tag uses the "CODEBASE" parameter, the picture's base URL will need to be obtained from "getCodeBase()". The image you want to load can be in a sub-directory of the base URL if you wish. You load the image by using the "getImage()" method which takes as its arguments the base URL and the name of the image along with a path to the image. In Code 10-1, we get the document base and then use that to retrieve the image. You will need to decide for yourself whether to use the document base or the code base within your applets, although using the code base does allow images from remote sites to be used.

```
public class DrawPicture extends java.applet.Applet {
  Image myImage;
  public void init(){
    URL baseURL = getDocumentBase();
    myImage =getImage(baseURL,"Pictures/myPicture.gif");
  }
}
```

CODE 10-1

The picture is drawn on the applet's drawing surface in the paint method using "drawImage()". In its basic form this takes an image and draws it with the top-left corner at the specified co-ordinates.

```
public void paint (Graphics g){
  int x=10;
  int y=10;
  g.drawImage(myImage,x,y,this);
}
```

CODE 10-1

The image can be drawn with a different width and height by still using the "drawImage()" method but adding a width and height parameter:

```
public void paint (Graphics g){
  int x=10;
  int y=10;
  int width=200;
  int height=200;
  g.drawImage(myImage,x,y,width,height,this);
}
```

Although this is a useful feature, try to avoid stretching your image too much, as the distortion can be unpleasant. If the original image is very large and you are going to draw it small, it would be better to create a smaller version of the image on the server. This will avoid having to load too many bytes over the network. Also, be wary of expanding an image too much, as the final picture will be very pixelated. In general, try to avoid scaling your image too much in Java; specialised graphics packages are much better at the conversion and will give far superior results.

CHAPTER 11

A Multi-tasking Applet

Why would we want an applet to use multi-tasking? Wouldn't it slow the applet down trying to do more than one thing at a time? Well, no, even in its basic form an applet does more than one thing at once – the applet is busy cleaning up unused variables whilst at the same time running the code you have written. If an applet weren't multi-tasking then it could not use the user interface components described in the Part B.

Java implements multi-tasking through the use of "threads". When an applet is started, a thread is created for it to use (plus some others that you do not see) and it is free to start or stop as many threads as it needs.

Note

Do not start threads and leave them running just for the sake of it. If you start too many without stopping them, they will eat up all the processor time of someone viewing your page, making the page impossible to view!

To make an applet multi-tasking we need to define a number of methods within the body of the applet. We have already seen the init and paint methods in use: for a multi-tasking applet we need to define also a start method, a stop method and a run method. The start method of an applet is executed after the init method and usually creates the new threads of the applet. The stop method is executed just before the applet stops and usually makes sure that all threads have stopped. The run method of the applet is executed when you start a thread.

Let's look at a skeleton multi-tasking applet by creating an applet that generates two threads for itself. The first change we need is to add the words "implements Runnable" to the class definition. This tells the compiler that this will be a multi-tasking applet and that it must specify the start, stop and run methods. We then define two variables to hold our references to the threads we will create. This allows us to control the threads we have created later in the applet. The example in Code 11-1 shows a blank init() method that would initialise any variables, load images and sounds or do any other work that will be needed before the applet starts.

```
public class Multithread extends java.applet.Applet implements Runnable{

   Thread myThread1;
   Thread myThread2;

   public void init(){
      //Set up any variables etc
   }
```

CODE 11-1

Next we define the start method. This is executed after the init method has finished and creates the threads we want. For each thread we first check that the reference is blank (this is not strictly necessary but is good practice just in case, especially if you are working on an applet generated by someone else). We then use the "new" operator to create the reference to the thread, and use the start method of the thread to run it. When the start method executes the start method of the thread it will execute the run method of the thread whilst the applet continues to start the next thread, "myThread2".

```
public void start(){
   if (myThread1 == null){
      myThread1= new Thread(this);
      myThread1.start();
```

```
    }
    if  (myThread2 == null){
        myThread2= new Thread(this);
        myThread2.start();
    }
}
```

CODE 11-1

After the start method we define the run method for the applet – this is
the method that does the actual work in the applet. The run method shown
here checks its own identity so that it can execute different tasks in each
thread. So thread "myThread1" will only execute the statements inside the
body of the first "if" statement, and "myThread2" will only execute the
statements in the body of the second "if" statement.

```
public void run(){
    if (Thread.currentThread()==myThread1){
      //Do the stuff in thread 1
    }
    if (Thread.currentThread()==myThread2){
      //Do the stuff in thread 2
    }
}
```

CODE 11-1

When the applet stops (for example when the user leaves the web page)
the stop method of the thread is executed. For each thread we check to see if
the thread has been created by checking to see if the reference variable is set
to "null". If it is set to null we use the stop method of the thread to halt its
execution. It is always a good idea to check the status of a thread before
acting on it, because it could have been changed by some other thread in the
applet. After stopping the thread we make sure that it has been destroyed by
setting its reference variable to "null". Note that the stop method of the
applet is called when the applet stops, and it is the applet that needs to stop
its threads. The threads would continue to try to execute after the applet
stops if we did not explicitly stop them.

```
public void stop(){
    if  (myThread1 != null){
      myThread1.stop();
      myThread1= null;
    }
    if  (myThread2 != null){
      myThread2.stop();
      myThread2= null;
    }
  }
}
```

CODE 11-1

An example run method

Suppose we would like our applet to display a counter at the top-left of the drawing area that is updated once a second whilst the applet is running. In the run method we need some mechanism to be able to judge the passage of time within the applet. This can be done using a "sleep" command within the run method. This command tells the thread to do nothing for a period of time and then wake up and continue execution. If we place a call to the sleep method within a loop, the thread will wake up regularly and execute some code. The sleep method takes as its argument the number of milliseconds to sleep for. In our case we will increment some counting variable and then issue a "repaint" command to tell the applet to redraw the drawing surface.

```
public void run(){

  if (Thread.currentThread() == myThread1){
    while(true){
      try{
        Thread.sleep(1000);
      }catch (Exception ignored){
        return;
      }
      Count ++;
      repaint();
    }
  }
}
```

CODE 11-2

The "repaint" tells the applet to use its paint method to redraw the screen. It is important to note that "repaint" does not tell the applet to redraw the surface now; rather, it informs the browser that the contents of the drawing surface have changed and need to be updated as soon as possible. If the applet is busy or the computer is tied up with a different application, several repaints may occur before the "paint" method is actually called.

```
public void paint(Graphics g){
  g.drawString(""+Count,20,20);

}
```

CODE 11-2

Notes

In the example run method you will notice that the sleep method is surrounded by a try and catch statement. These are part of the Java error-handling mechanism and will be covered much later in the book. For now you need to know that sleep commands always need the try/catch statement pair.

If you try using the methods in Code 11-2 you will need to import the AWT library with a

```
import java.awt.*;
```

statement at the top of the file. You will also need to define an integer Count variable inside the class definition.

The "drawString()" method inside the paint method uses an empty string to force the integer to be displayed as if it were a string. An alternative method would be to convert the string to an object and then use the "toString()" method of the integer class.

```
g.drawString((new  Integer(Count)).toString(),20,20);
```

Although the sleep method takes as its arguments the number of milliseconds to sleep for there is no guarantee that it will not sleep longer. The argument is simply the smallest time that the thread will sleep. However, for most applications the sleep time does not have to be precisely guaranteed.

Using multi-tasking to create animations

As we have seen in our previous example, by using multi-tasking we can create a sort of animation, a counter that changes every second. As a practical example, let's create an applet that draws a logo and animates a ghost floating across the logo's surface. Before you begin you will need to use a graphics package to create your logo, and get the "ghost.gif" from the FTP site "http://snowflake.mcs.dundee.ac.uk/ft/Java". Alternatively, you can create your own "ghost.gif using a graphics package.

Within the "init()" method we will load the images we are going to use, the background logo and the ghost logo. We will also need to initialise some variables to hold the current location of the logo on the screen and the width of the applet. We start the ghost logo at a location just to the left of the applet, where it won't be seen, by setting the initial location to be minus the width of the logo.

```java
import java.awt.*;
import java.net.*;

public class code113 extends java.applet.Applet implements Runnable{

    Thread myThread1;

    int x_location;
    int y_location;
    int AppletWidth;
    Image Background;
    Image Foreground;

    public void init(){
      URL baseURL=null;
      baseURL = getCodeBase();
      Background = getImage(baseURL,"Pictures/Background.gif");
      Foreground = getImage(baseURL,"Pictures/ghost.gif");
      x_location = (-1)*Foreground.getWidth(this);
      y_location = (int)this.size().height/2;
      AppletWidth=this.size().width;
    }
```

CODE 11-3

Our start and stop methods only need to create and destroy one thread:

```
public void start(){
   if (myThread1 == null){
      myThread1= new Thread(this);
      myThread1.start();
   }
}
public void stop(){
   if (myThread1 != null){
     myThread1.stop();
     myThread1= null;
   }
}
```

CODE 11-3

Our paint method simply needs to draw the background logo and then the foreground logo on top of it at the current location. The foreground logo should be transparent (as the "ghost.gif" is) in order for it to appear in front of the background, but not square.

```
public void paint(Graphics g){
   g.drawImage(Background,0,0,this);
   g.drawImage(Foreground,x_location,y_location,this);
}
```

CODE 11-3

The run method sleeps for around 0.1 of a second, then updates the value of the x location (resetting it to an initial value if the logo goes off the right edge of the applet). After it has updated the x location it calls for a repaint.

```
public void run(){
   if (Thread.currentThread() == myThread1){
     while(true){
       try{
         Thread.sleep(100);
       }catch (Exception ignored){
         return;
       }
       x_location=x_location +2;
       if (x_location > AppletWidth)
         x_location =(-1)*Foreground.getWidth(this);
       repaint();
     }
   }
}
```

CODE 11-3

By altering the manipulation of the x and y location values in the run method you can change the behaviour of the foreground logo.

How to stop the applet flickering

The animation we have seen so far flickers terribly even on the fastest machine. The reason is quite simple: before the paint method is called, the applet redraws the background in the current background colour. This is done in an applet method called "update". If you add your own method called "update", this will override the standard behaviour and stop the background from being redrawn.

```
public void update (Graphics g){
  paint(g);
}
```

CODE 11-4

Adding the update method to our logo-animating applet works just fine because the paint method takes care of redrawing the background. However, if you add this method to the counting animation from earlier on you will see a problem. The text is written to the drawing surface, but the previous text is not deleted, because the background has not been cleared. If you use the update method you will need to redraw the background of any objects you are drawing on the surface.

```
public void paint(Graphics g){
  g.setColor(Color.white);
  g.fillRect(20,10,30,10);
  g.setColor(Color.black);
  g.drawString(""+Count,20,20);
}
```

CODE 11-5

Even after overriding the "update" method, your applet will still flicker. In order to reduce the flickering to a minimum, we need to implement a technique known as "double buffering". In this technique our paint method draws its objects to a buffer that does not appear on the screen, and then paints this buffer to the applet in one go. Thus, provided your applet screen area is not too big, the entire applet's surface will be redrawn very quickly, hiding all the work your paint method needs to do to achieve the desired result. If your applet is very big, then your graphics card will take time to transfer the contents of the off-screen drawing area into the video card memory, and you may still get some flickering.

In order to implement double buffering, we first create an off-screen image and then create a graphics reference for that image. It is this graphics reference that you draw on – the off-screen image is painted to the screen.

You can either create the image and the graphics reference for the entire class to manipulate, or create them in the paint method. Here is an example paint method that creates our off-screen graphics image and then transfers it to the screen.

```
public void paint(Graphics g){
  Image offscreenImage;
  Graphics offscreenGraphics;
  offscreenImage = createImage(this.size().width, this.size().height);
  offscreenGraphics = offscreenImage.getGraphics();
  offscreenGraphics.drawString("This is a test"+Count,20,20);
  g.drawImage(offscreenImage,0,0,this);
}
```

CODE 11-6

In this example we create our graphics image the same size as the applet by using a "this.size()" method. All our drawing is referenced to our "offscreenGraphics" – in this case a string is painted on the surface. After all the drawing is finished it is transferred to the applet's drawing surface using the "drawImage()" method.

Drawing only what is needed

In the previous part of this chapter it was mentioned that using double buffering largely removes any flickering from your applet, provided that the applet is not too big. If you do have a large surface area then it is probable that you only need to update a small portion for each repaint. In our animation that showed a ghost floating over a logo, we redrew the background each iteration and then placed the ghost on top. However, this is wasteful: we only need to draw the background for the previous position of the ghost plus the ghost in its new position.

We can use the "clipRect()" function to limit the drawing area to the size of the image of the ghost:

```
clipRect(originX, originY, ghost.size().width, ghost.size().height);
```

All graphics operations will only be performed within this rectangle. If we draw a large background then only the portion contained within this area will be drawn.

There is a problem however: we do not know how many repaints have occurred when the paint method is called. Remember, a "repaint" only informs Java that the screen has changed. The applet does not have to honour the repaint if it is doing other things. In order to redraw the background over the last position of the ghost we need to store the last position of the ghost in the paint method.

```
public void paint (Graphics g){
  //Draw the background at the old position
  if (first != true){
    g.clipRect(0,0,this.size().width,this.size().height);
    g.clipRect(lastx, lasty, Foreground.getWidth(this),
Foreground.getHeight(this));
    g.drawImage(Background,0,0,this);
  }else{
    g.drawImage(Background,0,0,this);
    first =false;
  }
  //Draw the Foreground at the new position
  newx=x_location;
```

```
    newy=y_location;
    g.clipRect(0,0,this.size().width,  this.size().height);
    g.clipRect(newx,  newy,  Foreground.getWidth(this),
Foreground.getHeight(this));
    g.drawImage(Foreground,newx,newy,this);
    lastx=newx;
    lasty=newy;

}
```

CODE 11-7

Why do we set the clip rectangle to the entire size of the applet before setting it to the new rectangle? When a new clip rectangle is defined, the result of the operation is the intersection of the current rectangle and the newly defined area. If the two areas do not overlap the result will be an area of zero size!

Notice that in the example we use a local Boolean variable to determine if this is the first time the paint method is called. When the paint method is first called we need to draw the background in its entirety. We do not draw the entire background each time the paint method is called. This leads to a problem: if the applet is covered up by another window and then uncovered, the background is not redrawn. Solving this problem will need to wait until Part B, when we learn how to handle events. Code 11-7 has another problem, however: because it takes time to load the background image, the first paint will be called before the image is in memory. If you try and use the example code as it is, you will get a blank applet except for where the ghost has been painted. We will look at a mechanism for this over the next few pages.

A paint method for tracking images

As a final example, let's create an applet that tracks images as they load. This example will provide some feedback to the user whilst the images load. This will avoid an inconvenient blank applet that is often shown while loading images. As you may have observed, when an image is loaded using "getImage", the whole image may not be available for drawing until some time later. This is because the "getImage" method returns to your applet as soon as it can. It starts the retrieval of the actual image but the image may not be completely loaded for some time. If the "getImage" function did not behave this way, your applet would stop while the image was loaded. Because the image may be loaded from some point far away on the Internet, Java must be able to carry on whilst images load. Java provides us with the Media Tracker class library to determine when the image has finished loading and is ready for use.

First we construct a variable to hold our tracker, and then add images to the tracker as they are loaded.

```
import java.awt.*;
import java.net.*;

public class code118 extends java.applet.Applet {
  MediaTracker myTracker;
  Image bgImage;
  Image fgImage;
  URL baseURL;

  public void init(){
    baseURL=getDocumentBase();
    bgImage=getImage(baseURL,"bg.gif");
    fgImage=getImage(baseURL,"fg.gif");
    myTracker = new MediaTracker(this);
    myTracker.addImage(bgImage,0);
    myTracker.addImage(fgImage,0);
    System.out.println("Waiting");
    try {
      myTracker.waitForID(0);
    } catch(Exception et){
      return;
    }
    System.out.println("Image Loaded");
  }
}
```

CODE 11-8

The Init method shown loads two images and adds them to the tracker. The applet will then halt and wait for both images to be loaded before continuing with its execution. Notice that the wait method can generate errors and so these need to be caught using the try-catch statements. The second argument to the addImage method defines a tracker group; we could have placed each image in a different group and waited for each image in turn. The approach shown in this "init" method is not very useful – the applet simply halts whilst the images load, and gives no feedback to the user.

If we make our applet multi-tasking, we can move the wait operation to a thread in the "run" method. We can then give the user feedback on the progress of loading the images. Make sure the applet implements "Runnable" in the class definition.

Use the start method to generate two threads as shown in Code 11-1, one called clockThread, the other called mainThread. Add a stop method to make sure they die properly. In the definition of the class's variables add a Boolean variable called Loaded and set its initial value to false.

In the run method we deal with the clock thread by sleeping for 1 second and then incrementing a clock counter before calling repaint and starting over. In the main thread we wait for the images to be loaded using the media tracker. When the images are loaded we can stop the clockThread before calling a repaint.

```
public void run(){
  if (Thread.currentThread() == clockThread){
    while(true){
      try{
        Thread.sleep(1000);
      }catch (InterruptedException ignored){
        return;
      }
      Count ++;
      repaint();
    }
  }
  if (Thread.currentThread() == mainThread){
    try {
    myTracker.waitForID(0);
  }catch(Exception et){
      return;
    }
```

```
    clockThread.stop();
    Loaded = true;
    // Now do what you want with the images I.e. call a repaint
    repaint();
  }
}
```

CODE 11-9

In the paint method we handle the clock thread by writing a text string to the applet's drawing surface with an appropriate "waiting for images" message. If the current thread is the main thread and the loaded variable is true, then we can draw the appropriate images. We need the loaded variable because a repaint could be generated by the applet when the viewer is resized or moved, or exposed from behind another window.

```
public void paint(Graphics g){
  if (Loaded==false){
    g.drawRect(10,10,200,10);
    g.drawString("Waiting for images, waited for "+Count,20,20);
  }
  if ( (Loaded ==true)){
    g.drawImage(bgImage,0,0,this);
    g.drawImage(fgImage,0,0,this);
  }
}
```

CODE 11-9

CHAPTER 12

Loading and Playing Sounds

Just as Java can draw images on the applet's drawing surface, it can retrieve sounds from the Internet and play them via your sound card. At present Java is limited to playing Sun's .au format files but in the future that will be extended.

Here is a simple applet that will load a sound and play it when the applet starts. As before, we first import the class libraries we need and create a variable to hold our audio clip. As with images, we need to get the root URL of our applet before we can load the sound. We can then load the sound using "getAudioClip", using the document base and the name of the sound file. Playing the sound clip is simplicity itself: simply use the "play" method of the "AudioClip".

```
import java.applet.AudioClip;
import java.net.*;

public class Sound extends java.applet.Applet {

  AudioClip Bang;
  URL baseURL;
  public void init(){
    baseURL = getDocumentBase();
    Bang=getAudioClip(getCodeBase(),"Bong.au");
    Bang.play();

  }
}
```

CODE 12-1

Hint

If you are having trouble creating audio files in the proper format for Java, try a package called "Goldwave". This shareware package is the best audio tool I have come across and does a good job of converting .wav files to the .au file format Java needs. When saving the file, make sure that the sub-format is "nlaw", or the audio file will not play.

If you issue a call to an audio clip's play method before the clip has finished playing, the clip is restarted immediately from the beginning. You can stop a clip at any time by issuing a call to the clip's stop method.

```
MyClip.stop();
```

To make the sound clip repeat itself over and over, issue a call to the clip's loop method. The looping can be stopped using the stop method.

```
MyClip.loop();
```

Java allows multiple sounds to be played at any one time, so you can loop a sound in the background and then add other sounds on top. At present the Media Tracker we used for images is not implemented for sound clips. This means there is no way to determine if the sound has completely loaded before playing it.

CHAPTER 13

Passing Parameters to Your Applet

As we saw very early on, it is a good idea to make your applet as flexible as possible by passing parameters to it in the <applet> tag. This will allow other web page developers to use your applet and customise it to their own needs. For example, suppose you create an applet that takes some text and drops it from the top of the applet's window to the bottom. The text could be embedded into the code, as in Code 13-1:

```java
import java.awt.*;

public class code131 extends java.applet.Applet implements Runnable{
  Thread myThread1;
  int Count=0;
  String myMessage = "This is my message";

  public void init(){
    //Set up any variables etc
  }
  public void start(){
    if (myThread1 == null){
       myThread1= new Thread(this);
       myThread1.start();
    }
  }

  public void run(){
    if (Thread.currentThread()==myThread1){
      while (true){
        try{
          Thread.sleep(100);
        }catch (InterruptedException ignored){
```

```
        return;
        }
        Count ++;
        repaint();
        if (Count>this.size().height)
          Count=0;
      }
    }
  }
  public void stop(){
    if (myThread1 != null){
      myThread1.stop();
      myThread1= null;
    }
  }
  public void paint(Graphics g){
    g.drawString(myMessage,20,Count);
  }
}
```

CODE 13-1

This works very nicely, but what if you want to change the text or the speed at which it moves? Without using parameters you will need to change the code and recompile it. Furthermore, if you distributed this code, others could not change it without having access to a Java compiler. As we saw earlier, parameters in the applet tag have two arguments. These arguments are the name of the parameter and a value for the parameter.

For example, if we have the following applet tag –

```
<applet  code="java.class" width="450" height="150">
<param name=Text value="This is my text">
</applet>
```

– we retrieve a parameter using the getParameter method, passing the name of the parameter to the method. We would need to retrieve the parameter named "Text". The getParameter method always returns a string and is very fussy about the case of the name of the parameter. If no parameter is found that matches the argument then null is returned. It is always a good idea to check for this result and set your variables to some sensible value.

```
public void init(){
  myMessage =getParameter("Text");
  if (myMessage== null)
    myMessage="You Need to supply some message to display.";
}
```

If we want to pass our applet an integer parameter such as a delay factor
for the sleep, we still need to pass it over as a string and convert it to an
integer in our code.

```
<Applet code="Drop.class" width="450"  height="150">
<param name=Text value="Hello world.">
<param name=Speed value="10">
```

We convert the string to an integer using the "parseInt" method of
integers. The full "init()" method to retrieve the parameters in the above tag
is shown in Code 13-2. Of course, the "run" and "paint" methods will need
to be changed to use these new values.

```
public void init(){
  myMessage =getParameter("Text");
  if (myMessage== null)
    myMessage="You Need to supply some message to display.";
  intParam =getParameter("Speed");
  if (intParam== null)
    intParam="1";
  Speed = Integer.parseInt(intParam);
}
```

CODE 13-2

CHAPTER 14

Setting Applet Information

Some web browsers will allow the user to display information about any applets that a web page contains. Typically, this will be copyright information, or information about the author of the web page. To include this in your applet you need to include a "getAppletInfo" method in your applet. This simple method should return a string with the information you want to be displayed.

```
public String getAppletInfo(){
  return("This applet by Andy C, May 1996");
}
```

This method will display the string "This applet by Andy C, May 1996" in the information window of the web browser. Figure 14-1 shows the output from the appletviewer under Windows NT.

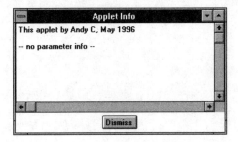

FIGURE 14-1

PART B

Using the AWT

Introduction to the Abstract Windows Toolkit (AWT)

Assuming you have been using a computer for a while now and are used to a Windows interface, you will be familiar with the concept of dialog boxes filled with a rich set of interface components. Nearly all dialog boxes have an "OK" button, some fields for text entry and possibly some boxes you can tick or clear. On top of that you will have used programs with pull-down menus, selection lists and scrollbars. In older languages adding these features can be rather difficult, but Java has built them into the Development Kit. Adding these components usually requires only a few lines of code. If you're lucky enough to be using an Integrated Development Environment (IDE, such as J++ or Symantech Café) then adding components is going to be even easier. It usually takes only a few mouse clicks and keystrokes to pick and place user interface components. The environment will usually generate the code for you and may even document it. However, if you read through this section you will be able to understand the code the IDE creates for you.

The AWT includes layout methods that allow your applet to be displayed in a similar way, regardless of the platform or browser it is being viewed upon. This avoids your Java program needing to be aware of the size of your applet, helping to make your applet platform- and browser-independent. This section of the book will take you through the basic components of the AWT and explain how to use them to control your applets. To use an AWT component, import the AWT class library in the import section, declare an AWT component variable and add it to your applet in the init() method of the applet.

Remember, you will gain more experience if you try the examples in this section for yourself. Enter the code using your favourite text editor and use the "javac" command to compile the source code. Examine the results using the applet viewer together with an appropriate ".html" file.

CHAPTER 15

Basic AWT Components

This chapter explains how to add all of the major elements to your applets: labels, buttons, text, checkboxes, pop-up menus and scrollbars. The following chapter will cover how to organise these components using layouts.

Adding labels to your applet

Labels are simple text fields that can be used to provide information to the user. The labels can not be changed by the user (although the applet can change them). You can declare an empty label and add the text later in the program with the setText method. We will use labels to illustrate how to add AWT components to your applet. Note that at the very start of the source code we import the AWT library to let the compiler know we are going to use user-interface components in our applet.

```
import java.awt.*;
public class code151 extends java.applet.Applet {
  Label TestLabel = new Label("This is a test Label");
  Label TestLabel2 = new Label();
  public void init(){
    add(TestLabel);
    TestLabel2.setText("This is a line of text");
    add(TestLabel2);
  }
}
```

CODE 15-1

In this example we declare a label using the "new" operator and initialise it to contain "This is a test Label". In the applet's init() method we use the "add" operator to add it to the applet's drawing surface. We create a second label in the source code, "TestLabel2". This is initially created as an empty label. We use the "setText" method of the label to initialise its contents in the "init" method of the applet. In this case we use the "setText" method before the label is added to the applet's drawing surface. The result is shown in Figure 15-1. There is no reason that a label's text can not be changed using the "setText" method at any point in the applet's lifetime. A little later in this chapter we will use the "setText" method together with the animation techniques from Part A to create a jiggly text applet.

FIGURE 15-1

Why not use the drawString method we met in Chapter 9? The drawString method needs co-ordinates relative to the top-left of the applet, so if we have added other AWT components then we can not guarantee the actual location of components. This would mean the output of the "drawString" may be badly aligned or even covered by another component. Using a label we can guarantee the alignment of the text with other components on the applet's drawing surface.

Because the size of the label depends on the layout (and the size) of the applet, the actual size of the label window may be greater than the size of the text it contains. You may wish to align the text within the window either left, right or centre.

```
import java.awt.*;

public class code152 extends java.applet.Applet {
  Label TestLabel = new Label("Test Left Label", Label.LEFT);
  Label TestLabel2 = new Label("Test Right Label", Label.RIGHT);
  Label TestLabel3 = new Label("Test Center Label", Label.CENTER);
  public void init(){
    add(TestLabel);
    add(TestLabel2);
    add(TestLabel3);
  }
}
```

CODE 15-2

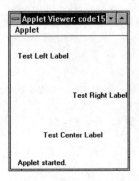

FIGURE 15-2

Note

With some early versions of Java and some browsers, Code 15-2 does not appear to work correctly: the text in the labels is not correctly aligned. You can fix this by using the grid layouts explained later in this section.

You can change the text in the label at any point in your program, or change the alignment of the text. The following applet adds three labels and changes the alignment and contents once a second to make a very jiggly applet! The code uses the runnable methods we looked at in Part A to create a multi-tasking applet. The applet creates the labels and adds them to the applet's surface in the "init" method. Most of the work, however, is in the "run" method. This method uses an infinite while loop to sleep for 1 second and then move the alignment and content of the labels. We use a counter and the "mod" operator to determine which alignment to use. The counter is incremented at the end of the run method, and is returned to zero if it exceeds the value of "3".

```java
import java.awt.*;
public class Jiggly extends  java.applet.Applet implements Runnable{

  Thread myThread;
  int Sleeper=1000;
  int Count=0;
  Label TestLabel = new Label("Test Left Label", Label.LEFT);
  Label TestLabel2 = new Label("Test Right Label", Label.RIGHT);
  Label TestLabel3 = new Label("Test Center Label", Label.CENTER);

  public void init(){
    add(TestLabel);
    add(TestLabel2);
    add(TestLabel3);
  }

  public void start(){
    if (myThread ==null){
      myThread=new  Thread(this,"MainThread");
      myThread.start();
    }
  }

  public void stop(){
    if (myThread !=null){
      myThread.stop();
      myThread=null;
    }
  }

  public void run(){
    if (Thread.currentThread()==myThread){
      while (true){
        try{
          Thread.sleep(Sleeper);
        }catch(InterruptedException ignored){
          System.out.println("Can't Sleep");
          return;
        }
        TestLabel.setText(Integer.toString(Count));
        TestLabel2.setText(Integer.toString(Count+10));
        TestLabel3.setText(Integer.toString(Count+20));
```

```
     if ((Count   % 3)==0){
       TestLabel.setAlignment( Label.LEFT);
       TestLabel2.setAlignment( Label.RIGHT);
       TestLabel3.setAlignment( Label.CENTER);
     }
     if ((Count   % 3)==1){
       TestLabel.setAlignment( Label.RIGHT);
       TestLabel2.setAlignment( Label.CENTER);
       TestLabel3.setAlignment( Label.LEFT);
     }
     if ((Count   % 3)==2){
       TestLabel.setAlignment( Label.CENTER);
       TestLabel2.setAlignment( Label.LEFT);
       TestLabel3.setAlignment( Label.RIGHT);
     }
     Count++;
     if (Count >3)
       Count=0;
     }
   }

  }
 }
```

CODE 15-3

Note

This code uses the "mod" operator to determine which alignment to use for this counter value. Remember, the mod operator returns the amount left over after division. Our counter is going to take the values 0,1,2,3. This table shows the results of the "mod" operator with each of these values:

Counter value	Counter mod 3
0	0
1	1
2	2
3	0

We use the "mod" operator with an "if" statement. When the result of the "mod" operator is 0, the code aligns label1 left, label2 right and label3 centre. The other "if" statements give different alignments for different results from the "mod" operator. Notice that, because of the way we have used the "mod" operator, the result will be 0 for two values of the counter. This gives the effect that the alignment stays in one state longer than the other states.

You should notice how the "setText" method uses the "toString" method to convert the integer variable "Count" to a string. The variable types Boolean, float and double all have similar methods to convert their values to a string representation. To convert a string to an integer, use the parseInt method from the Integer class:

```
int Value =Integer.parseInt("1234");
```

If you need to, you can retrieve the text of a label or its current alignment using the "getText" and "getAlignment" methods:

```
String TextofLabel = myLabel.getText();
int Alignment =myLabel.getAlignment();
if ( Alignment == Label.CENTER)
  System.out.println("Label is Centered");
if ( Alignment == Label.LEFT)
  System.out.println("Label is LEFT");
if ( Alignment == Label.CENTER)
  System.out.println("Label is RIGHT");
```

CODE 15-4

Buttons

Buttons are the simplest interface component that allow an applet user to interact with the applet. The user pushes the button with a mouse-click to initiate an event in the applet. For instance, suppose your game applet kept a record of the user's score, you might want to allow the user to post that score to a central server keeping a record of the high scores. You would add a button to the applet that initiates the code to post the score to the server.

```
import java.awt.*;
public class ButtonTest extends java.applet.Applet {

  Button TestButton = new Button("Post my Score Now !");
  public void init(){
    add(TestButton);
  }
}
```

CODE 15-5

This simple applet adds a button to your applet but does not do anything when the user activates the button. We need to add a method to "catch" the button-press and then take some appropriate action. In Java the button press is caught using an "action" method. We have created multi-tasking applets by using the "runnable" method in Part A and in the description of labels. However, the existence of the action method reveals that Java is inherently multi-tasking. When an event occurs, the applet starts the "action" method. After the action method finishes, the Java applet will return to finish whatever was happening when the event occurred.

FIGURE 15-3

The "action" method is passed the type of action and which object created the action. The "Event" parameter contains information about the type of User Interface component that generated the action. The "Object" parameter contains information about the actual component involved.

If we add the following method to our "ButtonTest" class we can catch the button and print a message to the console.

```
public boolean action(Event evt, Object arg){
  if (evt.target instanceof Button)
    if (arg.equals ("Post my Score Now !")){
      System.out.println("Caught the button");
      /* Do some other processing if we want */
      return true;
    }
  return false;
}
```

CODE 15-6

The action method in Code 15-6 first tests that it is a button that created the event using the "instanceof" operator. If it was a button, we test which button was pressed by checking the object argument. Notice that the "arg" contains the text that appears on the button. We use the "equals" method of the "arg" object to test the name of the button that was pressed. If it is the correct button, the method returns "true" to show that the button press has been dealt with. If it is not a button our applet recognises, the method returns "false" to allow other methods to process the button-press.

You can use the "setLabel" method to change the text on the button and the "getLabel" method to change the text. Unfortunately, at present there is no method to draw an image on a button without creating your own button class from scratch. Here is a simple applet that counts the number of times the button is pressed and displays the result on the button.

```java
import java.awt.*;

public class CountButton extends java.applet.Applet {
  Button TestButton = new Button("0");
  public void init(){
    add(TestButton);
  }

  public boolean action(Event evt, Object arg){
    if (evt.target instanceof Button){
      String ButtonLabel =TestButton.getLabel();
      int ButtonValue =Integer.parseInt(ButtonLabel);
      ButtonValue++;
      TestButton.setLabel(Integer.toString(ButtonValue));
      return true;
    }
    return false;
  }
}
```

CODE 15-7

Text fields and text areas

Although buttons allow your user to select an action, there are times when you need written information from the user. If you only need a single line from the user you can use the Text Field class. This object can be created either empty or with some initial text within it. You can specify the size of the text window or allow the Layout Manager to determine it for you. The program in Code 15-8 creates 4 text fields using each of the methods. The first is an empty text field of undetermined size. The second is empty but 25 characters wide. The third and fourth are initialised with the text "Enter your text here". The fourth text field is at least 25 characters wide.

```java
import java.awt.*;

public class TextFieldTest extends java.applet.Applet {
  TextField Text1 = new TextField();
  TextField Text2 = new TextField(25);
  TextField Text3 = new TextField("Enter your text here");
  TextField Text4 = new TextField("Enter your text here",25);

  public void init(){
    add(Text1);
    add(Text2);
    add(Text3);
    add(Text4);
  }
}
```

CODE 15-8

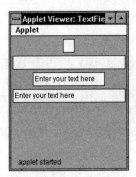

FIGURE 15-4

If you create an empty text field, the number of characters that will be shown will depend on the viewer that is used to show the applet. Although the window may only be 1 or 2 characters wide, text will scroll off to the left, allowing you to enter as much as you want. You can find the width of a text field using the "getColumns" method, as shown below. Even if the text field is visible, the "getColumns" method can report a width of zero. If the text field is one character wide it may be reported as zero width.

```
int Width=Text1.getColumns();
```

There may be occasions when you want to lock the contents of a text field after a user has entered some values. You use the setEditable method to do this:

```
myTextField.setEditable(true);        Allows users to enter values to this text field.
myTextField.setEditable(false);       Stops users entering text to this text field.
```

You may also want to be able to control whether the typed characters appear in the text window or some other character appears instead. This character is known as the "echo character". This facility is useful if you want to create a password-locked resource. The setEchoCharacter() method is used to set the echo character:

```
myTextField.setEchoCharacter('*');    Sets the echo character to "*".
myTextField.getEchoCharacter();       Gets the current echo character.
myTextField.echoCharIsSet();          Returns true if the echo character is set, otherwise it
                                       returns false.
```

Usually when using text fields a button is added to the applet for the user to let your applet know when to retrieve the text using the "getText()" method. The example below creates two text windows ("User" and "Password") and a button ("Finish"). The "Password" text window has its echo character set to '*'. When the button is pressed, the action method is activated. After the type of the event and the name of the button have been determined, the text window becomes uneditable using the "setEditable" method of text fields.

```
import java.awt.*;

public class TextButtonTest extends java.applet.Applet {

  TextField User = new TextField("Enter your User Name",25);
  TextField Password = new TextField("Enter your Password");
  Button Finish .= new Button("All Done");

  public void init(){
    add(User);
    add(Password);
    Password.setEchoCharacter('*');
    add(Finish);
  }

  public boolean action(Event evt, Object arg){
    if (evt.target instanceof Button)
      if (arg.equals ("All Done")){
        String s1= User.getText();
        String s2= Password.getText();
        User.setEditable(false);
        System.out.println("User" + s1 + "Password "+s2 );
        return true;
      }
    return false;
  }
}
```

CODE 15-9

FIGURE 15-5

One line of text is more than a little bit limiting if you require large amounts of text from the user. You could use multiple text fields to collect data that needs to be processed in separate strings. However, if you need a large block of text that is treated as a single entity then it is better to use a "text area". A text area can have as many lines as you like and will provide its own scrollbars for navigation. The area will even respond to the usual text-editing features of your environment such as Cut and Paste. The text area can be declared in a number of ways – the code shown creates a text window 25 lines deep and 40 characters across. You can also declare a text area with an initial string using TextArea(String) or with a string and initial size using TextArea(String, Height, Width).

```
import java.awt.*;

public class TextAreaTest extends java.applet.Applet {
  TextArea Area1 = new TextArea(25,40);
  public void init(){
    add(Area1);
  }
}
```

CODE 15-10

FIGURE 15-6

All the features available to TextFields (except for echo characters) are available to text areas. You can get the text with getText, set the text with setText and make the text read-only using the "setEditable" method. One of the nice features with text areas is that they allow the full cutting and pasting of text using the Cut and Paste features of Windows. Your Java program can also select text and cut and paste it to other locations within the text area. To select all the text in the text area use "selectAll()". Once selected, you get the selected text by using the "getSelectedText()" method. If the user selects text using the mouse you can find the start and stop position of the selection using "getSelectionStart()" and "getSelectionEnd()". You can use these two values with the "replaceText()" method to overwrite the selected area with new text. If the new text is a blank string then the selected text will be deleted. Text can be inserted in the text area using "insertText()", and added to the end of the area using "appendText()".

The applet in Code 15-11 creates a text area and three buttons: one button to delete the selected text; one button that adds a trademark sentence to the current location; and one button that adds a copyright statement to the end of the current text. As usual, the "action" method handles all the code to make the changes to the applet's behaviour when the buttons are pressed.

```java
import java.awt.*;

public class TextSelect extends java.applet.Applet {

  TextArea Area1 = new TextArea(25,40);
  Button Delete = new Button("Delete");
  Button Trademark = new Button("Add Trade Mark");
  Button Copyright = new Button("Append copyright");
  public void init(){
    add(Area1);
    add(Delete);
    add(Trademark);
    add(Copyright);
  }
  public boolean action(Event evt, Object arg){
    if (evt.target instanceof Button)
      if (arg.equals ("Delete")){
        int Start= Area1.getSelectionStart();
        int End =Area1.getSelectionEnd();
        Area1.replaceText("",Start,End);
        return true;
      }
      if (arg.equals ("Add Trade Mark")){
        int Start= Area1.getSelectionStart();
        Area1.insertText("(A trademark of  Blind Jeep Productions)",Start);
        return true;
      }
      if (arg.equals ("Append copyright")){
```

```
        Area1.appendText("This code is copyright \"Blind jeep
productions\"1995");
        return true;
     }
   return false;
  }
 }
```

CODE 15-11

Finally the current size of the text area can be retrieved by
"getColumns()" and "getRows()", both of which return an integer.

```
integer Columns = Area.getColumns();
integer Rows = Area.getRows();
```

Checkboxes and checkbox groups

Checkboxes are user-interface components that allow users to make a
selection from a number of choices presented to them. They can be used in
either of two ways – either the user can select as many items as they require,
or the user is confined to making only one choice from the selection. This
second type is sometimes known as a radio button system. This alludes to
the old style radios with preset channels assigned to buttons, of which only
one could be depressed at any one time.

Multiple-choice checkboxes are created with the "CheckBox()"
constructor or the "CheckBox(String)" constructor. The string represents
the label that will appear next to the checkbox, and can be changed using the
"setLabel()" method. Checkboxes of this type are always initialised in the off
state. To find out if a checkbox has been selected, use the "getState()"
method. The sample applet in Code 15-12 creates three checkboxes and a
button to retrieve the selection state of the boxes. The output of the applet
is shown in Figure 15-7.

```
import java.awt.*;
public class MultiCheck extends java.applet.Applet {
  Checkbox Choice1= new Checkbox("Peperami");
```

```
Checkbox Choice2= new Checkbox("Mushrooms");
Checkbox Choice3= new Checkbox("Peppers");
Button Done = new Button("Finished Pizza");

public void init(){
  add(Choice1);
  add(Choice2);
  add(Choice3);
  add(Done);
}

public boolean action(Event evt, Object arg){
  if (evt.target instanceof Button)
    if (arg.equals ("Finished Pizza")){
      if (Choice1.getState() == true)
        System.out.println("Add Peperami");
      if (Choice2.getState() == true)
        System.out.println("Add mushrooms");
      if (Choice3.getState() == true)
        System.out.println("Add Peppers");
      return true;
    }
  return false;
}
}
```

CODE 15-12

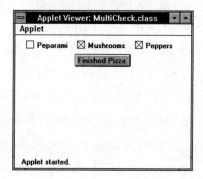

FIGURE 15-7

However, if we wanted the same applet to react whenever a checkbox changed, we would replace the action method with that shown in Code 15-13. This method checks the event target for instances of "checkbox" instead of instances of "button". If the event is an instance of "checkbox" we can then check which boxes are checked using the "getState()" method as before.

```
public boolean action(Event evt, Object arg){

  if (evt.target instanceof Checkbox){
    if (Choice1.getState() == true)
      System.out.println("Add Peperami");
    else
      System.out.println("Hold the Peperami");
    if (Choice2.getState() == true)
      System.out.println("Add mushrooms");
    else
      System.out.println("Hold the mushrooms");
    if (Choice3.getState() == true)
      System.out.println("Add Peppers");
    else
      System.out.println("Hold the Peppers");
    return true;
  }
  return false;
  }
}
```

CODE 15-13

To create a set of radio buttons we must first create a checkbox group and then add the checkboxes to it. The checkboxes are added to the group at construction time using the "Checkbox(String, CheckboxGroup, boolean)" method. This method insists that the initial state of the checkboxes is set at construction time. Although only one box should be initialised as true, the current version of the compiler will allow more than one to be initialised. However, only the last checkbox set to true will actually be crossed.

To find the current choice from the checkbox group, use the "getCurrent()" method. This returns a checkbox type so you can either use a "getLabel" method to get the text of the checkbox, or use a set of "if" statements to compare the returned value to the checkboxes you are interested in. Code 15-14 creates a checkbox group and adds three checkboxes to it. Both methods of getting the current value are shown in the action method.

```
import java.awt.*;

public class RadioButton extends java.applet.Applet {
```

```
CheckboxGroup myGroup= new CheckboxGroup();
Checkbox Choice1= new Checkbox("Peperami",myGroup,false);
Checkbox Choice2= new Checkbox("Mushrooms",myGroup,true);
Checkbox Choice3= new Checkbox("Peppers",myGroup,false);

public void init(){
  add(Choice1);
  add(Choice2);
  add(Choice3);
}
public boolean action(Event evt, Object arg){

  if (evt.target instanceof Checkbox){
    System.out.println(myGroup.getCurrent().getLabel());
    if (myGroup.getCurrent() == Choice1)
      System.out.println("Only Peperami");
    if (myGroup.getCurrent() == Choice2)
      System.out.println("Only Mushrooms");
    if (myGroup.getCurrent() == Choice3)
      System.out.println("Only Peppers");
    return true;
  }

  return false;
}
}
```

CODE 15-14

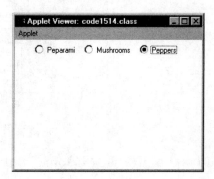

FIGURE 15-8

You can use the "setCurrent()" method to make a checkbox the current choice. The "setCurrent()" method takes a checkbox as its parameter:

```
myGroup.setCurrent(Choice1);
```

FIGURE 15-9

Pop-up menus and lists

If you are a computer user you will be familiar with the idea of menus similar to that shown in Figure 15-9, and might like to use them in your applets. Unfortunately, Java won't let you add this type of menu to the type of applet we have been writing so far. You will learn about this type of menu in Part C of the book. However, Java does support pop-up choice menus, which are sometimes known as pull-down menus. (Java 1.1 also allows floating menus to pop up when the mouse button is pressed. See Appendix B for details.) Before they are selected, they appear on the screen as shown in Figure 15-10. Once selected, they expand to show the full range of choices as shown in Figure 15-11.

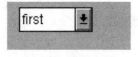

FIGURE 15-10

FIGURE 15-11

To create a pop-up menu, use the "Choice" constructor and add items by using the "addItem()" method. The "addItem" method takes as its argument a string that will represent the choice in the menu. To retrieve the item selected, you can use the "getSelectedItem()" method that will return the label of the selected item. Alternatively, the "getSelectedIndex()" method will return an integer value for the selection. The first item in the list has an integer value of 0 and the last item has a value 1 less than the number of items in the list. Code 15-15 creates a pop-up menu and adds four items to it. An action method retrieves the selected item using both the methods outlined above.

```
import java.awt.*;
public class PopupMenuTest extends java.applet.Applet {

  Choice myPopup = new Choice();

  public void init(){
    myPopup.addItem("first");
    myPopup.addItem("second");
    myPopup.addItem("third");
    myPopup.addItem("fourth");
    add(myPopup);

  }

  public boolean action(Event evt, Object arg){
  if (evt.target instanceof Choice){
    System.out.println(myPopup.getSelectedItem());
    System.out.println(myPopup.getSelectedIndex());
    return true;
  }
  return false;
  }
}
```

CODE 15-15

You can retrieve the number of items in the list using the "countItems" method:

```
int Numberof Items = myPopup.countItems
```

The pop-up menu choice allows the selection of only one item, but you can create a choice menu that allows multiple choices using the list class. This useful interface component has two constructors. The first creates an empty list of zero visible size, the second creates a list of known visible size that may allow multiple selections. Code 15-16 creates a list with three visible lines but four items in the list. This shows a window with three items visible and a vertical scrollbar to move up and down the list. The second argument to the list constructor determines whether the list allows multiple selections. The example code here sets this argument to true, thus allowing multiple selections.

```
import java.awt.*;

public class ListMenuTest extends java.applet.Applet {
  List myList = new List(3,true);
  public void init(){
    myList.addItem("first");
    myList.addItem("second");
    myList.addItem("third");
    myList.addItem("fourth");
    add(myList);

  }
}
```

CODE 15-16

FIGURE 15-12

However, in early versions of Java the list class does not generate an action when an item is selected. You might like to try adding an action to see if this is true for the version you are using. In order to get the selected choices, a button will need to be added to this applet. There are a number of methods to get the items selected – you could query each item in turn using the "isSelected()" method:

```
public boolean action(Event evt, Object arg){
  for (int I=0; I< myList.countItems();I++){
    if (myList.isSelected(I) == true){
      System.out.println("Selected"+I);
    }
  }
  return (true);
}
```

CODE 15-17

Alternatively, you can use either "getSelectedIndexes" to get the index number of the selected items, or getSelectedItems to get the strings of the selections. Code 15-18 uses both of these methods and inserts the results directly into arrays of appropriate types. The example then uses a "for" loop to print all the selected values to the console.

```
public boolean action(Event evt, Object arg){
  if (evt.target instanceof Button){
    if (arg.equals ("All Done")){
      int Values[]=myList.getSelectedIndexes();
      String Names[]=myList.getSelectedItems();

      for (int i=0; i<Values.length;i++)
        System.out.println(Values[i]+"    "+Names[i]);
      return true;
    }
  }
  return false;
}
```

CODE 15-18

As well as adding items to the list, you can remove items by using "delItem()", which takes a single integer argument, or "delItems()", which takes two integer arguments. These arguments specify the range of items to be removed. Remember that the first item in the list is number 0.

Scrollbars

Scrollbars are a common feature in all Graphical User Interfaces. The text area component we met earlier had scrollbars on the right and the bottom to allow for navigation through the text. However, we might want to create scrollbars on their own. The Java AWT does contain a scrollbar component that can be displayed either horizontally or vertically. A word of warning, however: in early versions of Java the implementation was not terribly good. What is worse is that the functionality varied from platform to platform. Over the next portion of this chapter we will see how to use scrollbars, and how to deal with some of the problems caused by early versions of the Development Kit.

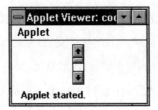

FIGURE 15-13

There are three constructors that can be used to create a scrollbar. The first operates with no arguments and creates a vertical scrollbar. The second uses one parameter to determine the orientation of the scrollbar. The third takes parameters that specify all the working aspects of the bar. Code 15-19 creates a vertical scrollbar using the third method. To create a horizontal scrollbar, change the first argument to "Scrollbar.HORIZONTAL". The second argument specifies the initial value of the scrollbar (with zero at the top). The third argument specifies the amount of scrollbar "handle" that is visible. The last two arguments specify the minimum and maximum value respectively. The result is shown in Figure 15-13.

```
import java.awt.*;

public class code1519 extends java.applet.Applet {

  Scrollbar myScroll = new Scrollbar(Scrollbar.VERTICAL,0,10,0,200);
  public void init(){
    add(myScroll);
  }
}
```

CODE 15-19

The physical size of the scrollbar can not be changed, unless it is used with a layout described in the next chapter.

At some point we will need to get the current value of the scrollbar. This is done with the "getValue()" method of the scrollbar class. However, we can not use the familiar "action" method; there is a more basic handler AWT for events, called "handleEvent". We will use this later in the section for trapping keyboard events. The method in Code 15-20 traps all events and tests for events from the scrollbar. We use a case statement to find out which type of event has been generated. Notice that when we have handled an event, we return from the method with a value of true. If we don't handle an event, we give the "parent" scrollbar a chance to handle the event by using "super.handleEvent(ev)". The term "parent" comes from the object-oriented nature of Java – you will learn more about this in the next section.

```
public boolean handleEvent(Event ev){
  if (ev.target==(Object)myScroll){
    switch (ev.id){
      case Event.SCROLL_LINE_DOWN:
        System.out.println("Scroll line down");
        return true;
      case Event.SCROLL_LINE_UP:
        System.out.println("Scroll Line up");
        return true;
      case Event.SCROLL_PAGE_DOWN:
        System.out.println("Scroll Page down");
        return true;
      case Event.SCROLL_PAGE_UP:
        System.out.println("Scroll Page up");
        return true;
    }
  }
  return super.handleEvent(ev);
}
```

CODE 15-20

We now have a method of catching changes in the value of the scrollbar. The applet in Code 15-21 creates three scrollbars and uses them to change the background colour of the applet whenever they are moved. The code uses the "getValue()" method from the slide bar class to get the current value of each scrollbar. Notice also that the "init()" method of the applet changes the amount the slider moves. The "setLineIncrement()" method changes the amount the value changes when the up or down arrows are pressed. The "setPageIncrement()" method changes the amount the value changes when the cursor is clicked in the space between the handle and the arrows.

```
import java.awt.*;

public class code1521 extends java.applet.Applet {

  Scrollbar redScroll = new Scrollbar(Scrollbar.VERTICAL,0,10,0,255);
  Scrollbar greenScroll = new Scrollbar(Scrollbar.VERTICAL,0,10,0,255);
  Scrollbar blueScroll = new Scrollbar(Scrollbar.VERTICAL,0,10,0,255);

  public void init(){
    redScroll.setLineIncrement(20);
    redScroll.setPageIncrement(50);
    greenScroll.setLineIncrement(20);
    greenScroll.setPageIncrement(50);
    blueScroll.setLineIncrement(20);
    blueScroll.setPageIncrement(50);
    add(redScroll);
    add(greenScroll);
    add(blueScroll);
  }

  public boolean handleEvent(Event ev){
    if ((ev.target==(Object)redScroll) ||
      (ev.target==(Object)greenScroll) ||
      (ev.target==(Object)blueScroll)){
      int red= redScroll.getValue();
      int green= greenScroll.getValue();
      int blue= blueScroll.getValue();
      setBackground(new Color(red,green,blue));
      repaint();
      return true;
    }
    return super.handleEvent(ev);
  }
}
```

CODE 15-21

There are a couple of additional methods for the scrollbar class that are worth a mention. You can change the current value of a scrollbar using the "setValue()" method. This method takes a single integer argument for the new value of the scrollbar. You can get the current page increment with the "getPageIncrement()" method and the current line increment with "getLineIncrement()". Both return an integer value. There are, of course, similarly named methods to get the minimum and maximum values and the orientation of the scrollbars. Examples are shown on the following page.

```
int Maximum = myScroll.getMaximum();
int Minimum = myScroll.getMinimum();

switch (myScroll.getOrientation()){
  case Scrollbar.VERTICAL: System.out.println("Bar is Vertical");
                        break;
  case Scrollbar.HORIZONTAL: System.out.println("Bar is Horizontal");
                        break;
}
```

CHAPTER 16

Using Simple Layouts

In the previous section we added user-interface components to our applet's surface without any concern for the components' placement. In fact, Java was taking care of the component placement using a default layout called "FlowLayout". This adds components onto the drawing surface from left to right until no more components will fit onto the same line. However, we might want to add our components using a different scheme to give a different appearance, and the AWT provides a number of these to customise your applet's appearance. These layouts are "FlowLayout", "GridLayout", "BorderLayout", "CardLayout" and perhaps the most useful, "GridBagLayout". Many of the Integrated Development Environments available at present use their own layout managers. These are not part of the standard Java Development Kit and will not be covered here.

FlowLayout

As stated above, the FlowLayout class adds components to the applet's surface from left to right. The default for this layout class is to add components so that they appear centred in the applet, as shown in Figure 16-1. You can change the default, so that components are added aligned to the left or to the right as shown in Code 16-1. The layout manager is created using the "new" statement with the FlowLayout constructor, and the layout is imposed on the applet's drawing surface using "setLayout" in the init method. If the applet window is too small to accommodate all components on one row, another will be created. Additional components will follow the alignment specified at construction.

```
import java.awt.*;

public class FlowLayoutTest extends java.applet.Applet {

  FlowLayout myLayout = new FlowLayout(FlowLayout.RIGHT);
  Button Button1= new Button("1");
  Button Button2= new Button("2");
  Button Button3= new Button("3");
  Button Button4= new Button("4");
  Button Button5= new Button("5");

  public void init(){
    setLayout(myLayout);
    add(Button1);
    add(Button2);
    add(Button3);
    add(Button4);
    add(Button5);
  }

}
```

CODE 16-1

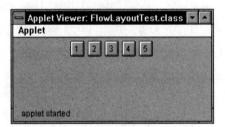

FIGURE 16-1

The separation between the components can be specified when the layout is constructed. Although the horizontal separation can be defined, it is constant between all components. The vertical separation between rows (if more than one row exists) can also be defined:

```
FlowLayout myLayout = new FlowLayout(FlowLayout.LEFT,20,30);
```

This small sample creates a flow layout, aligned left with a horizontal separation between components of 20 points and a vertical separation of 30 points.

GridLayout

The GridLayout manager class creates a grid for your components of a specified number of rows and columns. Components are added starting at the top-left and moving to the right until a row is full; additional components start on the next row down at the left-hand side. If there are not enough components to fill the grid then empty spaces are left, as shown in Figure 16-2. Notice also that the button components fill the entire area that is allocated to them. One of the constructors of the grid layout allows you to specify the gap between rows and columns of components:

```
GridLayout myLayout = new GridLayout(2,3);
```

This creates a grid layout with 2 rows and 3 columns, with the components filling the entire area available to them.

```
GridLayout myLayout = new GridLayout(2,3,10,20);
```

This creates a grid layout with 2 rows, 3 columns with a horizontal separation of 10 points and a vertical separation of 20 points.

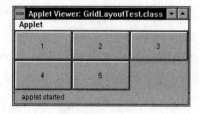

FIGURE 16-2

The current version of Java (version 1.1) has a feature affecting the number of components that can be added to the grid layout. For instance, if a layout is constructed to contain six components but by mistake a seventh is added, the layout manager will change either the number of rows or columns so that all components fit. This can actually be rather handy as it allows you to create a grid layout of two rows and no columns and let the compiler sort out how many columns are actually needed. Before you use this feature, check with your version of Java that it still works!

BorderLayout

Another simple layout manager class is BorderLayout, as shown in Figure 16-3:

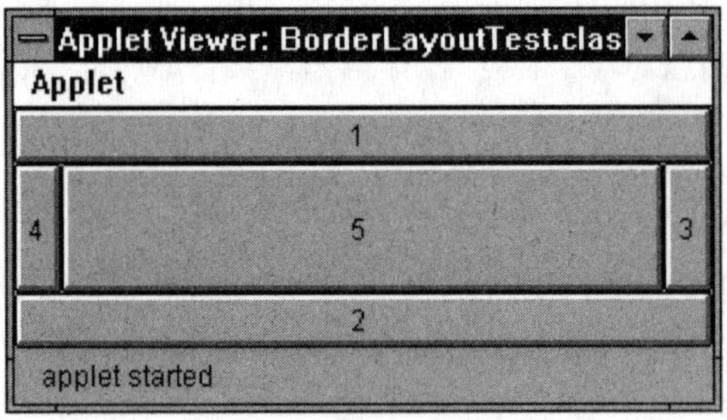

FIGURE 16-3

To use this layout manager, first create a layout using the new statement, set the applet's layout to this and then add components specifying where you want each component. You have the choice of north, south, east, west or centre. The centre component will take the space left over after the other components have been placed on the surface. If two components are placed at the same location then only the second will be visible. Note that the add statement is very fussy that the location is properly spelt, with the first letter capitalised.

```
import java.awt.*;

public class BorderLayoutTest extends java.applet.Applet {

  BorderLayout myLayout = new BorderLayout();
  Button Button1= new Button("1");
  Button Button2= new Button("2");
  Button Button3= new Button("3");
  Button Button4= new Button("4");
  Button Button5= new Button("5");
  Button Button6= new Button("6");
  Button Button7= new Button("7");

  public void init(){
    setLayout(myLayout);
    add("North",Button1);
    add("South",Button2);
    add("East",Button3);
    add("West",Button4);
    add("Center",Button5);

  }

}
```

CODE 16-2

You can define the spacing between components by using a BorderLayout (int,int) constructor. The first integer gives the horizontal gap, and the second the vertical gap.

Panels

All the applets you have seen so far have had a single drawing surface on which you lay a single layout manager. However, it turns out that this is not really very useful. For instance, you might want a group of buttons at the bottom of the applet in a flow layout. Above this you would like a grid with some text fields in a column. In order to be able to do this you need to use panels that create new drawing surfaces for the applet. Each panel surface can have its own layout manager. Panels are created in the same way as any other user-interface component. Just like any other component, they are added to the applet's drawing surface using the add method. Because panels are the same as other interface components, they follow the same rules. You

will need to specify a layout manager for the applet in order to get the panels
to display in the correct positions.

FIGURE 16-4

Here is an example that creates four text fields organised in rows at the
top of the applet, and three buttons in columns at the bottom. First we create
a grid layout of two rows and one column ("myLayout"). We then create
two panels ("TopPanel" and "BottomPanel") to place on the grid layout. The
text fields and buttons are constructed next. Within the init method the
applet's layout manger is set to the grid layout we created earlier. The top
panel's layout is set to a grid layout, and the bottom panel is set to a flow
layout. The buttons and text fields are added to the appropriate panels and
finally the panels are added to the applet's drawing surface.

```
import java.awt.*;

public class PanelTest extends java.applet.Applet {

    GridLayout myLayout = new GridLayout(2,1);

    Panel TopPanel =new Panel();
    Panel BottomPanel = new Panel();
    TextField TextField1= new TextField();
    TextField TextField2= new TextField();
    TextField TextField3= new TextField();
    TextField TextField4= new TextField();
    Button Button5= new Button("5");
    Button Button6= new Button("6");
    Button Button7= new Button("7");

    public void init(){
```

```
  setLayout(myLayout);
  TopPanel.setLayout(new GridLayout(4,1,5,5));
  BottomPanel.setLayout(new FlowLayout(FlowLayout.CENTER));
  TopPanel.add(TextField1);
  TopPanel.add(TextField2);
  TopPanel.add(TextField3);
  TopPanel.add(TextField4);
  BottomPanel.add(Button5);
  BottomPanel.add(Button6);
  BottomPanel.add(Button7);
  add(TopPanel);
  add(BottomPanel);

  }
  public boolean action(Event evt, Object arg){
    if (evt.target instanceof Button){
      System.out.println("Button !");
        return true;
    }
    return false;
  }

}
```

CODE 16-3

CardLayout

The CardLayout manager displays components as if they were a stack of cards with only the top card showing. You can move forward and backwards through the deck of cards or you can jump to the first or last card, or to any named card in the pack. Without using panels, card layouts are not very useful, as you would be limited to a single component on each card. The code shown in Code 16-4 creates a card layout with a button on each card that moves to the next card when pressed. The "action" method checks for an instance of a button and uses the "next" method of the CardLayout to move to the next card.

```
import java.awt.*;

public class CardLayoutTest extends java.applet.Applet {

  CardLayout myLayout = new CardLayout();
  Button Button1= new Button("1");
```

```
Button Button2= new Button("2");
Button Button3= new Button("3");
Button Button4= new Button("4");
Button Button5= new Button("5");
Button Button6= new Button("6");
Button Button7= new Button("7");

public void init(){
  setLayout(myLayout);
  add(Button1);
  add(Button2);
  add(Button3);
  add(Button4);
  add(Button5);

}
public boolean action(Event evt, Object arg){
  if (evt.target instanceof Button){
    myLayout.next(this);
    return true;
  }
  return false;
}

}
```

CODE 16-4

If panels are combined with card layouts, you can create a series of cards, each with its own layout and user-interface components. Code 16-5 creates a card layout for the main applet window, then creates three panels, each with its own border layout. Each panel has a label and two buttons for moving between cards. Notice in this example that when we add a panel to the card layout we add it with a name for use in the show method in the button action. One of the panels of this applet is shown in Figure 16-5. The code is slightly awkward to follow, so let's try and go through it. First a card layout is constructed, followed by three layout managers. A panel for each card is then constructed. Each panel will need two buttons to move to the other cards in the card layout. These buttons are constructed next. Notice that each button is given a unique name identifying its panel and the panel that it will switch to.

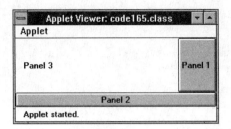

FIGURE 16-5

Within the "init()" method the layout for the applet is set to our card layout. Each of the panels is then assigned a border layout and the panels are added to the card layout. Notice that when the panels are added to the cards they are assigned a name (in the form of a string). Finally, a label is added to each of the panels in the centre.

```
import java.awt.*;

public class CardPanelTest extends java.applet.Applet {
  CardLayout myLayout = new CardLayout();
  BorderLayout myBorderLayout1 = new BorderLayout();
  BorderLayout myBorderLayout2 = new BorderLayout();
  BorderLayout myBorderLayout3 = new BorderLayout();
  Panel Panel1=new Panel();
  Panel Panel2=new Panel();
  Panel Panel3=new Panel();

  Button Panel1Button2= new Button("Panel 2");
  Button Panel1Button3= new Button("Panel 3");

  Button Panel2Button1= new Button("Panel 1");
  Button Panel2Button3= new Button("Panel 3");

  Button Panel3Button1= new Button("Panel 1");
  Button Panel3Button2= new Button("Panel 2");

  public void init(){

    setLayout(myLayout);
    Panel1.setLayout(myBorderLayout1);
    Panel2.setLayout(myBorderLayout2);
    Panel3.setLayout(myBorderLayout3);

    add("Panel1",Panel1);
    add("Panel2",Panel2);
    add("Panel3",Panel3);
```

```
        Panel1.add("South",Panel1Button2);
        Panel1.add("West",Panel1Button3);

        Panel2.add("East",Panel2Button1);
        Panel2.add("West",Panel2Button3);

        Panel3.add("East",Panel3Button1);
        Panel3.add("South",Panel3Button2);

        Panel1.add("Center", new Label("Panel 1"));
        Panel2.add("Center", new Label("Panel 2"));
        Panel3.add("Center", new Label("Panel 3"));

    }

    public boolean action(Event evt, Object arg){
        if (evt.target instanceof Button){
          if (arg.equals ("Panel 1"){
            myLayout.show(this,"Panel1");
            return true;
          }
          if (arg.equals ("Panel 2")){
            myLayout.show(this,"Panel2");
            return true;
          }
          if (arg.equals ("Panel 3")){
            myLayout.show(this,"Panel3");
            return true;
          }
        }
        return false;
    }
}
```

CODE 16-5

The action method of Code 16-5 is extremely simple. It simply checks for an instance of a button press. It then checks the name of the button using a series of "if" statements. When the correct button is identified, we use the "show()" method of the card layout class to display the correct panel. Notice that the show method uses the names we assigned to the cards when they where added in the "init()" method.

CHAPTER 17

The GridBag Layout

The layouts that we have been using up until now have been fairly simple and quite constrained. In the case of the border layout it only allows five components to be added. Some of the layouts make the components fill the specified area, giving ugly-looking components. The GridBagLayout class is a much more flexible layout manager that can align components vertically and horizontally. Further, the GridBagLayout manager does not require that components fill an area. To use a GridBag layout you must set constraints for each component that you add. These constraints tell the layout manager how to lay that component out on the drawing surface. To use a GridBagLayout, create a GridBagLayout object using the "new" operator. A variable to hold the constraints is also created using the "new" operator.

```
GridBagLayout myLayout = new GridBagLayout();
GridBagContraints Contraints = new GridBagConstraints();
```

Note

Although you may be adding many components to the GridBagLayout, you only need one constraints variable, which can be used over and over again.

Within the init method, use setLayout(my Layout) in the example below to make your GridBagLayout the layout manager. Before each component is added to the drawing surface, its constraints must be set in the GridBag constraints variable. The following example sets the constraints on a button and then adds it to the applet.

```
Constraints.gridx=GridBagConstraints.RELATIVE;
myLayout.setConstaints(Button1,Constraints);
add(Button1);
```

Let's take a look at the constraints that can be applied and how we can use them to create our own layouts.

Constraints.gridx and Constraints.gridy

These constraints set the grid location that the component will be added to. The grid bag looks like a rectangular grid layout with the location 0,0 at the top-left of the drawing surface. We can then place components at any grid location we like, leaving gaps if we wish. Code 17-1 adds four buttons, with the result shown in Figure 17-1. Each button is placed on the grid according to the x and y locations defined in the constraint for the button. Notice that we do not need to define the number of rows and columns for the grid. The layout manager will work out the size of the grid from the location of the components it contains.

```
public void init(){
  setLayout(myLayout);
  Constraints.gridx=0;
  Constraints.gridy=0;
  myLayout.setConstraints(Button1,Constraints);
  add(Button1);
  Constraints.gridx=2;
  Constraints.gridy=0;
  myLayout.setConstraints(Button2,Constraints);
  add(Button2);
  Constraints.gridx=0;
  Constraints.gridy=1;
  myLayout.setConstraints(Button3,Constraints);
  add(Button3);
  Constraints.gridx=1;
```

```
    Constraints.gridy=1;
    myLayout.setConstraints(Button4,Constraints);
    add(Button4);
}
```

CODE 17-1

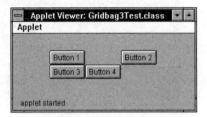

FIGURE 17-1

The x and y locations can be replaced with GridBagConstraints.RELATIVE. This constraint will place a component to the right of the previous component if specified in gridx, or below the previous component if specified in gridy. In order to get a horizontal stack of components you must specify a column address in the gridx constraint:

```
setLayout(myLayout);
Constraints.gridx=0;
Constraints.gridy=GridBagConstraints.RELATIVE;
myLayout.setConstraints(Button1,Constraints);
add(Button1);
myLayout.setConstraints(Button2,Constraints);
add(Button2);
myLayout.setConstraints(Button3,Constraints);
add(Button3);
```

CODE 17-2

Constraints.weightx and Constraints.weighty

In the previous example you will notice that the components are grouped together in the centre of the applet's drawing surface. You can use the weightx and weighty constraints to give the components more separation: these two constraints affect the spacing between columns and rows respectively. Normally the weights are specified as a number between 0 and

1.0, the larger the number the more space the component should get. If we specify both weights as 1.0 for all components then they will be laid out with maximum separation, as shown in Figure 17-2:

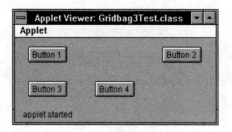

The separation for a row or column is related to the highest weight in that row or column. This means that in some circumstances even if you explicitly set the weight for one component, it may be overridden by other components in that row or column. Code 17-3 shows how to use weights to create columns with different degrees of separation.

```
public void init(){
  setLayout(myLayout);
  Constraints.weightx=0.0;
  Constraints.weighty=0.0;

  Constraints.gridx=2;
  Constraints.gridy=0;
  myLayout.setConstraints(Button2,Constraints);
  add(Button2);

  Constraints.weightx=0.5;
  Constraints.weighty=0.5;
  Constraints.gridx=1;
  Constraints.gridy=1;
  myLayout.setConstraints(Button4,Constraints);
  add(Button4);

  Constraints.weightx=1.0;
  Constraints.weighty=1.0;
  Constraints.gridx=0;
  Constraints.gridy=0;
  myLayout.setConstraints(Button1,Constraints);
  add(Button1);
  Constraints.gridx=0;
  Constraints.gridy=1;
```

```
myLayout.setConstraints(Button3,Constraints);
add(Button3);
Constraints.gridx=0;
Constraints.gridy=2;
myLayout.setConstraints(Button5,Constraints);
add(Button5);
Constraints.gridx=0;
Constraints.gridy=3;
myLayout.setConstraints(Button6,Constraints);
add(Button6);
}
```

CODE 17-3

The table below shows which buttons are affected by which weights. The appearance of the applet is shown in Figure 17-3.

Which Button	Weights	Separation	Is the Weight Overridden?
Button 2	Horizontal weight=0	Minimal separation	
	Vertical weight=1.0	Maximum separation	Overridden from button 1
Button 4	Horizontal weight=0.5	Medium separation	
	Vertical weight=1.0	Maximum separation	Overridden from button 1
Button 1, Button 3, Button 5, Button 6	Horizontal weight=1.0 Vertical weight=1.0	Maximum separation	

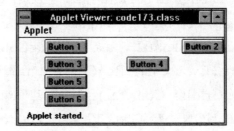

FIGURE 17-3

Constraints.gridwidthx and Constraints.gridheighty

These constraints allow a component to span multiple rows or columns. Be aware that if you specify that a component should span more than one column or row, the adjoining space must be clear of components. If there is a component in the adjoining row or column then the two will overlap, as shown in Figure 17-4. To make a component spread over two rows, set gridwidth to 2; to make it spread over two columns set the gridheight to 2.

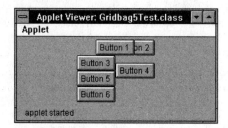

FIGURE 17-4

Note

In version 1.0 of Java you can only make a component spread over two columns if the component is in column 1.

Constraints.fill

Our examples of grid bag layout so far have allowed components' display areas to be just big enough to contain their text. If we want to make a component fill its grid cell then we can use the fill constraint. To make a component fill its cell horizontally, use GridBagConstraints.HORIZONTAL. To fill the cell vertically, use GridBagConstraints.VERTICAL, and to fill the cell completely use GridBagConstraints.BOTH. To turn filling off, use GridBagConstraints.NONE. In Code 17-4 we create three buttons using each of the possible constraints. The resulting applet is shown in Figure 17-5.

```
Constraints.fill=GridBagConstraints.BOTH;
Constraints.gridx=0;
Constraints.gridy=0;
myLayout.setConstraints(Button1,Constraints);
add(Button1);
Constraints.fill=GridBagConstraints.HORIZONTAL;
Constraints.gridx=0;
Constraints.gridy=2;
myLayout.setConstraints(Button5,Constraints);
add(Button5);
Constraints.fill=GridBagConstraints.VERTICAL;
Constraints.gridx=0;
Constraints.gridy=3;
myLayout.setConstraints(Button6,Constraints);
add(Button6);
```

CODE 17-4

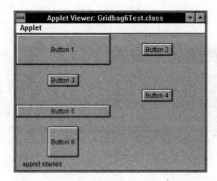

FIGURE 17-5

Constraints.ipadx, Constraints.ipady and Constraints.insets

The ipadx and ipady constraints allow you to specify that a component should be bigger than its default size. The ipadx constraint specifies how much wider on either side the component should be. Setting the ipadx value to 1 makes the component 2 pixels wider, one pixel on either side. The ipady constraint works in the same way to adjust the height of the component.

Constraints.insets

Insets determine the amount of space around a component added to the grid bag layout. You can specify the amount of space at the top, bottom, left or right all independently. Figure 17-6 shows a grid bag layout without weights or insets, while Figure 17-7 shows the effect of adding an inset to each component. Insets have to be defined using the AWT insets class, which is constructed using the "new" operator.

```
Constraints.insets=new  Insets(5,5,5,5)
```

The insets' parameters are:

1) Space above the component
2) Space to the left of the component
3) Space below the component
4) Space to the right of the component

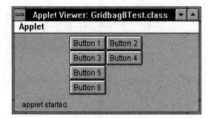

FIGURE 17-6

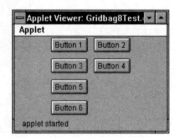

FIGURE 17-7

Constraints.anchor

When a component is added to the grid bag it could well be smaller than the display area allocated to it by the layout manager. Provided that it is a grid with weights greater than zero, it can be anchored to any point on the compass within its cell. The table below shows valid values for the anchor constraint, along with which weight needs to be greater than zero to allow the component to float to that compass point. Anchoring in the centre is the default setting.

GridBagConstraints.CENTER	Neither
GridBagConstraints.NORTH	weighty
GridBagConstraints.NORTHEAST	weighty and weightx
GridBagConstraints.EAST	weightx
GridBagConstraints.SOUTHEAST	weighty and weightx
GridBagConstraints.SOUTH	weighty
GridBagConstraints.SOUTHWEST	weightx and weighty
GridBagConstraints.WEST	weightx
GridBagConstraints.NORTHWEST	weightx and weighty

The following code shows how a button is added and anchored to the north, whilst all other buttons are anchored in the centre.

```
Constraints.weightx=1.0;
Constraints.weighty=0.0;

Constraints.gridx=0;
Constraints.gridy=0;
Constraints.anchor=GridBagConstraints.NORTH;
myLayout.setConstraints(Button1,Constraints);
add(Button1);

Constraints.anchor=GridBagConstraints.CENTER;
```

An example grid bag layout

The example program in Chapter 15 for scrollbars showed very small bars with no accompanying text. We would like to have the scrollbars as shown in Figure 17-8 – that is, with text for the functions of the bars.

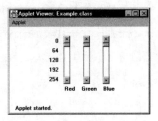

FIGURE 17-8

We will develop a grid bag layout to be used in the "init()" method: the "handleEvent" method can be stolen from Code 15-21. In the class definition, let's define the components we are going to use. We will use three scrollbars for the colour controls. The text will be added by using labels. In the code example below, we define some string constants for the value of the labels and assign these at construction time.

```
import java.awt.*;

public class code174 extends java.applet.Applet {

GridBagLayout Overall = new GridBagLayout();
GridBagConstraints gc = new GridBagConstraints();

Scrollbar redScroll=new Scrollbar(Scrollbar.VERTICAL,
                  0,
                  1,
                  0,255);
Scrollbar greenScroll=new Scrollbar(Scrollbar.VERTICAL,
                  0,
                  1,
                  0,255);
Scrollbar blueScroll=new Scrollbar(Scrollbar.VERTICAL,
                  0,
                  1,
                  0,255);

String    SideStrings[]={"0","64","128","192","255"};
String    BottomStrings[]={"Red","Green", "Blue"};

Label SideLabels[] = new Label[5];
Label BottomLabels[] = new Label[3];
```

Let's look at the applet layout one group component at a time. The five labels on the left of the scrollbars need to be in their own grid bag box. Although we will define the label to be right-aligned, we will also add a constraint on the grid bag so the label is anchored south-east. The labels below the scrollbars also need to be in their own boxes, but this time we align them in the centre. The code to create the labels and add them to the grid bag is shown below.

```
public void init(){

  setLayout(Overall);
    gc.gridx=0;
    gc.anchor=GridBagConstraints.SOUTHEAST;
    for (int i=0;i<5;i++){
      gc.gridy=i;
      SideLabels[i]=new Label(SideStrings[i],Label.RIGHT);
      Overall.setConstraints(SideLabels[i],gc);
      add(SideLabels[i]);

    }
    gc.gridy=6;
    gc.anchor=GridBagConstraints.NORTH;
    for (int i=0;i<3;i++){
      gc.gridx=i+1;
      BottomLabels[i]=new Label(BottomStrings[i],Label.CENTER);
      Overall.setConstraints(BottomLabels[i],gc);
      add(BottomLabels[i]);

    }
```

Each scrollbar will be in its own box and aligned in the centre. However, the scrollbars will need to reach from the top of the first label on the left to the bottom of the last label. To do this we need to set the gridheight constraint to be five for each scrollbar. However, this alone will not make the scrollbar reach from the top to the bottom. We need to set the fill constraint to VERTICAL to make the scrollbars fill the gap. We do not want the bars to fill out horizontally, however, since this will give them a fat appearance. Here is the code for adding the bars:

```
gc.gridx=1;
  gc.gridy=0;
  gc.gridheight=5;
  gc.anchor=GridBagConstraints.CENTER;
  gc.fill=GridBagConstraints.VERTICAL;
  Overall.setConstraints(redScroll,gc);
  add(redScroll);
  gc.gridx=2;
  Overall.setConstraints(greenScroll,gc);
  add(greenScroll);
  gc.gridx=3;
  Overall.setConstraints(blueScroll,gc);
  add(blueScroll);

}
```

If you do steal the "handleEvent()" method from Code 15-21, you will notice a problem. As the scrollbars are moved, the background colour changes, except for the colour of the labels. The labels have their own background colour. You can use the "setBackground" method to change the colour of the labels or you can use the fill constraint to make sure the labels fill their area, as in Figure 17-9.

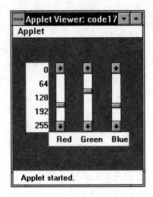

FIGURE 17-9

CHAPTER 18

Handling Mouse Events

We have already seen how to handle mouse events when the event refers to an action within an AWT component. However, events are generated whenever the mouse is moved, or when any of the buttons is pressed regardless of the location of the mouse. Your applet can catch these events and use them to make your applet even more interactive.

mouseDown and mouseUp

Whenever the mouse button is pressed, a mouseDown action is generated. Conversely, when the button is released, a mouseUp action is generated. These two actions are separated so you can detect when the mouse button is held down. This allows you to drag components or objects around the screen whilst the mouse button is pressed. You can then detect when the button is released and place the object on the applet's surface. To catch when a mouse button is pressed you add a "mouseDown()" method to your applet:

```
public boolean mouseDown(Event evtd, int x, int y){
  System.out.println("Mouse Down");
  return true;
}
```

The method receives an event plus integers representing the location of the mouse when the button was pressed. These two integers follow the normal convention for co-ordinates in the AWT, with the origin at the top-left. The Event variable contains detailed information about the mouseDown event, and you can use it to test which mouse button was pressed:

```
if (evtd.metaDown() == false)
  System.out.println("Left Button");
else
  System.out.println("Right Button");
```

Note

The Apple Macintosh mouse has only one mouse button, and a right mouse click is emulated by pressing the meta button at the same time as the mouse button. This explains why the test for the right mouse button looks for the meta key being pressed.

To detect the mouse button being released, add a similar method but replace the method name with mouseUp().

```
public boolean mouseUp(Event evtd, int x, int y){
  System.out.println("Mouse Down");
  return true;
}
```

If you have user-interface components on your drawing surface, they will still receive an Action event but the mouseDown or mouseUp event will not be generated.

Tracking the mouse

Four different events can be trapped to detect mouse movement. A "mouseMove" event is generated whenever the mouse is moved without the button being pressed. If a mouse button is pressed, a mouseDrag event will be generated. The number of events that your applet will receive whilst the mouse is moving will depend on the speed that the user moves the mouse. Slow movements will generate an event for each pixel that the mouse moves through. Fast movements, however, will only generate events for some of the pixels moved over, but you will get a value for the resting place of the mouse. To use the mouse tracking functions, add a mouseMove or mouseDrag method to your applet:

```
public boolean mouseMove(Event evtd, int x, int y){
  System.out.println("Mouse move"+evtd);
  return true;
}

public boolean mouseDrag(Event evtd, int x, int y){
  System.out.println("Mouse move"+evtd);
  return true;
}
```

Two other mouse methods are worth a mention – mouseEnter and mouseExit. These methods are called when the mouse enters or exits your applet. You can use them if you need to know if the mouse is in your applet or elsewhere on the screen.

```
public boolean mouseEnter(Event evtd, int x, int y){
  System.out.println("Mouse Enter"+evtd);
  return true;
}

public boolean mouseExit(Event evtd, int x, int y){
  System.out.println("Mouse Exit"+evtd);
  return true;
}
```

An example mouse-tracking applet

To tie together all the mouse methods, let's look at an example. The applet shown in Code 18-1 implements a "mouseDown()" method, a "mouseMove()" method and a "mouseDrag()" method. The applet is quite simple – it draws a square on the applet and manipulates it with the mouse. A left mouse click will increase its size; a right mouse click will decrease the size. Moving the mouse will cause the square to rotate around its centre. Moving the mouse with a button held down will cause the shape to follow the mouse. An example of the output is shown in Figure 18-1.

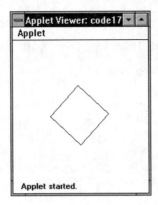

FIGURE 18-1

Let's walk through the code. The first thing that our class does is initialise some variable to hold current values for the position of the shape and its current rotation. The next section on Object Oriented Programming will show better ways of doing this, but for now we shall hold these values in our applet class. We are going to store the position of the corners of the shape in a Polygon class – the "init()" method creates an initial shape at (100,100) with zero rotation.

In the "make()" method we store the basic shape to be drawn in two integer arrays. In order to get the final shape, each corner will need to be first scaled to give its new size. Each point will then be rotated and finally translated to the current position on the applet surface. To scale the point, the x and y locations are multiplied by the Size variable. We rotate the shape around its centre using the following equations:

```
newx= oldx * Cosine(Theta) - oldy * Sine(Theta)
newy= oldx * Sine(Theta) + oldy * Cosine(Theta);
```

Notice that the shape is defined with its centre at location (0,0). This makes the calculation for rotation much easier. Whilst calculating the rotation, we take a temporary copy of the x location and use that for calculating the new value of y. If we don't do this then the value of x will have changed before it is used to calculate the new value of y. Finally we translate the shape to its proper location by adding the current position of the mouse to each co-ordinate.

The "paint()" method simply has to draw the polygon using the "drawPolygon" method introduced in the first section. Each of the mouse methods alters the current value of one of the controlling variables and then creates a new polygon using the "make()" method. They all end with a call to "repaint()" to update the applet's surface.

```java
import java.awt.*;

public class code175 extends java.applet.Applet {
  int Lastx=0;
  double CurrentTheta =0.0;
  int Currentx=100;
  int Currenty=100;
  Polygon points;;
  double Step=Math.PI/180;
  double Size=1.0;

  public void init(){
    points=make(,0.0);

  }

  public Polygon make(double theta){
    int x[]={-25,25,25,-25,-25};
    int y[]={-25,-25,25,25,-25};


    int tmpx;
    double sin=Math.sin(theta);
    double cos=Math.cos(theta);
    for (int i=0;i<5;i++){
      x[i]=(int)(Size*x[i]);
      y[i]=(int)(Size*y[i]);
      tmpx=x[i];
      x[i]=(int)((cos*x[i])-(y[i]*sin));
      y[i]=(int)((tmpx*sin)+(cos*y[i]));

      x[i]=x[i]+Currentx;
      y[i]=y[i]+Currenty;
    }
    return new Polygon(x,y,5);
  }

  public void paint(Graphics g){
    g.drawPolygon(points);
  }
```

```
public boolean mouseDrag(Event evtd, int x, int y){
  Currentx=x;
  Currenty=y;
  points = make( CurrentTheta);
  repaint();
  return true;
}

public boolean mouseMove(Event evtd, int x, int y){
  CurrentTheta=CurrentTheta+0.0087266;
  if (CurrentTheta >2*Math.PI)
    CurrentTheta=0.0;
  points = make( CurrentTheta);
  repaint();
  return true;
}

public boolean mouseDown(Event evtd, int x, int y){
  if (evtd.metaDown() == false)
    Size=Size+0.25;
  else
    Size=Size -0.25;
  repaint();
  return true;
}
}
```

CODE 18-1

Other information about the mouse event

There are a couple of other potentially useful pieces of information about the mouse clicks that are delivered along with the mouseDown event. The first is a variable called "when". This gives an indication of when the mouseDown event happened. This is really only useful for finding the time the "mouseDown" event happened in relation to the last "mouseDown" event. The variable is a long integer and there seem to be 1000 iterations of the variable every second.

The second variable available to the "mouseDown" event counts the number of simultaneous clicks on the mouse button leading up to this event. The count is cleared by a pause in the clicks greater than the time to clear the double-click buffer. That is, if a user double-clicks the mouse button then the count will be two. If the user treble-clicks the button at the same rate as needed for a double-click, the count will be 3. Because the variable is an integer, the maximum number of clicks that can be counted is around two million. You will however have a very tired user if you require them to perform that many clicks! The variable is known as "clickCount". The example method below illustrates using these two variables, albeit in a very trivial way.

```
public boolean mouseDown(Event evtd, int x, int y){
   System.out.println(""+evtd.clickCount+"    "+(evtd.when-Last));
   Last=evtd.when;
   return true;
}
```

CODE 18-2

Handling Keyboard Events

Just as mouse events can be handled through "mouseDown()" and "mouseUp()" methods, keyboard events can be handled through "keyDown()" and "keyUp()". Outline methods are shown below:

```
public boolean keyDown(Event evt, int Key){
   System.out.println("Down "+Key+"   "+evt);
   return false;
}

public boolean keyUp(Event evt, int Key){
   System.out.println("Up  "+Key+"   "+evt);
   return false;
}
```

For the numeric and character keys it turns out that the "Key" parameter is actually the ASCII value of the key that was pressed. All other keys have a code as shown in the table below.

F1 - F12	These represent the function keys along the top of a normal IBM-type keyboard
DOWN, UP	The Down and Up arrow keys
LEFT, RIGHT	The Left and Right arrow keys
HOME, END	The Home and End keys from the numeric keypad
PGUP, PGDN	The Page Up and Page Down keys

You can detect when the key press is accompanied by the Shift or Control key. If the user is using a Sun keyboard, you can also detect if the Meta key is held down. Code 19-1 shows simple ways of using the key presses and detecting the Control, Shift and Meta keys.

```java
import java.awt.*;
public class code191 extends java.applet.Applet {
  public boolean keyDown(Event evt, int Key){
    if (evt.controlDown() == true)
      System.out.println("Control Down");
    if (evt.metaDown() == true)
      System.out.println("Meta Down");
    if (evt.shiftDown() == true)
      System.out.println("Shift Down");

    switch (Key){
    case Event.F1:System.out.println("F1 Pressed");
      break;
    case Event.F2:System.out.println("F2 Pressed");
      break;
    case Event.F3:System.out.println("F3 Pressed");
      break;
    case Event.F4:System.out.println("F4 Pressed");
      break;
    case Event.F5:System.out.println("F5 Pressed");
      break;
    case Event.F6:System.out.println("F6 Pressed");
      break;
    case Event.F7:System.out.println("F7 Pressed");
      break;
    case Event.F8:System.out.println("F8 Pressed");
      break;
    case Event.F9:System.out.println("F9 Pressed");
      break;
    case Event.F10:System.out.println("F10 Pressed");
      break;
    case Event.F11:System.out.println("F11 Pressed");
      break;
    case Event.F12:System.out.println("F12 Pressed");
      break;
    }
    return false;
  }
}
```

CODE 19-1

The ASCII representation of characters

ASCII is an acronym for American Standard Code for Information Interchange. This is the usual way that characters are represented within computers. Although the code has been superseded by UNICODE in Java for the representation of characters in strings, the values from a standard keyboard are still in the ASCII code. This code represents every alpha-numeric key on the keyboard as a code between 0 and 127. The table below gives the values for most of the keys on the keyboard. Values below 32 are used for Control keys and can in some cases be generated by holding the Control key down at the same time as a character key. For instance, pressing the "m" key whilst holding down the Control key will generate a value of 13.

ASCII	Key	ASCII	Key	ASCII	Key	ASCII	Key
32	Space	56	8	80	P	104	h
33	!	57	9	81	Q	105	I
34	"	58	:	82	R	106	j
35	#	59	;	83	S	107	k
36	$	60	<	84	T	108	l
37	%	61	=	85	U	109	m
38	&	62	>	86	V	110	n
39	'	63	?	87	W	111	o
40	(	64	@	88	X	112	p
41	)	65	A	89	Y	113	q
42	*	66	B	90	Z	114	r
43	+	67	C	91	[	115	s
44	,	68	D	92	\	116	t
45	-	69	E	93	]	117	u
46	.	70	F	94	^	118	v
47	/	71	G	95	_	119	w
48	0	72	H	96	'	120	x
49	1	73	I	97	a	121	y
50	2	74	J	98	b	122	z
51	3	75	K	99	c	123	{
52	4	76	L	100	d	124		
53	5	77	M	101	e	125	}
54	6	78	N	102	f	126	~
55	7	79	O	103	g	127	DEL

**PART
C**

OOP and All That

What is Object Oriented Programming?

So what is this Object Oriented Programming (OOP) all about, what makes it so powerful and how can you use it to add functionality to your applets? If you have never programmed a computer before then you should find it the most natural way to program and will have a hard time to think why computers were ever programmed any other way. If you are used to non-Object Oriented Programming languages then you need to change your way of thinking just a little bit. Many of the features you have come to rely on are still there, some have slightly different names with new features and there are one or two new ideas to understand.

If you have come to Java from one of the other OOP languages (e.g. C++) then all of this is going to be very familiar. However, there are going to be things you have used often that simply don't exist in Java. You might want to skip over most of the start of this section and pick up again in Chapter 22 where we deal with the AWT and its relation to OOP techniques.

To put it simply, Object Oriented Programming makes the programmer think about the objects that are needed in order for the program to work. The objects in an OOP program are exactly the same as objects that you might come across in real life. Of course, it is much easier to create a virtual object than the real thing! With that in mind, let's look at a real object and explore the ideas of Object Oriented Programming.

If we think about a really simple object, such as a rectangle, we can begin to look at the properties of the object. A rectangle has a number of defining features that it must have to be called a rectangle:

- It must have 4 sides.
- The angle between adjacent sides must be 90°.
- Each parallel side must be equal in length.

However, for a rectangle there is one feature that can change without interfering with the defining features of the rectangle: the length of either pair of parallel sides.

Once we have defined our virtual rectangle there are a number of things we can do to the rectangle without actually changing it.

- We can change where in space the rectangle is.
- If we have a rectangle in 3-dimensional space we can change the roll, pitch and yaw of the plane of the rectangle, as shown in Figure 20-1.

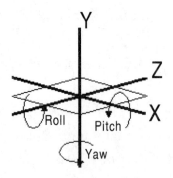

FIGURE 20-1

Once we have defined what a rectangle is and exactly what we can do to it, we can use that rectangle to build more and more complex shapes. If we create six rectangles and join them together correctly, we can create a rectangular box; with more we could model a 3-dimensional surface. What's more, once we have created a shape out of rectangles we could use those shapes to create other shapes. We can use our 3-dimensional rectangles as building blocks to create complex shapes.

This is how Object Oriented Programming works. We define a set of simple program objects. We define the exact specifications of what each object can do and how the objects can be modified. We then use these objects to create other objects for the entire program. However, the actual process of creating a Java program is usually slightly different. You need to identify the objects in the program, find relationships between the objects, and arrange them into hierarchies. We will leave the design of a Java program until later in this section, and for the moment concentrate on the techniques and vocabulary of OOPs.

Let us begin by defining a rectangle using Java. As we have already stated, all rectangles have properties in common. We can think of all possible rectangles as belonging to the same class of objects – the concept of class is at the root of OOPs. To create a class we need to provide it with a constructor; that is, a method that tells the class about the defining features that can change between instances of the class.

For rectangles, the defining features that change are the lengths of the two sets of parallel sides. A rectangle will always have four sides and four 90° internal angles: these are inherent properties and will never change.

In Code 20-1 we define a new class, "Rectangle", and create a constructor method for that class. Notice that the constructor has exactly the same name as the class. This constructor method is called whenever we want to create a new instance of the class. You can think of the constructor method as initialising the class and setting any initial values that the class will need. The constructor is similar to, but not the same as, the "init" method of applets. This class should be stored in a file "Rectangle.java". The constructor we have defined takes integer arguments and so defines our rectangles to be integer entities. That is, the rectangle can only have sides whose length can be defined by an integer. Note that although the constructor is defined as "public", it does not have a returning type. For now, we can define all our classes as public – this means that the class is "visible" to any other Java class. After you have entered the code into an editor and saved the file, you will need to compile it in the normal way using the "javac" compiler. This will produce a class file called "Rectangle.class".

```
class Rectangle {
  public int Side1;
  public int Side2;

  public  Rectangle(int Length_of_side_1, int Length_of_side_2){
    Side1= Length_of_side_1;
    Side2= Length_of_side_2;
  }
}
```

CODE 20-1

Now we have the "Rectangle.class", we can use a rectangle in another class. For instance, we might create our rectangle in the init method of an applet:

```
public class  UseRectangle extends java.applet.Applet{
  public void init(){
    Rectangle myRectangle=new Rectangle(100,100);
  }
}
```

CODE 20-2

When we create a new rectangle using the new operator, the constructor method of the rectangle class is executed. In this case the constructor copies the parameter of the constructor to the rectangle's "side" variables. We can create as many rectangles as we like with different sizes. Each rectangle we create is called an instance of the class rectangle. Each instance of rectangle is an entity by itself and in no way interacts with other instances of rectangles. There are techniques to link instances together, but we will not deal with them here. Because we have defined the variables of the rectangle to be public, the creator of the rectangle has access to the variables of the class through the dot notation we have used before. Thus, in the applet, "myRectangle.Side1" refers to the "Side1" variable of the myRectangle instance of the rectangle class. Our rectangle class has no access to its creator's variables or methods, nor does it have access to other instances of rectangle.

The rectangle method shown here is really useless: we can create it but we can not do anything with it. We might want to add methods to the rectangle which will allow users of the class to find out features of the rectangle. The features we are interested in might be the surface area or the length of the perimeter. We can add some methods to the rectangle that do the calculations we want. These calculations will use the same methods for all instances of rectangles, regardless of the value of the rectangles' variables. The example in Code 20-3 shows methods for the perimeter and the area.

```
class Rectangle {
  public int Side1;
  public int Side2;

  public Rectangle(int Length_of_side_1, int Length_of_side_2){
    Side1= Length_of_side_1;
    Side2= Length_of_side_2;
  }

  public int perimeter(){
    return (2*(Side1+Side2));
  }

  public int area(){
    return(Side1*Side2);
  }
}
```

CODE 20-3

We can now create rectangles and calculate their important features using our rectangle class by using the dot notation to call the area and parameter methods of our class. Notice that the details of calculating the properties of our rectangle are hidden from the user of the class. If we change the methods then all users of this class will be affected without having to change the users' codes. The following example shows how to create rectangles and use the rectangle methods.

```
Rectangle myRectangle = new Rectangle(10,2);
Rectangle myRectangle = new Rectangle(10.2, 8.6);
int Area = myRectangle.area();
int parimeter = myRectangle.perimeter();
```

The rectangle we have created is limited to integer values, although the second example above passes floating-point values to the constructor. These floating point values will be "cast" into integer values when the constructor is called. If we wanted to create a rectangle with non-integer side lengths, we could create a new class called, say, "FloatingRectangle", with its own methods and internal values. However, Object Oriented Programming provides us with a much more powerful technique called "Method Overloading". This technique allows us to create methods with the same name but different parameters. The type of the parameters passed to the method are taken into account by the compiler to make sure the correct method is used. Code 20-4 shows method overloading in action.

```
class Rectangle {
  int Side1;
  int Side2;
  float fSide1;
  float fSide2;

  public Rectangle(int Length_of_side_1, int Length_of_side_2){
    Side1= Length_of_side_1;
    Side2= Length_of_side_2;
  }

  public Rectangle(float Length_of_side_1, float Length_of_side_2){
    fSide1= Length_of_side_1;
    fSide2= Length_of_side_2;
  }

  public int integerperimeter(){
    return (2*(Side1+Side2));
  }
```

```
public int integerarea(){
  return(Side1*Side2);
}

public float floatingperimiter(){
  return (2*(fSide1+fSide2));
}

public float floatingarea(){
  return(fSide1*fSide2);
  }
}
```

CODE 20-4

In our new "Rectangle" class we have two constructors called Rectangle –
one takes two integer arguments, and the other takes two floating-point
arguments. When we create an integer, the type of the arguments determines
which constructor method is called and so which of the class's variables is
initialised. However, when we want to use the "area" and "perimeter"
methods, Java does not use the return type of the methods to determine
which method is used for the calculation. We have to create two methods –
one for floating-point numbers and one for integers.

```
Rectangle myRectangle = new Rectangle(10,10);
Rectangle mySecondRectangle = new Rectangle(7.5, 8.6);

int Area1 = myRectangle.integerarea();
float Area2 = mySecondRectangle.floatingarea();
```

When we use the methods for calculating the area we must ensure that the
correct method is used for the type of variable we are using. The compiler
will complain if we try and use the wrong method with the wrong variable
type. If we create an instance of an integer rectangle and then try and
calculate the floating point area, no errors will be generated but the result of
the calculation will be wrong. However, if we create our classes with care,
we can take care of this eventuality. Code 20-5 shows a class that records its
type for each instance. This record is used to make sure correct values are
returned regardless of its initialisation. The type of the rectangle is stored in

one of two Booleans. When the methods for calculating the area or perimeter are called, these Booleans are used to determine the type of calculation that will be performed.

```
class Rectangle {
  int Side1;
  int Side2;
  float fSide1;
  float fSide2;

  boolean integertype=false;
  boolean floatingtype=false;

  public Rectangle(int Length_of_side_1, int Length_of_side_2){
    Side1= Length_of_side_1;
    Side2= Length_of_side_2;
    integertype=true;
  }

  public Rectangle(float Length_of_side_1, float Length_of_side_2){
    fSide1= Length_of_side_1;
    fSide2= Length_of_side_2;
    floatingtype= true;
  }

  public int integerperimeter(){
    if (integertype ==true)
      return (2*(Side1+Side2));
    else
      return((int)(2.0*(fSide1+fSide2)));
  }

  public float floatingperimeter(){
    if (floatingtype ==true)
      return (2*(fSide1+fSide2));
    else
      return(2*(Side1+Side2));
  }
}
```

CODE 20-5

Our rectangle class creates rectangles that have no location in space; we do not know their co-ordinates or their orientation. If we wanted to add these features, we could simply add methods and variables to our rectangle class to handle our new requirements. But this would mean changing the source code of our rectangle class, a class we know works and is without bugs. If we added new code, we could conceivably break the old code by inserting some subtle bug. It would be nice if we could add the new features without changing the old code. If you like, it would be nice if our new code could "inherit" the features of the "Rectangle" class.

We can do this in Java by making "Rectangle" a sub-class of our new class. In terms of OOP programming, we extend the functionality of the class "Rectangle" with a new class "LocatedRectangle":

```
class LocatedRectangle extends Rectangle{
  int myOriginX;
  int myOriginY;

  public LocatedRectangle(int OriginX, int OriginY, int Width, int Height){
    super(Width, Height);
    myOriginX=OriginX;
    myOriginY=OriginY;
  }

  public LocatedRectangle(Point Origin, float Width, float Height){
    super(Width, Height);
    myOriginX=Origin.x;
    myOriginY=Origin.y;
  }

  public Point Origin(){
    return (new Point(myOriginX,myOriginY));
  }

}
```

CODE 20-6

In our constructor methods we make a call to our parent class (the "Rectangle" class) by using the "super()" operator. This sets up the width and height variables in our parent class. However, notice that the "Origin()" method returns a type "Point". We have not imported the AWT library (and don't want to in this case), so we will need to define our own point class. Our example below defines a point with integer values – we haven't bothered with the floating-point methods for now.

```
class Point{
  int x;
  int y;
  public Point(int x, int y){
    this.x=x;
    this.y=y;
  }
}
```

Because our new class extends the old "Rectangle" class, any users of the "LocatedRectangle" have access not only to the new class's methods but also to the old class's methods; we say it has inherited all the properties of its parent.

```
LocatedRectangle myRectangle = new LocatedRectangle(new
point(10,20),50.5,100.3);
  point Origin = myRectangle.origin();
  float Area = myRectangle.area();
```

When trying to locate a method in a class tree, Java starts at the bottom and moves up until it finds a method that matches the name and argument types of the method it is looking for. So Java looks first in the "LocatedRectangle" class for a method called "area". It will not find one, so it then looks in that class's parent, "Rectangle", and so on, until a match is found. If no match is found then a compiler error is generated.

Of course, the new "LocatedRectangle" class only defines the origin of the rectangle, and does not define anything about the rotation of the rectangle. We could add new constructor methods that define the rotation of the rectangle about its origin, or we could define a new class that extends the "LocatedRectangle" class to add the new functionality:

```
class RotatedRectangle extends LocatedRectangle{
  double myRotation;
  int x1,x2,x3,x4;
  int y1,y2,y3,y4;
  public RotatedRectangle(int OriginX, int OriginY, double Rotation, int
Height, int Width){
    super(OriginX, OriginY,Height,Width);
    myRotation=Rotation;
    CalculateCorners(OriginX, OriginY, Rotation,Height,Width);
  }
```

```
    private void CalculateCorners(int OriginX, int OriginY, double
Rotation,int Height, int Width){
    double sin=Math.sin(Rotation);
    double cos=Math.cos(Rotation);

    x1=OriginX;
    y1=OriginY;
    x2=(int)(cos*Width)+x1;
    y2=(int)(Width*sin)+y1;
    x3=(int)((cos*Width)-(Height*sin))+x1;
    y3=(int)((Width*sin)+(cos*Height))+y1;
    x4=(int)(-Height*sin)+x1;
    y4=(int)(cos*Height)+y1;
    }

    public void getPoints(Point points[]){

    points[0]=new Point(x1,y1);
    points[1]=new Point(x2,y2);
    points[2]=new Point(x3,y3);
    points[3]=new Point(x4,y4);

    }
  }
```

CODE 20-7

Notice in our example that we have created a constructor method that only deals with integer heights and widths: if we wanted to distribute this class for others to use, we would either have to make this restriction known in the documentation, or create the constructors needed for the other cases. Our "RotatedRectangle" makes use of the point class defined earlier. The getPoints method transfers our local corners into an array of points.

We have defined a method CalculateCorners to work out the location of the rectangle in two-dimensional space, which is defined as private. Making a method private means that only the other methods in this class can see the method. Any class that creates instances of the "RotatedRectangle" can not use the CalculateCorners method; we have hidden the implementation of the class from any of its users. There is no reason for classes that use the "RotatedRectangle" class to call the method that calculates the corner locations, so we hide it.

This is common practice in Object Oriented Programming, which makes the distribution of class libraries more efficient. The interface to the class library is published for other programmers to use, but the implementation is hidden. Programmers using the class library can override any of the methods that have been published. The user can extend any of the classes but can not change the workings of the original library.

Just to round things off, here is an applet that uses our rectangle class library in a very rudimentary way:

```
public class UseRotatedRectangle extends java.applet.Applet{
  public void init(){
    Point myPoints[]=new Point[5];
    RotatedRectangle myRectangle=new RotatedRectangle(100,100,Math.PI/
2.0,200,300);
    System.out.println(""+myRectangle.integerperimeter());
    myRectangle.getPoints(myPoints);
    for (int i=0;i<4;i++)
      System.out.println(""+myPoints[i].x+"   "+myPoints[i].y);
  }
}
```

CODE 20-7

Instance parents

As we have seen, when we extend a class the new class inherits all the properties of its parent: it inherits all its public variables and methods. However, when a class is used by another class it becomes in effect a child of the class that uses it. This is different to extending a class: we are creating a reference to an instance of the class. In Code 20-7 we created an instance of a "RotatedRectangle" and thus had access to the "getPoints()" method. The class that creates the instance of the child has access to all the public methods and variables of the child. The child, however, does not have direct access to the methods and variables of its parent. However, the creator can allow its instance children access to its variables. A special variable called "this" is implemented in Java and refers to the current object; that is, it refers to the object in which the code word "this" is used. Since the "this" operator refers to the current class or object, if the parent passes the "this" reference to its children, the children can have access to the parent through the dot operator. We can pass this reference to the class either in the constructor or in some other method of the class. In Code 20-8 the class "Accessor" is expecting a reference to its parent in the constructor method:

```
public class Accessed extends java.applet.Applet{
  int A=0;
  Accessor myArray[] = new Accessor[10];
  public void init(){
    for (int i=0;i<10;i++)
      myArray[i]=new Accessor(this);
    System.out.println(A);
  }
}

class Accessor{
  Accessed myParent;
  public Accessor(Accessed Parent){
    myParent=Parent;
    Change();
  }

  private void Change(){
    myParent.A++;
  }
}
```

Code 20-8

In this case we create a class "Accessor" that has access to its creator through the variable myParent. The constructor for "Accessor" needs a reference in its parameter list. When we create an instance of the Accessor class, we pass it a reference to the parent using the "this" reference. Our "Accessed" applet creates an array of ten "Accessor" classes. As each is constructed, it makes a call to the private "Change()" method. The "Change()" method increments the parent's variable A. After all have been created, the "A" variable has a value of 10.

Once an instance class has access to its parent's public data, it can also have access to the parent's other children's public data. Code 20-9 shows an "Accessor" class that has its own variable "B". When the class is constructed it expects a handle on its parent and a number indicating where in the array it is. The constructor method then increments the "B" variable of the other previous instances of the class.

```
public class Accessed209 extends java.applet.Applet{

  int A=0;
  Accessor myArray[] = new Accessor[10];
  public void init(){
    for (int i=0;i<10;i++)
      myArray[i]=new Accessor(this,i);
    System.out.println(A);
    for (int i=0;i<10;i++)
      System.out.println(""+myArray[i].B);
  }
}

class Accessor{
  Accessed209 myParent;
  int B=0;
  public Accessor(Accessed209 Parent, int MyNumber){
    myParent=Parent;
    for (int i=0; i<MyNumber;i++){
      myParent.myArray[i].B++;
    }
  }
}
```

CODE 20-9

Static data: Sharing information between instances of a class

There is a method to share data throughout all instances of a class. If a variable is defined as "static", then only one instance of that variable is created and shared amongst all instances. In Code 20-10, a simple class "StaticTest" is defined with one static variable initialised to zero. After 10 instances are created in the applet, just one instance of the "B" variable is set to 10. After this, all instances of the "B" variable have a value of 10.

```
public class UseStatic extends java.applet.Applet{

  StaticTest myArray[] = new StaticTest[10];
  public void init(){
    for (int i=0;i<10;i++)
      myArray[i]= new StaticTest();
```

```
    myArray[4].B=10;
    for (int i=0;i<10;i++)
      System.out.println(""+myArray[i].B);
  }
}

class StaticTest{
  static int B=0;
  public StaticTest(){
  }

}
```

CODE 20-10

Notice that it does not matter if you create one instance of the "StaticTest" class and adjust the value of the "B" variable – all other instances created later will have the new value. Furthermore, if any methods within the "StaticTest" class change the static variable, it will be changed across all instances.

As well as static variables, you can also have static methods. These methods are common across all instances of a class. Any changes made by a static method will be made across all instances of that class. However, static methods can only make changes to static variables within the class or variables local to the static method. Code 20-11 shows a static method within a class. This class doesn't do very much, but gives an example of the syntax.

```
class StaticMethodTest{
  static int B=0;
  public StaticMethodTest(){
  }

  public static void ChangeIt(){
    int C=30;
    C=40;
    System.out.println("C=  "+C);
    B=20;
  }

}
```

CODE 20-11

Note

Sharing data through all instances of a class creates global data. Within computer science, global data is somewhat frowned upon. This is because it has been shown that global data can very easily generate errors in your program. However, used with great care, you might find sharing data between instances of a class useful, as long as you are aware of the problems it can cause.

Object Oriented design

Designing a program in an Object Oriented environment is a process of iteration. A first draft design is produced and then continually refined before the final design emerges. It is always good practice with any project to produce a specification of the program before any coding takes place. Write this specification with as much detail as possible, giving full details of exactly what you expect the program to do. In an Object Oriented environment you will take this specification and look for suitable candidates for objects. You will then take each of the objects and define the behaviour and the attributes for each of them. At this point you may find relationships between the classes you have defined, and so may be able to organise them into hierarchies.

Some specifications for programs will suggest objects almost immediately as you read them. Usually this happens if the program is somehow modelling the real world, for instance a program handling ticket sales for a cinema multiplex may have a class such as "customer" and another "film". Other specifications will be much more obscure, with few clues as to the best candidates for classes.

Let's take a specification as an example, and generate a design and finally some code to implement our specification. Suppose we wanted to create a program to handle our music collection. The music collection probably has CDs and cassette tapes and possibly some older vinyl records. Any item in our collection will have a title and an artist plus a track listing. We might want to include some other details such as the music label, possibly the producer of music and so on.

At first sight, it looks as if we have some good candidates for objects in the shape of CDs, tapes and records. We could create a class for each of these types of object; each one would keep a record of its title, its track listing, producer, and so on. But wait, what's the difference between each of these types of object? In reality, the only difference is that cassette tapes (and vinyl records) have two sides, whereas the CD only has one. What we really need is a class of objects that embodies all the common characteristics of these objects, which can then be extended (where needed) for the special cases. So we could define a class of object named MusicRecording which holds the title of the recording, the artists, the producer and the label name. We can then extend this class to produce a CD class, a Cassette class and a Vinyl class. Figure 20-2 shows our hierarchy.

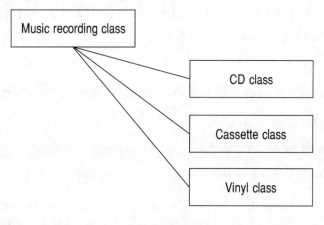

FIGURE 20-2

Now we have defined a simple class hierarchy, we need to know what these classes are going to do.

Obviously, we will need some method to set the data the objects are going to hold, and some accessor methods to retrieve these values. Which of this data has to be filled at construction time? Is there any data which, if it were not present, would mean the instance of the class would be meaningless? It would seem that it would be meaningless to have a music object without a title, though probably all the other data are optional and so can be set at a later time in the life of the object. Those items of data which are common between each of the objects should be held at the top level of the class hierarchy, the MusicRecording class. The question occurs as to where would be the best place to hold the track listing. For a CD, each track has a track number and a title, while for the cassette and vinyl record the track listing has a track number, a title and an associated side. For our first step let's hold the track listing at the top of the hierarchy and then hold the association of the side number at the lower levels.

Our first-level design might look something like this:

For the MusicRecording class:
- We will need a constructor which sets the title of the recording.
- We will need methods to set and retrieve the performer's name, the record label, and the track list.

For the CD Class:
- We need to override the constructor method but no others.

For the Cassette class:
- We will need to override the constructor method and the methods concerned with setting and retrieving the track listing.

Let us first create the MusicRecording class with its constructor. The title, performer and producer will be stored in strings, with the title being set in the constructor.

```
class MusicRecording {
  private String Title;
  private String Performer;
  private String Producer;
```

```
public MusicRecording(String newTitle){
  Title = newTitle;
}

}
```

We can now add the methods to set and access the performer and producer data. We could leave out any methods to access the values of producer and performer and allow the creator of the MusicRecording class to access these values through the dot operator. However, at a later date we might want to change the method for storing these values – if we have accessor methods we can change the implementation without having to change any of the classes that use the Recording class.

```
public void SetPerformer(String newPerformer){
  Performer=newPerformer;
}

public void SetProducer(String newProducer){
  Producer = newProducer;
}

public String getPerformer(){
  return(Performer);
}
public String getProducer(){
  return(Producer);
}
```

We now need to turn our attention to the storage of the track listing – we will store them as an array of strings. This means we need to define the maximum number of tracks that can be stored in our class. It makes sense that the method we create for storing the strings should do something sensible if the maximum number of tracks is exceeded. Our method will return a Boolean value, true if the strings were stored successfully and false if the storage was unsuccessful. Our initial class will be able to store only 10 tracks. Add the Tracklist to the variable list of the method:

```
String TrackList[]=new String [10];
```

Now add the method to the class definition:

```
public boolean SetTrackList(String newTrackList[]){
  if (newTrackList.length > 10)
    return false;
  for (int i=0; I<newTrackLength.length;i++){
    TrackList[i]=new String();
    TrackList[i]=newTrackList[i];
  }
  return true;
}
```

We will also need methods to get the track list and to get an individual track number:

```
public String[] getTrackList(){
  return(TrackList);
}

public String getTrack(int Tracknumber){
  return (TrackList[Tracknumber]);
}
```

Our initial "MusicRecording" class is now complete. We can now create the other classes that will extend the "MusicRecording" class's capabilities, starting with the CD class. This class does nothing new, but if we find later that we need to add new capabilities, we can add them here without major upheaval to the "MusicRecording" class.

```
class CD extends MusicRecording{
  public CD(String Title){
    super(Title);
  }
}
```

For the vinyl records and cassettes the class constructor method will be the same as the CD class, but we will need to override the setTrack List method. This method will need to take two arguments, the track list and an accompanying array to give the side information. The array for storing the side information will be an integer array allowing for double albums and cassettes. That is, the A side of cassette 1 will be represented by the number

1, the B side by the number 2. The A side of cassette 2 will be number 3 and the B side number 4.

```
class Cassette extends MusicRecording{
  int SideInformation[] = new int[10];
  public Cassette(String Title){
    super(Title);
  }

  public boolean SetTrackList(String newTrackList[], int
newSideInformation[]){
    if (newTrackList.length > 10)
      return false;
    for (int i=0; i<newTrackList.length;i++){
      TrackList[i]=new String();
      TrackList[i]=newTrackList[i];
      SideInformation= newSideInformation[i];
    }
    return true;
  }
}
```

We will also need to override the getTrackList method, which will need to return the name of the tracks and the track siding list. We could create two methods, one for the track listing and one for the side listing, but this would mean we would need to treat cassettes and vinyl records differently to CDs. Our original specification was flawed: we really need an object to hold an instance of a track, holding the title and the side information. We will need to define the new class and go back to our previous classes to see how they change.

The Track class will need a constructor that sets the track title. We will also need to make a constructor that creates an instance with the title and the side information. For simplicity's sake we will make these values public, and so accessible through the dot notation.

```
class Track {
  public String Title;
  public int Side=0;

  public Track(String newTitle){     '
    newTitle= Title;
  }
```

```
  public Track(String newTitle, int newSide){
    Title = newTitle;
    Side = newSide;
  }
}
```

Notice that we give "Side" an initial value when the class is constructed, to protect against a class accidentally using a "Side" instance that has not been properly instantiated. We need to alter the methods of the classes we have already defined to use this new class. In the MusicRecording class, change the definition of TrackListing to:

```
Track TrackList[]= new Track[10];
```

And change the SetTrackList method to:

```
public boolean SetTrackList(Track newTrackList[]){
  if (newTrackList.length > 10)
    return false;
  for (int i=0; i<newTrackList.length;i++){
    TrackList[i]=new Track(newTrackList[i].Title, newTrackList[i].Side);

  }
  return true;
}
```

We will also need to change the methods for retrieving track lists and individual tracks:

```
public String getTrack(int Tracknumber){
    return (TrackList[Tracknumber].Title);
  }

  public Track[] getTrackList(){
    return(TrackList);
  }
```

Now, because the track class contains all the information about a track, we do not need to override the "setTrack" method for cassettes and vinyl records. We will, however, have to add methods which retrieve the side information for a track.

```
class Cassette extends MusicRecording{

  public Cassette(String Title){
    super(Title);
  }

  public int getSide(int TrackNumber){
    return (TrackList[TrackNumber].Side);
  }
}
```

The Vinyl class can be the same as the Cassette class.

```
class Vinyl extends MusicRecording{
  public  Vinyl(String Title){
    super(Title);
  }
  public int getSide(int TrackNumber){
    return (TrackList[TrackNumber].Side);
  }
}
```

Note

The experienced programmer may well reel in horror at the use of arrays to hold some of the information here, when a linked list might be a more appropriate technique. Well, of course it would, but the purpose of this example is to demonstrate class hierarchies and the design methods used.

CHAPTER 21

The OOP Philosophy

All well-designed languages have a well-thought-out philosophy backing them up. Java is no exception; based heavily on other Object Oriented programming languages, it continues the philosophy of Object-based programming. Developing a Java program is a matter of thinking about objects, what they do and how they interact. We will spend this chapter looking at the main philosophical principals of Object Oriented design, how they are implemented in Java and how they will help us to create well-designed and robust programs.

Object Oriented philosophy is based upon three key ideas: Abstraction, Encapsulation and Inheritance. We will look at each in turn, first generally and then more specifically, as we consider their implementation in Java.

Abstraction

If a programming language implements any level of abstraction, it is allowing you to ignore some detail of the implementation. This detail has been taken care of by the language designers and the writers of the compiler. If you consider the most basic of programming languages, an assembler, this language hides the individual steps the processor must carry out to execute the assembler statement. A high-level language such as C hides the individual assembler statements from the programmer but also hides some concepts.

Languages such as C and Pascal implement procedural abstraction; that is, they allow you to hide some of the detail of a process by blocking code together into procedures that other programmers can use. If another programmer has a description of the interface to your procedure they can make use of it without being aware of the detail of the implementation.

These traditional languages also allow for a level of data abstraction: when you refer to a floating-point number you do not refer to the hexadecimal code that goes up to make that number. Furthermore, these languages allow the definition of new data types to be built by using structures which can be referred to by name and moved about without having to deal with the internals of the structure.

Object Oriented languages combine these two abstractions – procedural and data – into one object-level abstraction. When we think of an object, we think of the data the object contains and exactly what the object can do. Java implements the object-level abstraction through classes – as we have seen, a class contains data and methods to manipulate that data. Once a class has been created, we can use that class without being aware of the internal structure of the data or of the procedures the class implements to deal with the data.

Encapsulation

Encapsulation is the process of hiding the implementation from the users of the class. We separate the private internal workings of the class from the public interface that we advertise for others to use. Traditional programming languages such as C implement a certain amount of encapsulation by using modules to gather procedures (and to some extent data) together. The module defines a public interface to the internal data, and the use of global variables is kept to a minimum to avoid interaction between the modules. By using modules the programmer hopes to implement a high degree of "locality", so that changes to one part of the program do not ripple through to other parts of the program. A program with a low degree of locality will be difficult to maintain: changes will ripple through the program, meaning not only more work for the programmer but also a high chance of introducing new faults.

Java allows the programmer to determine the visibility of methods and data through the public and private keywords. Java itself does not enforce the programmer to implement a high level of localisation; it's just as easy to create a bad program in Java as in any other language.

Note

There are other levels of protection — these will be dealt with in Part E of this book.

Inheritance

We have already seen inheritance in action in the design example of the previous section, where the Cassette class inherited the properties of the MusicRecording class. Inheriting from a parent class allows you to share the parent's methods, or you can override these methods and replace their behaviour. If the behaviour of the parent is acceptable to the child then there is no need to override it, cutting down on the amount of code that you need to write. If the majority of code is in the base class then the child classes can concentrate on specific behaviour for the child. As we will see, the Abstract Windows Toolkit class library handles almost all the details of creating user interfaces. We can extend these objects and add specific behaviour such as defining the preferred size of windows or creating effects by overriding the paint method.

Unlike other Object Oriented programming languages, Java only allows you to inherit properties from a single parent class (C++ allows you to inherit from as many classes as you like). This could be thought of as limiting, but in practice it will force you to think about the class hierarchy more clearly. It is believed that the multiple inheritance ability of C++ leads to poorly understood code that is difficult to maintain. However, Java does allow a form of multiple inheritance in the form of interface inheritance. The example in Part A which created threaded applets did so by inheriting the "runnable" interface. The interface defines the methods that its children must implement, but does not define any behaviour. The children must override the methods the interface defines to provide a behaviour for those methods. The "runnable" interface used for the multi-threading applets insists that a start, a stop and a run method are defined in the applet. The Java compiler will complain if these methods are not overridden in your program.

CHAPTER 22

Objects and
the AWT

Now that we have covered the technologies and methods of Object Oriented Programming, we can discover how to use them to interface with the Abstract Windows Toolkit. In our earlier sections on the AWT we added components to the drawing surface of the applet and interfaced to them from within the applet's class description. By using OOP methods we can define new classes that extend the objects in the AWT. This will allow us to define new methods and override existing methods in the AWT objects.

Extending the Canvas class

The Canvas class is an extension of the component class in the AWT class library, whose sole purpose is to provide you with a drawing surface. However, in order to draw on a canvas you need to extend the class and override the paint method. We first need to define the class and its constructor. The only thing the constructor is required to do is to make a call to its class parent through the "super()" method. The call to "super()" must be the first statement in the constructor method. Remember also that the AWT library will need to be imported at the start of a file containing the new class.

```
class myCanvasType extends Canvas {
  myCanvasType(){
    super();
  }

  public void paint(Graphics g){
  }
}
```

We can create our canvas using the normal method for a new class and add it to our applet in exactly the same way that other user interface components are added in the init method of the applet.

```
public void init(){
    myCanvasType myCanvas= new myCanvasType();
    add(myCanvas);
  }
```

CODE 22-1

Code 22-1 does absolutely nothing: we need to add some bones to it to get it to do some work for us. Suppose we wanted a canvas to draw an image that we had previously loaded. We pass the image to the canvas in the constructor and display it in the paint method.

```
class myCanvasType extends Canvas {
  private Image myImage;
  myCanvasType(Image newImage){
    super();
    myImage=newImage;
  }

  public void paint(Graphics g){
    g.drawImage(myImage,0,0,this);
  }
}
```

CODE 22-2

If you try Code 22-2, you will find that although the canvas is created, nothing is drawn on the screen – in fact, the paint method is never called. The reason is simply that the canvas has been created with zero size. The simplest remedy is to add the canvas to a grid layout manager in the init method of the applet. This will force the canvas to be the size needed to fill the grid.

```
myCanvas= new myCanvasType(myImage);
setLayout(new GridLayout(1,1));
add(myCanvas);
```

This unfortunately only works if the layout on which the canvas is created is a grid layout. The other layout types will not force the canvas to a certain size. We need to be able to control the size of our canvases reliably. Fortunately, the AWT provides us with a mechanism for controlling the minimum size and the preferred size of an AWT component by adding the methods "minimumSize()" and "preferredSize()". These methods return a dimension object that contains the height and width of the component. You should set the dimension of your canvas to a value in the constructor of the extended canvas class.

```
class myCanvasType extends Canvas {
  private Image myImage;
  private Dimension myDimension;

  myCanvasType(Image newImage){
    super();
    myImage=newImage;
    myDimension = new Dimension(50,50);

  }
  public Dimension minimumSize(){
    return myDimension;
  }

  public Dimension preferredSize(){
    return myDimension;
  }

  public void paint(Graphics g){
    g.drawImage(myImage,0,0,this);
  }
}
```

CODE 22-3

You can use the getWidth and getHeight methods of the image to ensure that the size of the canvas is just big enough to hold the image. Be aware, however, that unless the image has fully loaded then the width will be reported incorrectly. Use the Media Tracker methods from Part A to make sure the image is loaded before your canvas is created.

```
myCanvasType(Image newImage){
   super();
   myImage=newImage;
   myDimension = new Dimension(myImage.getWidth(this), myImage.getHeight(this));
}
```

Note
The code shown below is a very simple applet to use the Canvas class we have just defined. The applet loads an image and tracks it, although it does not implement the runnable interface as described in Part A.

```
import java.awt.*;
import java.net.*;

public class code223 extends java.applet.Applet {

  myCanvasType myCanvas;
  private URL ImageURL;
  private Image myImage;


  public void init(){
    MediaTracker tracker= new MediaTracker(this);
    ImageURL = getDocumentBase();
    myImage = getImage(ImageURL,"ghost.gif");
    tracker.addImage(myImage,0);
    try {
      tracker.waitForID(0);
    }catch (InterruptedException e){
      System.out.println("Caught interrupt Exception"+e.getMessage());
      return;
    }
    myCanvas= new myCanvasType(myImage);
    add(myCanvas);

  }
}
```

Extending the Frame class

The Frame class allows you to create windows that float outside of the web browser being used to view your applet. Applets that use a frame have a number of advantages, not least the fact that you can add menus to the menu bar. Figure 22-1 shows a simple frame running on a Windows NT (3.51) machine:

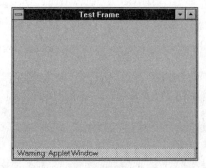

FIGURE 22-1

The surface of the frame is independent of the painting surface of the applet – you can draw things on the applet while the frame displays other information. Creating a frame is similar to creating a canvas: we need to create a class to extend the normal frame and then create an instance of the frame using the "new" operator.

```
import java.awt.*;

public class FrameTest extends java.applet.Applet{
  myFrame Window= new myFrame("Test Frame");
  public void init(){
    Window.show();
  }
}


class myFrame extends Frame {
  myFrame(String title){
    super(title);
  }
}
```

The first thing that must be performed in the constructor for "myFrame" is a call to the constructor of the class's parent, through a call to super(). All frames that are displayed (on any platform) have a bright yellow bar along the bottom with the words "Warning Applet Window" written in it. This is a security feature: any applet with a frame must display this message. This is to prevent an unscrupulous programmer creating an applet which looks like a logon prompt, with the intention of catching people's passwords. This is a very crude feature and may be improved at a later date. Notice also that frames are hidden when created – you need to use the "show()" method to make them visible.

If you try viewing the frame from a Netscape browser you will notice that, when you leave the page with the applet, the frame does not disappear. In fact, you can not get rid of the frame at all, even using the close menu item. The only way to get rid of the frame is to close down your web browser! This might be a useful feature in some cases, but really we want the frame to die gracefully when the browser leaves the page. When the applet is closed, the frame will receive a "Window_Destroy" event. We must trap events and test for this one to close the window when the applet dies.

```
public boolean handleEvent(Event ev) {
  if (ev.id==Event.WINDOW_DESTROY) {
    this.hide();
    return true;
  }
  return super.handleEvent(ev);
}
```

Notice that if the event does not match the "Window_Destroy" event, we pass the event to our parent in the class tree. We use the hide method of the component when we receive the destroy event to remove the frame from the display, but it is still available for use later on. You can use the dispose method to remove the frame completely.

```
public boolean handleEvent(Event ev) {
  if (ev.id==Event.WINDOW_DESTROY) {
    this.dispose();
    return true;
  }
  return super.handleEvent(ev);
}
```

You will notice that the frames we have created so far have varied in size each time the applet is run. The window manager for the machine that is running the applet decides what size to create the frame. We can use the "minimumSize()" and "preferredSize()" methods that were introduced in the Canvas class to control the size of frame we want. However, in order to make the frame the actual size we want, we need to "resize()" the window after it is shown. Add the "preferredSize()" and "minimumSize()" methods to your frame class and call the resize in the init of the applet after the call to "show()" the frame. However, if your frame will have a number of components on it, all arranged according to a layout, you will have to calculate the size of the frame from the size of the components.

```
public void init(){

    Window.show();
    Window.resize(Window.preferredSize());
  }
```

You can control whether a frame is allowed to be resized or not by using the setResizable method of the frame class. This method takes a Boolean argument, which if true allows the frame to be resized. If the window is not resizable, the grab bars around the frame disappear.

```
this.setResizable(false);
myFrame.setResizable(true);
```

The first example is used within the frame class itself; the second can be used by any class using the frame.

The title of the frame is usually set when the frame is created, although it can be changed at a later time using the "setTitle" method. You can create a frame with no title by using the same constructor but with no string argument.

```
myFrame.setTitle("This is the new title");
```

Setting the cursor style

The appearance of the cursor can be changed within a frame to one of fourteen different styles. Besides the default cursor there are eight cursors for use in resizing the window, a crosshair cursor, a hand cursor, a text cursor, a move and a wait cursor. Of course, the actual appearance of each of these cursors will depend on your operating system and the cursor selection you have chosen to use. The cursor is chosen using the "setCursor" method of the frame class, using one of the following variables as an argument.

CROSSHAIR_CURSOR	DEFAULT_CURSOR
E_RESIZE_CURSOR	HAND_CURSOR
MOVE_CURSOR	NE_RESIZE_CURSOR
NW_RESIZE_CURSOR	N_RESIZE_CURSOR
SE_RESIZE_CURSOR	SW_RESIZE_CURSOR
S_RESIZE_CURSOR	TEXT_CURSOR
WAIT_CURSOR	W_RESIZE_CURSOR

Within a frame class the cursor is set thus:

```
this.setCursor(CROSSHAIR_CURSOR);
```

The current cursor appearance can be determined using the "getCursorType" method of the frame class; the value will be one of the predefined variables shown above.

Adding menus

In Part B we mentioned that applets could not have menus of the sort familiar to all Windows users at the top of the applet. Frames allow a menu bar with drop-down menus to be added at the top. These menus can behave exactly as you are used to in other Windows applications, but can also be extended so as to allow nested menus as shown in Figure 22-2.

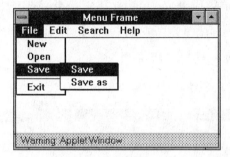

FIGURE 22-2

To use menus we must first create a menu bar to hold the menus. We can then add the top-level menu choices that will drop the menu down when activated. Code 22-4 creates a frame with a menu bar called "myMenuBar" and then adds three top-level menus – "Files", "Edit" and "Search".

```
class myFrame extends  Frame {

  MenuBar myMenuBar= new MenuBar();

  myFrame(String title){
    super(title);
    Menu FileMenu= new Menu("File");
    myMenuBar.add(FileMenu);
    Menu EditMenu = new Menu("Edit");
    myMenuBar.add (EditMenu);
    Menu SearchMenu = new Menu("Search");
    myMenuBar.add (SearchMenu);
    setMenuBar(myMenuBar);
  }
}
```

CODE 22-4

It is customary to include a Help menu in any menu bar; some systems allow the Help menu to appear on the right of the frame's window. The Help menu item is added in an identical way to the other items, but the "setHelpMenu" method is used to make it appear on the right of the menu bar.

```
Menu HelpMenu = new Menu("Help");
myMenuBar.add (HelpMenu);
myMenuBar.setHelpMenu(HelpMenu);
```

Currently, under Windows NT and Windows 95 the Help menu appears with the other menu items, but under Openwindows on the Sun system it appears over to the right as intended.

WINDOWS NT   WINDOW 95   OPENWINDOWS

FIGURE 22-3   FIGURE 22-4   FIGURE 22-5

Once the top-level menu items have been added to the frame, the drop-down items can be created and added. The drop-down elements are added as "MenuItems". An item is added to a top-level menu item by using the "add" method for that item. Create each menu item in turn and then add it to the top-level menu.

```
Menu FileMenu= new Menu("File");
myMenuBar.add(FileMenu);
MenuItem NewMenu = new MenuItem("New");
MenuItem OpenMenu = new MenuItem("Open");
MenuItem SaveMenu = new MenuItem("Save");
MenuItem ExitMenu = new MenuItem("Exit");

FileMenu.add(NewMenu);
FileMenu.add(OpenMenu);
FileMenu.add(SaveMenu);
FileMenu.add(ExitMenu);
```

If you want to create sub-menus from the drop-down menus (Figure 22-6), create the root menu item as a "menu" instead of a "MenuItem". This type of menu item has a small arrow to the right of it to indicate that either another menu or a dialog box will appear when this item is selected.

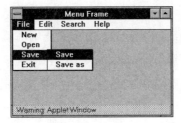

FIGURE 22-6

```
Menu SaveMenu = new Menu("Save");
FileMenu.add(SaveMenu);
MenuItem Save2Menu = new MenuItem("Save");
MenuItem SaveasMenu = new MenuItem("Save as");

SaveMenu.add(Save2Menu);
SaveMenu.add(SaveasMenu);
```

You will sometimes want to put a separator into the menu to indicate important items or to group items together. A separator can be added to the current location in any menu by using the addSeparator method when adding menu items to the menu bar. For our File menu bar, if we wanted to add a separator before the Exit item, we must add it after the Save menu item. The complete menu-building code is shown below.

```
Menu FileMenu= new Menu("File");
myMenuBar.add(FileMenu);
MenuItem NewMenu = new MenuItem("New");
MenuItem OpenMenu = new MenuItem("Open");
Menu SaveMenu = new Menu("Save");
MenuItem ExitMenu = new MenuItem("Exit");

FileMenu.add(NewMenu);
FileMenu.add(OpenMenu);
FileMenu.add(SaveMenu);
MenuItem Save2Menu = new MenuItem("Save");
MenuItem SaveasMenu = new MenuItem("Save as");
SaveMenu.add(Save2Menu);
SaveMenu.add(SaveasMenu);
FileMenu.addSeparator();
FileMenu.add(ExitMenu);
Menu HelpMenu = new Menu("Help");
myMenuBar.add (HelpMenu);
myMenuBar.setHelpMenu(HelpMenu);
setMenuBar(myMenuBar);
```

Retrieving menu selections

You can retrieve menu selections in much the same way as you did in Part A for buttons and the other simple User Interface components. In the "myFrame" class, override the action method and check for instances of menu items – a check on the value of the argument will determine the action to be carried out. For example, the method in Code 22-5 traps the Exit menu item and destroys the frame. If no menu item is recognised, the method returns false, so classes further up the tree can deal with the action.

```
public boolean action(Event evt, Object arg){
  if (evt.target instanceof MenuItem)
    if (arg.equals ("Exit")){
      this.dispose();
      return true;
    }
  return false;
}
```

CODE 22-5

Disabling menu items

You can stop a user from selecting a menu or menu item by disabling it, which turns it grey to indicate that it can not be used. You can enable the item again by using the enable method. As an example, let's create our File menu but with the "Save" option turned off until the "Save as" option has been used. Because we have defined the save2Menu as local to the init method, we need to move it to inside the class definition. We can then disable it just after we add it to the menu bar, and enable it in the action method when the "Save as " menu item is selected. Code 22-6 shows a complete skeleton for a frame with menu items.

```
import java.awt.*;
public class code226 extends java.applet.Applet{
  myFrame Window= new myFrame("Menu Frame");
  public void init(){
    Window.show();
    Window.resize(Window.preferredSize());
```

```
     }
   }

class myFrame extends Frame {
  private Dimension myDimension;
  MenuBar myMenuBar= new MenuBar();
  MenuItem Save2Menu = new MenuItem("Save");

  myFrame(String title){
    super(title);
    myDimension = new Dimension(300,200);
    Menu FileMenu= new Menu("File");
    myMenuBar.add(FileMenu);
    MenuItem NewMenu = new MenuItem("New");
    MenuItem OpenMenu = new MenuItem("Open");
    MenuItem ExitMenu = new MenuItem("Exit");
    FileMenu.add(NewMenu);
    FileMenu.add(OpenMenu);
    Menu SaveMenu = new Menu("Save");
    FileMenu.add(SaveMenu);
    MenuItem SaveasMenu = new MenuItem("Save as");
    SaveMenu.add(Save2Menu);
    Save2Menu.disable();
    SaveMenu.add(SaveasMenu);
    FileMenu.addSeparator();
    FileMenu.add(ExitMenu);
    Menu EditMenu = new Menu("Edit");
    myMenuBar.add (EditMenu);
    Menu SearchMenu = new Menu("Search");
    myMenuBar.add (SearchMenu);
    Menu HelpMenu = new Menu("Help");
    myMenuBar.add (HelpMenu);
    myMenuBar.setHelpMenu(HelpMenu);
    setMenuBar(myMenuBar);
  }

  public boolean handleEvent(Event ev) {
    if (ev.id==Event.WINDOW_DESTROY) {
      this.dispose();
      return true;
    }
    return super.handleEvent(ev);
  }

  public Dimension minimumSize(){
    return myDimension;
  }

  public Dimension preferredSize(){
    return myDimension;
  }

public boolean action(Event evt, Object arg){
  if (evt.target instanceof MenuItem)
    if (arg.equals ("Exit")){
```

```
      this.dispose();
      return true;
    }
    if (arg.equals ("Save as")){
      Save2Menu.enable();
      return true;
    }
  return false;
  }

}
```

CODE 22-6

Check box menu items

There are instances when a menu item needs to display a tick next to it to indicate that an option is enabled: these are called check box menu items in Java. An example is shown in Figure 22-7:

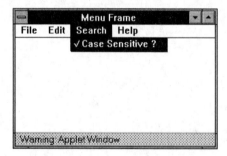

FIGURE 22-7

Check boxes can be created in the same way as normal menu items and are always created with the check box turned off. The state can be changed by using the "setState()" method and of course retrieved by the "getState()" method. Code 22-7 adds a check box menu item to the Search menu and checks the status when it changes in the action method.

Create the menu item:

```
CheckboxMenuItem CaseSensitive = new CheckboxMenuItem("Case Sensitive ?");
```

Add it to the menu bars:

```
SearchMenu.add(CaseSensitive);
```

And finally handle the event in the action method:

```
public boolean action(Event evt, Object arg){
  if (evt.target instanceof MenuItem)
    if (arg.equals ("Save as")){
      System.out.println("Caught the Exit menu item");
      Save2Menu.enable();
      return true;

    }
    if (arg.equals ("Case Sensitive ?")){
      if(CaseSensitive.getState() == true)
        System.out.println("Case sensitive search");
      else
        System.out.println("Case insensitive search");
      return true;
    }
  return false;
  }
}
```

CODE 22-7

Windows

Windows are the basis of pop-up menus; they resemble frames but have no title bar and so can not be moved around by the user. Windows have to be created in relation to a frame, and as with frames it's best to override their preferred size. This will allow accurate control of the size of the window. The window can hold any of the normal user-interface components and layout methods, but defaults to the border layout. The window is created by referring to the frame name:

```
myWindow newWindow=new myWindow(FrameName);
newWindow.show();
newWindow.resize(newWindow.preferredSize());
```

You extend the window class in the normal fashion to give the window its functionality. This class creates a window and adds an edit area to it.

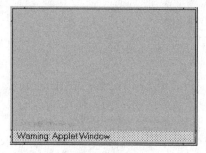

Warning Applet Window

FIGURE 22-8

```
class myWindow extends Window {

  private Dimension myDimension;
  private TextArea myTextArea= new TextArea("",25,80);

  myWindow(Frame myFrame){
    super(myFrame);
    setLayout(new GridLayout(1,1));
    this.add(myTextArea);
    myDimension = new Dimension(200,200);
  }
  public boolean handleEvent(Event ev) {
    if (ev.id==Event.WINDOW_DESTROY) {
      this.dispose();
      return true;
    }
    return super.handleEvent(ev);
  }
  public Dimension minimumSize(){
    return myDimension;
  }
  public Dimension preferredSize(){
    return myDimension;
  }
}
```

CODE 22-8

Dialog boxes

Dialog boxes are not greatly different from windows. They must be associated with a frame and are generally used to retrieve information from the user. The advantage of dialog boxes is that they can be made modal. A modal dialog box will not let the user use the frame until the dialog box has been disposed of. Typical uses of a modal dialog box include login boxes or warning messages that must be read before the user can continue.

A problem arises when using dialog boxes, especially modal ones. If the dialog box is disposed of after it is closed, any data in the dialog box will be disposed of as well. Java has an efficient garbage collector that cleans up the memory when objects are disposed of and are no longer in use. There are two techniques to use a dialog box and to retain the data after the dialog box has been disposed of.

1) Extend the dialog class with your own class and create the user interface components in the parent. These components will still be available to the parent after the dialog has closed.

2) Extend the dialog box with your own class and create the user interface components in the constructor of the class. However, you will need to pass the data to the inheritance parent before the dialog box is closed.

Let's see how to use these two methods to create modal dialog boxes and retrieve data from them.

Method 1

First we create an extended dialog box. The general form is much the same as for frames and windows. As before, we override the "minimumSize()" and "preferredSize()", but we add an action to dispose of the dialog box.

```
class myDialogType extends Dialog {
  private Dimension myDimension;

  public myDialogType(Frame newFrame, String Title, boolean modal){
    super(newFrame,Title,modal);
    myDimension = new Dimension(200,200);
  }

  public Dimension minimumSize(){
    return myDimension;
  }
```

```
public Dimension preferredSize(){
  return myDimension;
}

public boolean action(Event evt, Object arg){
  if (evt.target instanceof Button)
    if (arg.equals ("Done")){
      this.dispose();
      return true;
    }
  return false;
}

}
```

Now we have created the dialog box, we can use it in an applet. Once we have created an instance of the new dialog class, we add the text fields and add a button to indicate when the user has finished with the dialog. We must first create a frame to associate with the dialog box. However, we do not need to show the frame so the dialog box appears to be associated with the applet's drawing surface. The dialog box is created with the "new" operator with references to the parent frame, a string for the dialog name and a Boolean value to control the modality. If this Boolean is true, the dialog box will be modal, otherwise it will not. Once the dialog box has been constructed we create a layout manager and add a couple of text fields for the users to add data. Because the dialog is modal, once it has been shown the user can only interact with it and no other windows belonging to the applet.

```
public class code229 extends java.applet.Applet
{
  Frame myFrame= new Frame("Test Frame");
  TextField Name= new TextField(25);
  TextField Address = new TextField(25);

  public void init()
  {
  myDialogType myDialog = new myDialogType(myFrame, "Test Dialog",true);
  GridLayout dialogLayout= new GridLayout(3,1);
  myDialog.setLayout(dialogLayout);
  myDialog.add(Name);
  myDialog.add(Address);
  myDialog.add(new Button("Done"));
```

```
    myDialog.show();
    myDialog.resize(myDialog.preferredSize());

    String TextName= Name.getText();
    String TextAddress =Address.getText();
    System.out.println("Name:  "+TextName);
    System.out.println("Address:  "+TextAddress);
    }
}
```

CODE 22-9

If you try Code 22-9 you will notice that it always reports the text areas are empty. What's more, the "println()" statement executes before the user has had a chance to enter any data. This is because, although the dialog box is modal, it doesn't pause the applet. We need to add a method in the dialog box that tells the applet when to retrieve the data. The dialog box class code will change to include a reference to the inheritance parent in the constructor. A call will be made to a method in the parent (called getData in this example) in the action method to actually get the data. Add a global variable for the inheritance parent and change the constructor class to accept the reference to the inheritance parent. Our example is shown below (the name of the applet has been changed to "code2210").

```
class myDialogType extends Dialog {
  private Dimension myDimension;
  code2210 myParent;

  public myDialogType(code2210  parent,Frame newFrame, String Title,
boolean modal){
     super(newFrame,Title,modal);
     myDimension = new Dimension(200,200);
     myParent=parent;
  }
```

Now we change the action method to call a method in the parent to retrieve the data.

```
public boolean action(Event evt, Object arg){
   if (evt.target instanceof Button)
     if (arg.equals ("Done")){
  myParent.getData();
```

```
      this.dispose();
      return true;
      }
    return false;
    }
```

Finally, the applet class will need a method to retrieve the data:

```
public void getData(){
  String TextName= Name.getText();
  String TextAddress =Address.getText();
  System.out.println("Name:  "+TextName);
  System.out.println("Address:  "+TextAddress);
}
```

CODE 22-10

Method 2

We are going to create our dialog box and add text fields in the constructor. We will then pass the values from the text fields to the parent in the action method. Because we are going to return more than one text field, we will create a class to hold the data. Here is a simple class to hold the Name field and the Address field.

```
class details{
  public String myName;
  public String myAddress;
  public details(String Name,  String Address){
    myName=Name;
    myAddress=Address;
  }
}
```

The class defines two public variables for holding the Name and Address fields. We can now create the dialog class with its associated action method and text fields. The action method calls a method in the parent named "printDetails()" with a details class for a parameter. We create the instance of the details class as usual with the new operator, but use the returned values from the text fields as parameters.

```
class myDialogType extends Dialog {
  private Dimension myDimension;
  code2211 myParent;
  TextField Name = new TextField(25);
  TextField Address = new TextField(25);

  public myDialogType(code2211 parent,Frame newFrame, String Title, boolean
modal){
    super(newFrame,Title,modal);
    myDimension = new Dimension(200,200);
    myParent=parent;
    GridLayout dialogLayout= new GridLayout(3,1);
    setLayout(dialogLayout);
    add(Name);
    add(Address);
    add(new Button("Done"));
  }

  public Dimension minimumSize(){
    return myDimension;
  }
  public Dimension preferredSize(){
    return myDimension;
  }

  public boolean action(Event evt, Object arg){
    if (evt.target instanceof Button)
    if (arg.equals ("Done")){
      details myDetails =new details(Name.getText(),Address.getText());
      myParent.printDetails(myDetails);
      this.dispose();
      return true;
    }
    return false;
  }

}
```

We now need a simple applet to construct the dialog box and accept its
data through a "printDetails()" method.

```
import java.awt.*;
public class code2211 extends java.applet.Applet
{
  public void init()
  {
  Frame myFrame= new Frame("Test Frame");
    myDialogType myDialog = new myDialogType(this,myFrame, "Test
Dialog",true);
    myDialog.show();
    myDialog.resize(myDialog.preferredSize());
  }
```

```
public void printDetails(details myDetails){
  System.out.println(myDetails.myName);
  System.out.println(myDetails.myAddress);
}
}
```

CODE 22-11

CHAPTER 23

Protecting Classes and Methods

Throughout this book we have seen classes and methods described as public and private, with no further explanation except that it has something to do with security. The security we are referring to here is not to do with access to your machine's resources over the Internet, but the security of your classes when they are used by other developers. Unless you can protect the variables and methods that your classes use, you can not guarantee that your classes will work correctly when used by another programmer.

If we look at the rather contrived class in Code 23-1, the variable "myVariable" should only ever have the value of 1. If the class is used properly by only calling the constructor and only ever reading "myVariable", the class will behave as expected. However, if the class is used as in Code 23-2 then myVariable can have any value, because:

- Direct access is allowed to my variable
- Access is allowed to the "ShouldBePrivate" method

```
class NotSecure{
  int myVariable;

  NotSecure(){
    myVariable=1;
    ShouldBePrivate(1);
```

```
    }

    void ShouldBePrivate(int Controller){
      myVariable =Controller*myVariable;
    }

  }
```

C<small>ODE</small> 23-1

```
class UseNotSecure{
  UseNotSecure(){
    NotSecure myUnsecureOne=new NotSecure();
    System.out.println("Unsecure now :"+myUnsecureOne.myVariable);
    myUnsecureOne.myVariable=100;
    System.out.println("Unsecure now :"+myUnsecureOne.myVariable);
    myUnsecureOne.ShouldBePrivate(-2);
    System.out.println("Unsecure now :"+myUnsecureOne.myVariable);
  }
}
```

C<small>ODE</small> 23-2

When the "UseNotSecure" class is constructed it will print the following to the console:

```
Unsecure now :1
Unsecure now :100
Unsecure now :-200
```

When the "NotSecure" class is created, its variable is initialised to 1. The "UseNotSecure" class then changes the value to 100, and finally uses the "ShouldBePrivate()" method to change the value again. If any methods in the "NotSecure" class rely on the variable having a value of 1 then it will fail.

It is common practice for a team of programmers to "slice up" the task amongst themselves. Each person in the team "publishes" the interface to the other members of the team. Any language that intends to distribute its code amongst a number of authors needs to be able to protect its variables and methods from unintended usage.

Java allows programmers to protect their code through four levels of protection: private, package, protected and public. These modifiers are applied to the variable, class or method definition. Our Unsecure class above should have made use of the private modifier to protect its variable and method:

```
class Secure{
  private int myVariable;

  public Secure(){
    myVariable=1;
    IsPrivate(1);
  }

  private void IsPrivate(int Controller){
    myVariable =Controller*myVariable;
  }

}
```

CODE 23-2

Any class that uses the "Secure" class has access to the constructor method but does not have any access to the variable or the "IsPrivate" method. However, there is no way to obtain the current value of "myVariable" from outside the class. We can create an "accessor" method that can be used to retrieve the value of the variable, but does not allow the variable's value to be changed.

```
public int GetVariable(){
  return myVariable;
}
```

It might seem like a lot of effort to create accessor methods for all variables that your classes might like to share, but it really is worth the effort. By using accessor methods with private variables and methods, you can make your class entirely secure from unwanted side-effects. With the current versions of the Java compiler and web browsers available, the use of accessor methods does slow your applets down a little. However, in the near future the compiler and browser will be so optimised that accessor methods will be as fast as any other method of variable access.

There are two other levels of protection: packages and private. We will leave these until Part E, when we find out more about packages and the need for more subtle security. For now, it is best to use private variables wherever you can and only make public variables and methods if you absolutely have to.

PART D

Networking

Java's class libraries come complete with a rich set of tools to send and retrieve information across the Internet. These range from the ability to display web pages to posting data as if entered into an input form. Java will also allow you to interact with the network at a very basic level. This section will lead you through the possibilities, from creating a URL, to using this URL to display remote Web pages posting data across the Internet. We will create sockets to send and receive information to remote servers.

Whenever you want to use the network support in Java you must import the java.net library at the start of the Java source code.

```
import java.net.*;
```

CHAPTER 24

Creating and Working with URLs

The URL (Uniform Resource Locator) is the primary means by which web browsers and Java are able to find objects around the World Wide Web. A URL is composed of up to four components:

- The Protocol
- The Server address
- The Port number
- The File name

The protocol refers to the type of data transfer that this URL will carry out; examples are HTTP, FTP and Gopher. Java will use the protocol field to determine the type of transfer to carry out exactly what needs to be done to fetch files across the Net. Notice that although Java recognises a number of protocols for URL connection, it does not define the methods necessary to handle all the protocols. The server is the Internet name of the machine that the file resides upon. All servers have a number of ports; HTTP transfers normally happen over port 80, but for security reasons some servers use a different port number. Finally, the file name is given, which includes the full path to the file on the file system.

Java treats the URL as a complete entity, not the sum of its parts, but it can be created from strings and integers representing the URL. To create a

URL, use the "new" operator with string representations of the URL components:

```
myURL = new URL("http","snowflake.mcs.dundee.ac.uk","test.html");
```

This would create a new URL pointing to "http://snowflake.mcs.dundee. ac.uk/test.html". If a different port number is needed, an integer representing the port is inserted between the host and the file:

```
myURL = new URL("http","snowflake.mcs.dundee.ac.uk",80,"test.html");
```

A URL can be created from a string representing the whole thing:

```
myURL = new URL ("http://snowflake.mcs.dundee.ac.uk:80/test.html");
```

Finally, a URL can be created from another URL and a string representing the relative path to the file required. As we will see later, you can retrieve the current address where the applet resides using the getDocumentBase method; we can use this to retrieve documents from a server relative to the location of the applet:

```
myURL = new URL(getDocumentBase(),"Test.html");
```

All the URL constructor methods can generate an error if there is a problem with the URL it is trying to construct. For this reason the URL constructors have to be surrounded by the try and catch statements we encountered in Part A.

```
try {
  myURL = new URL(getDocumentBase(),"Test.html");
}catch (Exception et){
// Handle the error here
}
```

If an error does occur in the URL, how you deal with it depends on where the URL data was generated. If it comes from the applet's user, there could be a problem that can be solved by asking the user.

If you already have a URL object, the URL class library provides methods to retrieve the component parts of the URL:

myURL.getProtocol()	Returns the protocol of the URL as a string
myURL.getHost()	Returns the Host of the URL as a string
myURL.getPort()	Returns the port number in this URL as a string
myURL.getFile()	Returns the file name in the URL including the full path in the file system

---

Note

Although you can use Java to access network resources, in general applets are restricted to talking to resources that are located on the server that holds the applet's class. Any applet that uses a URL for its connections is limited in this way. If you use sockets (as we do later in the section) then the restriction is relaxed, but the Java code becomes much more complicated. Notice that in order to be able to make some of the connections used in the code shown here, the security features of your browser may have to be relaxed. You should experiment with the settings of your browser and take note of how they affect the operation of the code in this section of the book.

Showing an HTML page

Because Java is so integrated into the Internet environment, it is relatively easy to display a document in the parent browser's window. If the browser is Netscape or Internet Explorer (or another browser capable of displaying frames), Java can control the contents of the frames currently on show in the page.

The Java applet class libraries include the showDocument method, which takes a URL as an argument and displays the output either on the browser's surface or in a frame within the browser. The following code sample displays the contents of a URL on the browser's surface. As we have seen, the method to generate a URL needs to be encapsulated in a try-catch statement to trap any errors that may be generated. If an error occurs, it will be ignored by the empty catch statement; the sample assumes that the URL is correct and is currently reachable. Unless the applet that uses this statement is in its own independent Java frame (window), the browser will cease to display the applet that generates the showDocument.

```
import java.net.*;
public class code241 extends java.applet.Applet{
  public void init() {
    try {
      this.getAppletContext().showDocument(new  URL("http://
alpha.mic.dundee.ac.uk/ft/ft.cgi?-1,ft"));
    }catch(Exception eT){};
  }
}
```

CODE 24-1

Notice that, in order to use the "showDocument" method, we need to get a handle to where the applet is running. We use the "getAppletContext" method to retrieve a context from the web browser. If a second argument is added to the showDocument method, it is taken as the name of a currently displayed browser frame. The document from the "showDocument" method is displayed in the named frame. If the frame does not exist then a new browser window is created and the document is displayed there instead. Using browser frames like this means that the applet does not need to be displayed in its own frame to use the "showDocument" method. The following code sample will attempt to display a URL in a frame called BottomFrame in the current browser page

```
import java.net.*;

public class code242 extends java.applet.Applet{
  public void init() {
    try {
      this.getAppletContext().showDocument(new  URL("http://
alpha.mic.dundee.ac.uk/ft/ft.cgi?-1,ft"),"BottomFrame");
    }catch(Exception eT){};
  }
}
```

CODE 24-2

To use this sort of statement effectively, we need to set up a collection of HTML documents that deal with the frames. We need one document to handle the frames. We need another to hold the applet, and a third to be shown to the user whilst the bottom frame is loading. The code below shows suitable HTML for the three pages.

```
<html>
<head>
<title>Test of ShowDocument
and frames</title>
</head>
<frameset rows="30%,*">
<frame scrolling="no"
src="code242.html"
name="Header">

<frame  scrolling="yes"
src="blank.html"
name="BottomFrame">
</frameset>

<noframes>
You need  Netscape 2 or
above </noframes>
</html>
```

```
<title>Test</title>
<hr>
<applet
code="code242.class"
     width=200
     height =200
>
</applet>
```

```
<title>Blank</title>
<h1>Loading Something
</h1><hr>
```

THE FRAME HTML   THE APPLET HTML   THE DEFAULT LOADING HTML
                              (CODE242.HTML)   (BLANK.HTML)

We can use this ability to create a simple applet with buttons that link to other web pages. Code 24-3 does just that. You will need to use it in conjunction with framed HTML pages similar to those shown above. The applet stores the names of some sites as an array of strings. Part of the address is also stored as an array of strings. The names of the sites are used as labels on the array of buttons. In the button action method, a check is made to find which button was pressed. The "showDocument()" method is then used to display the page.

```
import java.net.*;
import java.awt.*;

public class code243 extends java.applet.Applet{
  String Sites[]={"Java Soft",
```

```
        "How Do I",
        "Gamelan",
        "The Java centre"};
String Urls[]={     "javasoft.com",
        "digitalfocus.com/faq/howdoi.html",
        "gamelan.com/index.shtml",
        "java.co.uk"};

public void init() {
  GridLayout myLayout = new GridLayout(2,2);
  setLayout(myLayout);
  Button myButtons[]= new Button[4];
  for (int i=0; i<4;i++){
    myButtons[i]=new Button(Sites[i]);
    add(myButtons[i]);
  }
}



public boolean action(Event evt, Object arg){
  if (evt.target instanceof Button)
    for (int i=0;i<4;i++){
      if (arg.equals (Sites[i])){
        System.out.println(Sites[i]);
        try {
          this.getAppletContext().showDocument(new  URL("http://
www."+Urls[i]), "BottomFrame");
        }catch(Exception eT){};
      return true;
    }
  }
  return false;
}
}
```

CODE 24-3

Retrieving the page and Codebase URLs

There are two important parameters that your program may need to be
aware of if it is to interact with the original location of the applet. The
document base of the applet is the URL of the page that holds the applet,
without the actual page name. Thus, if a page is stored at "http://
snowflake.mcs.dundee.ac.uk/xxx/qfort/qfort.html" then the document base is
"http://snowflake.mcs.dundee.ac.uk/xxx/qfort/". You can use the document
base to refer to any other object stored in the same location as the document

that holds the applet. You use the getDocumentBase method from the applet class library to retrieve the base document URL. Remember to import the applet class library using "import java.applet.*" at the beginning of any file that uses these methods.

```
baseURL = getDocumentBase();
```

If an applet has a different codebase set using the codebase parameter tag (see Part A) you can use the "getCodeBase" method to retrieve its value. If the codebase parameter has not been set in the applet tag, the method returns the document base. (However, see Apppendix B for more useful methods of checking with Java resources and version 1.1.)

```
baseURL = getCodeBase();
```

The document base method can be used to retrieve the name of the machine that originated the applet and the port number that is used for HTTP transfers on that machine. These two values are important if you want to pass information back to the originating machine. The machine name is returned as a string and the port number as an integer.

```
home = getDocumentBase().getHost();
port = getDocumentBase().getPort();
```

Retrieving text from a server

By using the URL class library and the file *io* libraries it is possible to retrieve text from a remote server. For security reasons Java does not allow you to put text onto a remote server using this method; you can use the CGI interface as described later in this section to do this. However, using the CGI post does mean you will need to have direct access to the server to install a handling program.

In the following code sample we assume that a URL has already been created. A stream is then opened by the openStream method and a data input stream is attached. Each line from the remote file is then read into an array of strings until the read statement returns a null string. (You will need to import the io library to use the data input stream.)

```
public String myStory[] = new String[100];
String myString="";
  try{
    myInputStream = myStoryURL.openStream();
  }catch (IOException et){
    System.out.println("Can not open that file");
  }
  myData = new DataInputStream(myInputStream);
  I=0;
  do{
    try{
      myString = myData.readLine();
    }catch (Exception et){
      System.out.println("Can not read from  that file"+et);
    }

    if (myString !=null)
      myStory[I]=myString;
      I++;
    }while (myString != null);
  }
```

Each line of data is stored in the string array; it can be used by a paint method to draw the text to an applet's surface. Because loading text from a remote server may take some time, it is a good idea to encapsulate the file-reading functions in a class of their own, implementing the "runnable" interface. Remember also that because of the security limitations of Java, the applet will need to be stored on the same server as the text that will be loaded. The following code sample shows an applet that uses a class to retrieve code from a remote server. The code to actually retrieve the text is exactly the same as the sample above and is implemented in the run statement of the "GetText" class.

```
import java.awt.*;
import java.net.*;
import java.io.*;

public class Code241 extends java.applet.Applet {
  GetText myText;
```

```
  public void init(){
    URL myURL;
    String FileName ="http://snowflake.mcs.dundee.ac.uk/cookies/cookie1.txt";
    try{
      myURL=new URL(FileName);
      myText = new GetText(myURL,this);
      myText.start();

    }catch (Exception et){
      System.out.println("URL is invalid"+et);
      System.exit(-1);
    }

    repaint();
  }

  public void paint(Graphics g){
    if (myText.Loaded == true){
      g.setColor(Color.black);
      for (int I=0; I<myText.Maxi;I++){
        g.drawString(myText.myStory[I],10,10+10*I);
      }
    }
  }
}

class GetText implements Runnable{

  InputStream myInputStream;
  DataInputStream myData;
  URL myStoryURL;
  Thread myThread;
  Code241 myParent;
  boolean Loaded=false;
  int Maxi;
  String myStory[] = new String[100];

  GetText(URL StoryURL,Code241 Parent){
    myStoryURL =StoryURL;
    myParent=Parent;
  }

  public void stop(){

    if (myThread !=null){
      myThread.stop();
      myThread=null;
    }

  }

  public void start(){
    if(myThread ==null){
      myThread=new Thread(this,"myThread");
      myThread.start();
```

```
      }

   }
   public void  run(){
     String myString="";
     int I=0;
     try {
       myInputStream = myStoryURL.openStream();
     }catch (IOException et){
       System.out.println("Can not open that file");
     }
     myData = new DataInputStream(myInputStream);

     do{
       try{
         myString = myData.readLine();
       }catch (Exception et){
         System.out.println("Can not open that file"+et);
       }

       if (myString !=null)
         myStory[I]=myString;
         I++;
     }while (myString != null);
     Maxi=I-1;
     Loaded=true;
     myParent.repaint();
     I=0;
   }

   }
```

CODE 24-4

The code as shown has wired into it a maximum number of lines of text that can be stored. The text is stored as an array of 100 strings. Instead of using an array of strings, another approach is to use a "string buffer" class to store the data. This class creates a buffer that can grow with the requirements of the data, allowing virtually unlimited storage. Replace the array definition with:

```
StringBuffer myStory = new StringBuffer();
```

Once this is done, you can change the loop-reading strings to append the data that has been read to the string buffer.

```
do{
  try{
    myString = myData.readLine();
  }catch (Exception et){
    System.out.println("Can not open that file"+et);
  }
  if (myString !=null)
    myStory.append(myString);

}while (myString != null);
```

To use the buffer in a "drawString" graphics method, the string buffer class must use the "toString" method to convert the buffer to a string. Using the string buffer class does have the disadvantage of losing access to the individual lines of text, as the drawString method displays the text as one long line. However, text retrieved this way is suitable for entry into a "text field" user-interface component which will optimise the text layout.

To draw the entire string to the surface as one long line, do the following:

```
g.drawString(myText.myStory.toString(),10,10);
```

(This method will display any control characters, such as "carriage returns" or "line feeds", as strange-looking symbols in the string.)

You can add the text to a text area using the "insertText" or the "appendText" methods. Although these will not display any control characters, the line will be added as a single line.

CHAPTER 25

Creating and Using Sockets

Sockets are the foundation on which most of the Internet is built: using sockets, your computer can communicate with web servers, gopher servers and FTP servers. Java allows you to create socket objects in your program and use them to send and receive data from a central server. Sockets have always been extremely complicated to use, but Java has hidden much of the detail away in the java.net library and the java.io libraries. Sockets are ports on network servers that your Java program can connect to in order to send or receive information. Each port on a server will have a particular number and often will do a known job. For instance, whenever your web browser connects to a site to retrieve a document, it usually attaches to port number 80. Telnet sessions usually use port 23, while mail is often delivered through port 25. Typically, however, you will be communicating with an application that you have written that runs on a server you have access to. The application will use a port number that you define, and only your applets will communicate through that port. You need to be careful that the port number you choose does not affect the server you are using. You will need to talk to whoever maintains the server before trying to use sockets.

To create a socket, you need to know the host name you are going to connect to and the port number you wish to communicate with. To be able to send and receive data from the socket you will need to create a data stream, the simplest of which is the InputStream for input and the OutputStream for Output. To use sockets and any of the input or output stream methods you will need to import java.net.* and java.io.* at the start of the class file. When using sockets, a large number of errors can be generated from the network; most of these need to be caught by encapsulating the network statements in a "try catch" clause. The examples we present will catch the errors and print a suitable message to the console. If possible, you should try and handle the exceptions in a more responsible manner in your own code – it will save time on debugging and prevent the user from getting frustrated if you use the errors to give meaningful feedback. Handling errors is dealt with in more detail in Part E.

In the following example a connection is made to port 13 on the machine kappa.mic.dundee.ac.uk, which returns the date and time to the applet. While the data is being transferred one byte at a time, it is written to the console using a "System.out.print" statement. When no more characters are available (signified by the read statement returning a value of -1) the socket is closed.

```
import java.net.*;
import java.io.*;

public class SocketTest extends java.applet.Applet{
  Socket mySocket;
  InputStream myInput;

  public void init(){
    try {
      mySocket= new Socket("kappa.mic.dundee.ac.uk",13);
    }catch (Exception et){
      System.out.println("Applet has thrown  exception"+et);
    }
    try {
      myInput=mySocket.getInputStream();
    }catch (Exception et){
      System.out.println("Applet has thrown  exception"+et);
    }
    int ch=0;
    while(true ){
```

```
    try{
      ch= myInput.read();
    }catch (Exception et){
      System.out.println("Applet has thrown exception"+et);
    }
    if (ch==-1) break;
    System.out.print(""+(char)ch);

  }
  try{
    myInput.close();
  }catch (Exception et){
    System.out.println("Applet has thrown  exception"+et);
  }
 }
}
```

CODE 25-1

The code appears complicated because of all the try and catch wrappers that are needed to catch errors. If we strip away the error-handling we can see more clearly the steps to create the connection and read the date and time.

```
import java.net.*;
import java.io.*;

public class SocketTest extends java.applet.Applet{

  Socket mySocket;
  InputStream myInput;

  public void init(){
    mySocket=new  Socket("kappa.mic.dundee.ac.uk",13);
    myInput=mySocket.getInputStream();
    int ch=0;
    while(true ){
      ch=myInput.read();
      if (ch==-1)
        break;
      System.out.print(""+(char)ch);
    }
    myInput.close();
  }
}
```

This code won't compile correctly but shows the creation of a socket using the new statement. If the socket is successfully connected to the remote machine, an input stream associated with the socket is created. The program then reads characters from the input stream one at a time until the read statement returns -1 when no more input is available. When the read statement returns -1, the while statement breaks and the socket is closed using the close method. If you compile and view the complete applet as it stands, you will connect to port 13 of a Sun server and receive the date and time from the server. The print statement converts the integer returned from the read into a character and displays it.

How to post to a CGI interface

Data-entry forms have become commonplace on web sites around the world: they pop up as visitors' books, on-lines sales forms, etc. Java can use its user-interface components and its network-handling functions to simulate a data-entry form and send that data to a server. However, with the power of Java the data can be generated from the user's actions rather than data directly entered by the user. For instance, a Java game program could send the user's score to a web server for inclusion in a high score table. A shopping program could keep a list of the user's purchases locally (with the user's machine not connected to the server) and only send the order when the user is finished and prepared to make a connection to the Internet.

Two things are needed in order for this type of data transfer to work: the client's Java program must "Post" the data to a server, and the server must have a program available to receive the data. (See a CGI reference book to find out about writing programs to handle the data that the Java program will send.) The Java program opens a socket in the normal way and creates an input stream and an output stream. A data output is attached to the output stream and a data input is attached to the input stream. The data to be posted is sent down the data output stream. An optional response from the server is retrieved from the data input stream. The data retrieved for the user interface components of the applet needs to be encoded before it can be sent to the server.

Without going into details (refer to the documentation for HTML 2.0 for complete details; a good text can be found at http://hopf.math.edu/html2.0), the POST method is split into two parts – a header and the data from the form.

Building the header

The first line of the header should be the string "POST", followed by the name of the CGI program on the server to handle the data. This is followed by the string "HTTP/1.0\r\n". If the name of the program on the server to handle the data is "Handler.cgi", then the first line will read:

```
"POST Handler.cgi HTTP/1.0\r\n"
```

Note

Remember from Part A that \r is carriage return and \n is line feed.

The second line of the header should be the string "Content-type:", followed by a string representation of the encoding form, and lastly a carriage return and line feed. For the POST method the encoding form string should be "application/x-www-form-urlencoded", which gives the second line as:

```
"Content-type:  application/x-www-form-urlencoded\r\n"
```

The third line contains information about the length of the data. The first part is the string "Content-Length:"; this should be followed by a string representation of the length of the data. Once the data has been encoded into the proper form, you can use the length method of the string class to obtain the length.

Encoding the data

The data from a form is combined together into a single string with no spaces, and with non-alphanumeric characters replaced by a hexadecimal pair representing the character. Each field of the data-entry form is represented by the name of the field followed by an '=' sign, followed by a string representing the data of the field. Any spaces in either the name of the field or the data of the field should be replaced by the '+' sign. So if we have a field whose name is "UsersName" and the user fills the field with "Andrew E Cobley" then the field is represented in the data string by:

```
"UsersName=Andrew+E+Cobley"
```

Each field you want to send is separated in the final string by the '&' character. If the '&' character appears in the data, it needs to be replaced by its hexadecimal representation "%26". Any line breaks in the data need to be changed to the hexadecimal representation of carriage return and line feed, i.e. %0D%0A. In the following method, the name of a field and its value are converted to a string suitable for posting: it first combines the name and value fields, and then steps through the string converting any non-& characters to their hexadecimal form and spaces to the '+' character.

```java
public String ToPostString(String Name, String Value){
  String WholeString = Name+"="+Value;
  String ConvertedString="";
  if (WholeString.length() >0){
    for (int i=0; i<WholeString.length();i++){
      if (WholeString.charAt(i) == ' '){ // Check for space
        ConvertedString=ConvertedString + "+";
      }else if ( WholeString.charAt(i) =='&'){
        ConvertedString = ConvertedString + "%26";
      } else
        ConvertedString= ConvertedString + WholeString.charAt(i);
    }
  } ConvertedString= ConvertedString + "&";
  return  ConvertedString;
}
```

The method shown converts any space characters to the "+" character, but does not convert non-alphanumeric characters to their hexadecimal forms. To create the entire data string for the post, call this method for each field you want to add, building up the data string:

```
DataString= ToPostString("Field1", Value1);
DataString=DataString +"&"+ToPostString("Field2", Value2);
```

To post the data

As we noted earlier, for security reasons Java will only allow you to post data back to the server that supplied the Java applet. Within the init method of the applet, you should use the document base to get the server's name and the port number that the server is using for the HTML protocol. The name of the server is a string and the port number an integer. Remember to make these variables "global"; that is, they should be available to all methods in the applet.

```
Home = getDocumentBase().getHost();
Port = getDocumentBase().getPort();
```

We can now create a method to post the data. However, because the server processing the post should send a reply, our method will have to handle this reply. For our example we will assume that you have created a method that retrieves the data from the user-interface components and combines them into a single data string before calling our post method. Our method will create a socket, get data input and output streams, and add the appropriate data streams to the input and output. We use the data stream because it allows us to read or write a string to the socket simply. As we saw in the last section, the methods to create these entities need to be enclosed in try and catch statements. For clarity, our example will leave these statements out, so you will need to add them yourself if you want to use this method. Here is the start of the method:

```
public void PostData(String Data){
   Socket Sock;
   OutputStream StreamOut;
   InputStream StreamIn;
   DataOutputStream DataOut;
   DataInputStream DataIn;
   String InString;

   Sock=new Socket(Home,Port);
   StreamOut=Sock.getOutputStream();
   StreamIn=Sock.getInputStream();
   DataOut=new DataOutputStream(StreamOut);
   DataIn=new DataInputStream(StreamIn);
```

We have now created all the socket objects we need to carry out the post. The first thing that needs to be sent is the header; we have hard-coded the name of the program to accept the data into this header:

```
   DataOut.writeBytes("POST accept.cgi HTTP/1.0\r\n");
   DataOut.writeBytes("Content-type: application/x-www-form-
urlencoded\r\n");
   DataOut.writeBytes("Content-length:" + Data.length() + "\r\n");
```

Once the header is sent, the actual data can be transferred.

```
   DataOut.writeBytes("\r\n");
   DataOut.writeBytes(Data);
   DataOut.writeBytes("\r\n");
```

A post method is expected to receive data back from the content handler – this is usually a string confirming the transfer of the data. We can receive this data in our post method, and use it for reposting the data or to confirm success to the user. The code shown here reads each line in turn and adds it to the "InString" string.

```
   String line;
   boolean Body = false;
   while ((line = DataIn.readLine()) != null){
     if (Body)
       InString + = "\n" + line;
     else if (line.equals(""))
       Body = true;
   }
   System.out.println("Returned"+InString);
```

After the post is complete, the sockets and data channels should be closed properly using the appropiate close method. (Again, our code is shown without the appropriate try/catch clauses.)

```
DataOut.close();
DataIn.close();
Sock.close();
```

Note

You can find all the example code from this book on the World-Wide Web, at `http://www.computerstep.com/1874029482.htm`. This contains all the try-catch statements, and is free from errors; download it from there if you want to actually use these examples to post to a CGI server program. The source code for a simple data-handler has been included here too. Three versions are provided, two written in C and one in PERL. Of the two C programs, one is suitable for most UNIX systems and the other for Microsoft Windows (NT or 95). The source for Microsoft has been compiled using Microsoft's C++ compiler and has been tested on a Windows NT 4.0 server.

CHAPTER 26

Communication Between Applets on One HTML Page

If you have got more than one applet on a page then it is conceivable that applets will need to communicate with each other – for instance, to keep all the applets' backgrounds the same colour. You can get a handle to which applets are on the current page by using the getApplets method of the AppletContext class.

Because it is impossible to know how many applets share the page with the current applet, the getApplets method returns an Enumeration class. The Enumeration class maintains a list of objects that can be as large as needed. Code 26-1 gets a list of the applets on the current page and makes each applet print an "I'm here" statement. Notice that the code imports the util package to support the Enumeration class.

```
import java.util.*;
import java.applet.*;

public class Multitest extends java.applet.Applet{

  public void init(){
    Enumeration Applets;
    Applets=getAppletContext().getApplets();
    while (Applets.hasMoreElements()){
      Applet Latest=(Applet)Applets.nextElement();
      Class object=Latest.getClass();
      ((Multitest) Latest).ImHere();
    }
  }
```

```
public void ImHere(){
  System.out.println("I'm here");
}
}
```

Code 26-1

Code 26-1 first retrieves a list of all applets on the current page and stores them in an enumeration. An enumeration contains a list of objects that can be retrieved one at a time. The list can be used once only; when the end is reached, the list does not exist anymore. For each applet on the page, the code retrieves the applet object from the enumeration. A descriptor of the class of the applet object is created, and using a cast (in this case to Multitest) calls the "ImHere" method.

If you include Code 26-1 twice in an .HTML document and then view it with the appletviewer, you will see "I'm here" printed 4 times. Because the applet retrieves a list of all the applets on the page, the list includes itself. So each applet will tell itself to print "I'm here" as well as the other applet on the page. Beware, however, of placing the "getApplets" in the init() section of an applet, as the other applets on the page may not have finished initialising when the current applet tries to retrieve the list. This will cause the list to be incorrect, possibly missing some applets and even having incorrect information about the other applets.

If you want to send messages between the applets on a page, your program will need to know the class names of the applets on the page, and each applet will need to have its name set in the <applet> tag. Furthermore, any class that is going to receive a message will need to have a method ready to receive messages.

In the example below we have two applets on a page, Namedtest and Namedtest2. Namedtest is going to receive messages sent by Namedtest2. The Applet tags are shown in the sample HTML below. The applet to receive the messages is shown in Code 26-2 – it simply contains a method called ImHere which will be called by the other applet sharing the web page.

```
import java.applet.*;

public class Namedtest extends java.applet.Applet{

  public void init(){
  }

  public void ImHere(String Who){
    System.out.println("I'm Here "+Who);
  }
}
```

CODE 26-2

In the applet class to send messages, we use the getApplet method from the appletContext class to create a new applet from the named applet:

```
Applet Latest = getAppletContext().gateApplet("Test1");
```

This will create a new instance of an Applet class (called "Latest"), which will reference the other applet on the page. In order to use the "Latest" instance to call the "ImHere" method in the Namedtest applet, it needs to be cast into that class:

```
(Namedtest)Latest.ImHere("Hello");
```

This why we need to know the class names of the other applets on the page before we can use them for inter-applet communications. The entire code for the second applet is very simple and is shown in Code 26-3 below. Notice that it gets a parameter from the HTML and sends that string to the first applet:

```
import java.util.*;
import java.applet.*;

public class Namedtest2 extends java.applet.Applet{

  public void init(){
```

```
   String Who= getParameter("WHO");
   Applet Latest= getAppletContext().getApplet("test1");
   ((Namedtest)Latest).ImHere(Who);
  }
}
```

CODE 26-3

The HTML code for the two applets is shown below, complete with the
parameter statements in the <Applet> tag.

```
<title>Test of applet communication</title>
<Applet code="Namedtest.class"
 width="175"
 height="276" Name="test1">
 <PARAM name=WHO value="Test1">
</Applet>
<Applet code="Namedtest2.class"
 width="175"
 height="276" Name= "test2">
 <PARAM name=WHO value="Test2">
</Applet>
```

PART E

Advanced Topics

CHAPTER 27

Modifers, Class Security and Packages

The need for protection

Back in Part C we saw that variables and methods can be "protected" from unwanted access by using the private modifier. This protection allows the programmer to make sure that access to a variable (or method) can be limited and controlled so that unforeseen side effects can be avoided. This chapter will expand on these simple ideas to allow more subtle levels of protection to be implemented. To begin with, let's recap on the material from Part C.

If we look at the rather contrived class in Code 27-1, the variable "myVariable" should only ever have the value of 2. The "NotSecure" class sets "myVariable" to 1 and uses the "ShouldBePrivate" method to multiply it by 2. To use the methods in the class the proper constructor should be called and the variable should only ever be read. However, the "UseNotSecure" method violates these intentions causing "myVariable" to have a value of -200. The "UseNotSecure" method causes problems because it:

1: Allows direct access to "myVariable"

2: Accesses the "ShouldBePrivate" method directly

```
class NotSecure{
  int myVariable;

  NotSecure(){
    myVariable=1;
    ShouldBePrivate(2);
  }

  void ShouldBePrivate(int Controller){
    myVariable =Controller*myVariable;
  }

}

class UseNotSecure{
  UseNotSecure(){
    NotSecure myUnsecureOne=new NotSecure();
    myUnsecureOne.myVariable=100;
    myUnsecureOne.ShouldBePrivate(-2);
  }
}
```

CODE 27-1

As we have seen before, Java allows programmers to protect their code through four levels of protection: private, package, protected and public. These modifiers are applied to the class, method or variable definition. Our insecure class should have made use of the private modifier to protect its variable and method:

```
class Secure{
  private int myVariable;

  public Secure(){
    myVariable=1;
    IsPrivate(1);
  }

  private void IsPrivate(int Controller){
    myVariable =Controller*myVariable;
  }

}
```

CODE 27-2

Any class that uses the "Secure" class has access to the constructor method but does not have any access to the variable or the "IsPrivate" method. However, there is no way to obtain the current value of "myVariable" from outside the class. We can create an "accessor" method that can be used to retrieve the value of the variable, but does not allow the variable's value to be changed. The accessor method is defined as public, so any class has access to it. However, because the author of this class defines the behaviour of the accessor method, the unwanted effects can be avoided.

```
public int GetVariable(){
  return myVariable;
}
```

If we do want to allow users of the class to change private variables, then an accessor method can be written that allows safe changes to be made. The code below shows an accessor method that only allows the private variable to be set within a narrow range. The method returns true if the variable is changed and false if it is not.

```
Public boolean SetVariable(in newValue){
    if ( (newValue >0) && (newValue <10){
       myVariable=newValue;
       return true;
    }
    return false;
}
```

Accessor methods are a very powerful way to protect your classes, but they might seem like a lot of effort, at least to begin with. However, if you start to share your code with other programmers, then the use of accessor methods will start to make sense; it is a good idea to start using them as soon as possible to become comfortable with their use.

Other levels of protection

The private and public levels of protection are the extremes of protection that Java allows. Two other levels of protection exist to fine-tune the security of your methods; these are "protected" and "package". Actually, "package" is the default level of protection and does not even have a keyword at present. If a class, method or variable is defined without a modifier (private, public or protected) then it is said to have a security level of "package". A class, variable or method that has a "package" level of security is only visible to other classes in the same package. A package groups related files together, as we will see shortly. If the source codes for more than one class are in the same directory (or file) as each other then they are said to be of the same package. Provided no other modifiers are used (such as public or private), the classes will be visible to each other. If we want to join classes from other directories into this package then we must use the "package" statement as described later in this chapter.

The final level of protection is "Protected". On its own, this level allows any member of the same package access to the variable or method, as well as classes outside the package that extend the class. When combined with the private keyword, this level of protection only allows children of that class to have access. This level of protection is useful in allowing other programmers access to the methods and variables of the class only when they extend the class. (Some development environments may not support the "private protected" level of protection. Check with the documentation or try out the sample program before you commit yourself to using this level of protection. In fact, in later versions of Java – 1.1 and above – the "private protected" level of protection is not supported.) This gives protection against casual usage of the class, but does allow programmers to access some of the internals if they need to. The applet in Code 27-3 shows an example of a protected variable and an attempt to access it. The "ProtectedClass" will not allow the applet to access the "ProtectedVariable" because the applet does not extend the protected class.

```
    import java.applet.*;

  public class TestProtected extends java.applet.Applet{
    ProtectedClass ProtectedClassObject;
    public void init(){
      ProtectedClassObject= new ProtectedClass();
      System.out.println("Variable is "
+ProtectedClassObject.ProtectedVariable); // This will not work
    }
  }

  class ProtectedClass{
    private protected int ProtectedVariable=1;
    ProtectedClass(){
    }
  }
```

CODE 27-3

In the following example we create a new class that extends the
"ProtectedClass". This new class has access to all the protected methods and
variables of the "ProtectedClass", and uses this access in an "Accessor"
method to allow the applet access to the protected variable.

```
    import java.applet.*;

  public class AccessTest extends java.applet.Applet{
    AccessProtected AccessClassObject;
    public void init(){
      AccessClassObject= new AccessProtected();
      System.out.println("Variable is "+AccessClassObject.AccessObject);
    }
  }

  class ProtectedClass{
    private protected int ProtectedVariable=1;
    ProtectedClass(){
    }
  }

  class AccessProtected extends ProtectedClass{
    AccessProtected(){
    }
    int AccessObject(){
      return (super.ProtectedVariable);
    }
  }
```

CODE 27-4

One final level of protection exists to stop yourself or others from extending a class any further. If the keyword "final" is placed before the class definition then this class can not be extended. Code 27-5 shows the final keyword in action:

```
final class FinalClass{
  int ProtectedVariable=1;
  FinalClass(){
  }

}
class AccessFinal extends FinalClass{
  AccessFinal(){
  }

  int AccessObject(){
    return (super.ProtectedVariable);
  }
}
```

Code 27-5

If you try to compile this program snippet, you will receive a short message telling you that you "Can't subclass final classes". By making a class "final" you can guarantee that no other programmer can override your class and cause unexpected side-effects. The writers of the Java libraries have made extensive use of the final modifier to ensure that we (as mere mortals!) can not cause havoc in our programs by overriding their carefully constructed code. Not surprisingly, you can have final methods and final variables. Final variables can not be changed and have to be set at the time of construction. These are great if you want to use a constant in your class and absolutely do not want it to be changed. Final methods can not be overridden even if the class itself has been extended. Again, this is useful for making sure that other programmers (or yourself) can not cause unexpected effects by overriding your methods. Just for completeness, the following code shows the use of the final statement for variables and methods.

```
class CalculateArea{
  final double PI=3.141519;
  double radius;
  CalculateArea(){}
  void SetRadius(double radius){
    this.radius= radius;
  }
  final double ShowArea(){
    return(radius*radius*PI);
  }
}
```

Packages

Java provides a rather useful mechanism for collecting related classes together into a unit known as a package. You have already used packages whenever you have used the import statement. When you use the import statement, you are retrieving "library" classes from the standard Java packages. If you use a statement such as "import java.awt.*", you tell the Javac compiler that you are going to use some of the classes in the "awt" package, so it should look in that package to find them. The compiler does not import all classes from the package – only the ones that it needs for your program.

You can create your own packages and import them in the same way. However, if you want to use them in an applet, the "classpath" statement of the <applet> tag will need to be set correctly to point to the root directory of the packages. To signal that a class is part of a package you include the package statement at the very start of the ".Java" file.

If we create two files in a directory called "MyFirstPackage" as shown in Code 27-6 and 27-7, and compile them using Java, we can import them into an applet as shown in Code 27-8, provided:

- The classpath statement is set in the <applet> tag (or your CLASSPATH variable contains a pointer to the current directory)
- The applet is stored in the directory above the "MyFirstPackage" directory as shown in Figure 27-1.

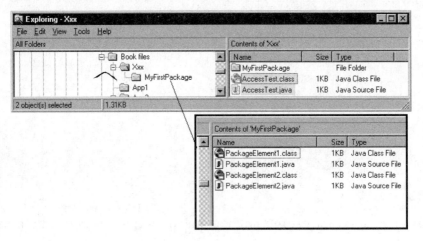

FIGURE 27-1

```
package MyFirstPackage;

public class PackageElement1{
  public PackageElement1(){
    System.out.println("Created
Package element 1 instance");
  }
}
```

CODE 27-6

```
package MyFirstPackage;

public class PackageElement2{
  public PackageElement2(){
    System.out.println("Created
Package element 2 instance");
  }
}
```

CODE 27-7

```
  import MyFirstPackage.*;
public class TestPackages extends java.applet.Applet{
  public void init(){
    PackageElement1 element1= new PackageElement1();
    PackageElement2 element2= new PackageElement2();
  }
}
```

CODE 27-8

These examples do not do much but print a line of text when an instance of the class is created, but they do show the principles of creating a package.

1: The package statement must be the very first statement in a Java file; it is followed by the package name you are creating.

2: The packages must be stored in a directory of exactly the same name as the package (including the case of the letters in the name).

3: The constructor of the class should be public if you want other classes to create instances of this class.

4: Once you have imported a package into a class with the "*" wild card, you can use any element of that package.

By using packages you can collect your classes together to form a library. However, Java allows you to go one step further: you can group your classes together into a hierarchy, placing related files together. For instance, suppose you were creating a library of classes for use in an accountancy package: you could join all the invoice-handling classes in one group, all the VAT-handling classes in another, and perhaps all the order-handling classes together. Java allows you to do this by placing the related files in a sub-directory and using the package statement to reflect this fact. Suppose we had a group of related classes in a sub-directory under our "MyFirstPackage" directory. If this directory is called "mySubFiles" then the package statement at the start of the files should be "package MyFirstPackage.mySubfiles;". Java insists that the subdirectory be named exactly the same as the sub-package name.

By grouping the files together like this, we can allow users of our library more flexibility as to which parts of the library they want to use. As an example, suppose we are creating a library of classes to manipulate images. The library will implement techniques such as contrast enhancement, edge detection, image comparison, etc. To make things easier we would want our classes to manipulate a neutral image format. We would want to provide classes to convert from popular file formats to our neutral format. However, our users may want to use only some of these converters and only some of the conversion techniques. By grouping all the converters and manipulators into sub-directories under our own main library we can let the library users select the components they want. Our directory structure may look like that in Figure 27-2.

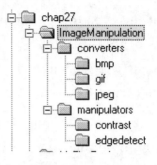

FIGURE 27-2

The Java file for each class in the library will announce which package it is in at the start of the source code. Thus, for example, the GifConverter class would begin:

```
package ImageManipulation.converters.gif;
```

Any program that wants to use our library could import the whole thing with "import ImageManipulation". Alternatively, it could import only the section you want by specifying the full path, as follows:

```
import ImageManipulation.converters.gif.*;  // Import all the gif converters
import ImageManipulation.maniplulators.contrast.*;  // Import all the
       contrast enhancement  classes.
```

The code below shows two ways that the library elements could be used. The first Import statement imports the entire library. (Actually, only the classes used are imported but this statement tells the compiler to look for any class in the package.) The second import statement imports the edge detection part of the library directly. Now, when we want to use one of the class libraries, we have a choice of how to address the class. Any class that is part of the edge detection sub-directory can be addressed directly as shown for the variable edg1. Any other class for the library needs to be addressed with the full path to the class, as shown for the myConverter variable.

```
import ImageManipulation.*;
import ImageManipulation.manipulators.edgedetect.*;

public class PackageTest extends java.applet.Applet{

  public void init(){
     ImageManipulation.converters.gif.ConvertGif myConverter = new
ImageManipulation.converters.gif.ConvertGif();
     EdgeDetect edg1= new EdgeDetect();
  }
}
```

Using packages may seem like a lot of trouble, but if you are intending to make libraries available to other programmers (as Sun have done with the Java libraries) then it really does make sense to create a sensible library structure. You will appreciate it and so will your library users.

Packages and the protected level of security

Now we have dealt with packages, we can take a look at using the protected level of security. Within our packages we will want to protect some of the classes, variables and methods so that they can not be altered by our package users. We could simply set the security to private for those methods and variables that need it, and leave everything else public. However, suppose one of the classes in the library wants to limit access to a variable so that only classes that extend it can access it: we can use a protected variable, as shown in Code 27-9. This variable is visible to any other class in the package and also to variables outside the package that extend it. The applet in Code 27-10 shows an illegal access (commented out), and the correct way to access the variable.

```
package ImageManipulation.manipulators.edgedetect;
public class EdgeDetect{
  protected int myProtected=2;

  public EdgeDetect(){
  }
}
```

CODE 27-9

```
import ImageManipulation.*;
import ImageManipulation.manipulators.edgedetect.*;
public class PackageTest extends java.applet.Applet{
  public void init(){
  EdgeDetect edg1= new EdgeDetect();
  /* edg1.myProtected=5;   ************** Can't do this protected */
    extendedEdgeDetect edg2= new extendedEdgeDetect();
    System.out.println(edg2.WhatIs());
  }
}


class extendedEdgeDetect extends EdgeDetect{
  public extendedEdgeDetect (){
    super.myProtected=5;
  }
  public int WhatIs(){
    return(super.myProtected);
  }
}
```

CODE 27-10

The Java language has one more trick up its sleeve to help us with the design of our programs. Interfaces are designed as a way for us to create "skeleton" classes that define the methods a class using the interface has to implement. The interface itself does nothing, but it may include some variables for the class that implements it to use. The code below shows a simple interface with the definitions of three methods:

```
public interface MyFirstInterface{
  void Amethod();
  int AnotherMethod();
  void YetAnotherMethod(int Avariable);
}
```

We might like to try and use this interface like this:

```
public class UseInterface2 extends java.applet.Applet implements
MyFirstInterface {
  public void init(){
  }
  public void Amethod(){}
  public int AnotherMethod(){
    return(1);
  }
}
```

This applet implements the interface and tries to define empty methods for two of the methods in the interface. These two blank methods will compile correctly, but the overall compilation will fail with an error similar to:

```
UseInterface.java:1: class UseInterface must be declared abstract. It does
not define void YetAnotherMethod(int) from interface MyFirstInterface.
```

When we define an interface, we define the methods that any class that implements this interface must implement. That is, any class that implements this interface must create a method with an actual body, even if the body is empty. Our applet example did not create a body for the method "YetAnotherMethod" and so generated an error at run time. By using an interface, we can define all the methods for a class library, and indeed the entire structure of the library, without having to write the bodies for these methods. This is extremely useful at the design stage of a program: we are interested in the structure of the classes, but we are not prepared to write the bodies – that will be done at a later stage.

Interfaces behave in a similar manner to classes. One interface can extend another and each interface can contain its own variables. However, these variables are constants; any class using the interface has access to the variables' values but can not change them. These variables are effectively "final" variables and will give the same errors as a final variable if you try and change their value or forget to initialise them in the interface definition. The small class below extends the first interface and defines an integer variable.

```
public interface MySecondInterface extends MyFirstInterface{
  int AVariable =2;
  public int ASecondMethod();
}
```

It turns out that our applets can create their own empty methods that the class's children will have to implement. These methods are known as abstract methods. Let's try a small example of their use. Suppose we have a simple interface with one method defined in it, as follows:

```
public interface DoingStuff {
  void DoSomething();
}
```

We could create a class that implements this interface but leaves the "DoSomething" method abstract for definition by a child of the class. Note that the "DoSomething" method is defined as abstract, but so is the class. This will mean that the class can not be instantiated but can be extended. The constructor calls a method "StartDoingStuff", which could be overridden by any child classes.

```
abstract public class ProcessStuff implements DoingStuff{
  ProcessStuff (){
    StartDoingStuff();
  }
  public void StartDoingStuff(){
    DoSomething();
  }
  abstract public void DoSomething();
}
```

So now we want to use the "ProcessStuff" class. Any class that uses it will need to create a "DoSomething" method and should call the parent through the use of super().

```
class myProcessStuff extends ProcessStuff{
  myProcessStuff(){
    super();
  }
  public void DoSomething(){
    System.out.println("Well I'm Doing Something");
  }
}
```

Finally, we can use this new class in an applet which when it is executed will print "Well I'm Doing Something" to the standard output.

```
public class UseProcess extends java.applet.Applet {
  myProcessStuff myProcess;
  public void init(){
    myProcess=new myProcessStuff();
  }
}
```

CHAPTER 28

Exceptions

Throughout this book we have been using try-catch statements to surround certain Java package methods without explaining why. The try-catch statements are part of Java's error-handling mechanism. Errors are defined as an unexpected result from a statement in Java, possibly due to external and unavoidable reasons. For instance, we used sockets in the last section to connect to a remote machine to receive the date and time, but what would be the result if the remote host were not available because of a power failure? The program has to be able to detect these events and handle them in a sensible manner. In older languages, errors are usually handled by checking the return value from a procedure. Usually, this is an integer value, possibly with negative numbers indicating an anomalous condition; but if negative numbers are a valid result, it can become impossible to find a suitable value to indicate that an error has occurred.

Java provides a mechanism for handling these unexpected results, called exceptions (a sub-class of the throwable class). These are classes in their own right, and can only be used for anomalous results; there is no need to "put aside" values to handle errors. You will need to be able to handle exceptions when they arise in the Java package library. Once you start creating your own packages and class libraries, you will need to be able to generate your own exceptions for classes you create.

We have already seen how to handle exceptions in a simple manner using the try-catch statements, usually by catching all exceptions thrown by a method and warning of the error with a system.out.println statement.

```
try{
  SomeStatement;
}catch (exception et){
  System.out.println("Something wrong happened");
}
```

This will catch any errors thrown by "SomeStatement" and print a warning. Some classes can throw a number of different errors, and we can catch each one separately. For instance, the socket class can throw either an "IOException" or "UnknownHostException", which we might like to handle separately. We can specify in the "catch" statement which exception this catch would like to handle. In the following example we catch the error thrown when an attempt is made to connect to an non-existent host.

```
try {
  Socket mySocket= new Socket("Some.Host", 90);
} catch (UnknownHostException et){
  System.out.println("Sorry that host does not exist");
}
```

CODE 28-1

However, if you do not catch all exceptions that a method can throw, the Java compiler will generate an error. To catch more than one error the "catch" statements can be stacked up, with each "catch" handling a different exception.

```
try {
  Socket mySocket= new Socket("Some.Host", 90);
} catch (UnknownHostException et){
  System.out.println("Sorry that host does not exist");
} catch (IOException et){
  System.out.println("Oops, an IOException occured");
}
```

CODE 28-2

You can choose to catch a specific exception explicitly and leave all other exceptions to a "catch all" catch statement.

```
try {
  Socket mySocket= new Socket("Some.Host", 90);
} catch (UnknownHostException et){
  System.out.println("Sorry that host does not exist");
} catch (Exception et){
  System.out.println("Some other Exception");
}
```

CODE 28-3

When an exception is caught, execution does not stop in the catch statement, but will continue with the statement after the closing bracket. If statements later in the program depend on the successful operation of the try statement, then they too will fail if they are allowed to attempt execution. You should include these statements within the try statement. In the previous section we showed how to connect to a remote machine and read the date and time from it. However, the code we used for the streams will fail in an ungraceful manner if the socket can not be created. That is, if the socket fails, the program will still try to connect input streams and read from them; these too will fail and generate error messages. If we rewrite the code as shown in Code 28-4, only the method that fails will generate a message, and the program will not attempt to execute methods dependent on the failing method.

```
public class SocketTest extends java.applet.Applet{
  Socket mySocket;
  InputStream myInput;

  public void init(){
    try {
      mySocket= new Socket("kappa.mic.dundee.ac.uk",13);
      try {
        myInput=mySocket.getInputStream();
        int ch=0;
          while(true ){
            try{
              ch= myInput.read();
```

```
        }catch (Exception et){
          System.out.println("Applet has thrown  exception"+et);
        }
        if (ch==-1) break;
          System.out.print(""+(char)ch);
      }
      try {
        myInput.close();
      }catch (Exception et){
        System.out.println("Applet has thrown  exception whilst
closing"+et);
      }
    }catch (Exception et){
      System.out.println("Applet has thrown  exception whilst getting
input stream"+et);
    }
  }catch (Exception et){
    System.out.println("Applet has thrown  exception whilst creating a
socket"+et);
    }
  }
}
```

CODE 28-4

However, we might want a piece of code to execute regardless of which
error is generated, even if we want different behaviour for each type of
error. In fact, we might want to execute a piece of code even if the try
statement succeeded. For instance, if we have successfully opened a service
on a remote machine, and then some other error occurs, we would want to
close the service gracefully. We can do this with a "finally" statement. This
is placed at the end of the catch statements and will always run regardless of
the success or failure of the try statement. So in the following code –

```
try {
  SomeStatements;
}catch (Exception et){
  SomeFailureStatements;
}
finally {
  AlwaysDoThis;
}
```

– "SomeStatements" will be attempted. If they fail, then "SomeFailureStatements" will be executed. After either or both of these have been run, the "AlwaysDoThis" statement will be executed.

Generating exceptions

Once your use of Java begins to increase, it is only a matter of time before you build a class in which some exceptional conditions can occur. You will want to let any class using this class be aware when the exceptional condition has arisen – i.e., you will want to generate an exception. To create a class which can generate exceptions you will have to define which exceptions are thrown, using the "throws" statement in the method which has the exceptional condition. This method can be the constructor of the class or some other method. You can use any of the normal exceptions that Java has defined for us or create your own. Code 28-5 will generate an IOException if the constructor is called with a parameter of 0.

```
class Thrower {
  Thrower (int Arg) throws IOException {
    if (Arg ==0){
      IOException Et = new IOException();
      throw Et;
    }
  }
}
```

CODE 28-5

However, reusing an exception that has already been defined is not really a sensible decision; in the example, an IOException does not really describe the nature of the fault. We really need an exception called "CanNotCreateWithZeroException" error. Because an exception is just a class defined in the Java call library, we can extend the class and inherit its properties. As with the AWT, the first statement in the constructor should call the parent class through the "super" statement.

```
class CanNotCreateWithZeroException extends Exception{
  CanNotCreateWithZeroException(String message){
    super(message);
  }
}
```

Our thrower class can now use this new exception as if it were built into Java. The "Throw" statement works as a kind of break statement – none of the code after it is executed.

```
class Thrower {
  Thrower (int Arg) throws CanNotCreateWithZeroException  {
    if (Arg ==0){
      CanNotCreateWithZeroException Et = new
CanNotCreateWithZeroException("Damn, Cannot create with zero");
      throw Et;
    }
  }
}
```

Any class that tries to use the Thrower class will need a try-catch statement pair to catch the "CanNotCreateWithZeroException" error, or else a compiler error will be generated. Thus we can ensure that any programmer using our class will have to handle the exception in some manner, even if it is just by generating an error message. However, when you start using Java for professional applications you will need to be more conscientious: handle exceptions in the most responsible manner you can, and your applications will be robust.

```
try {
  Thrower myThrower= new Thrower(0);
} catch(CanNotCreateWithZeroException et){
  System.out.println("Can not create with a zero");
}
```

A class can throw more than one type of exception, either from different methods within the class or from a single method. Supposing you have created two exception classes by extending the exception class, the throws statement simply has to mention both of these in the exceptional method. Code 28-6 shows the creation of two exceptions, and a method that can throw these exceptions. Notice that exceptions can throw a listed method definition separated by commas.

```
class MultiThrower {
  MultiThrower (int Arg) throws CanNotCreateWithZeroException,
CanNotCreateWithOneException {
    if (Arg ==0){
      CanNotCreateWithZeroException Et = new
CanNotCreateWithZeroException("Damn, Cannot create with zero");
      throw Et;
    }

    if (Arg ==1){
      CanNotCreateWithOneException Et = new
CanNotCreateWithOneException("Damn, Cannot create with One");
      throw Et;
    }
  }
}


class CanNotCreateWithZeroException extends Exception{
  CanNotCreateWithZeroException(String message){
    super(message);
  }
}

class CanNotCreateWithOneException extends Exception{
  CanNotCreateWithOneException(String message){
    super(message);
  }
}
```

CODE 28-6

We have seen how to handle an exception with a try-catch statement pair, usually by generating a error message. But what happens if we want to pass the exception back to whatever called this method? In other words, our method doesn't want to handle the error but wants to let whatever called it handle it. Once an exception has been caught, it can be passed back up the chain simply by rethrowing it. The following example tries to create a new Thrower with 0 as an argument: it will catch the error and pass it up to whatever tries to create it.

```
public class reThrower{
  public void reThrower throws CanNotCreateWithZeroException(){
    try {
      Thrower myThrower= new Thrower(0);
    } catch(CanNotCreateWithZeroException et){
      System.out.println("Can not create with a zero");
      throw(et);
    }
  }
}
```

CHAPTER 29

Threads

Way back in Part A we discovered that Java was a multi-tasking language, and found out how to achieve animation by making an applet implement the runnable interface. When we created a multi-tasking applet, we created a new "Thread" variable and then provided start, stop and run methods in the applet. These methods checked which thread they where running and altered their behaviour appropriately.

There is, however, another method of creating threads in your program. A thread is just another class of object in Java; you can create your own class and extend the "thread" class. In order for your thread class to do any work, it must override the run method of the standard thread class. Code 29-1 shows a very simple thread class.

```
class myThreadClass extends Thread{
  String myName;
    int i;
  myThreadClass(String name){
    super();
    myName=name;
  }
  public void run(){
    for ( i=0; i<10;i++){
      System.out.println("Thread " +myName+" Count "+i);
    }
  }
}
```

CODE 29-1

As usual, the class's constructor calls the constructor of the parent class "Thread" by using the "super()" method. The constructor shown also keeps a local copy of the name for use in the print statement of the run method. Our run method simply uses a "for" loop to output a counter to the standard output. Notice that unlike implementing a runnable interface (as we have usually done in previous sections) we do not need to provide stop and start methods. Now we have created a class that will run in its own thread, we can use it from within an applet (or application) in the same way that we would use any other class. We create a new instance of the class using the "new" operator. However, the class does not start to run until a call is made to the start method of the parent "Thread" class. It is this call to the "start" method that actually kicks the run method off. Code 29-2 creates two instances of the thread class and then runs them.

```
public class test extends java.applet.Applet{
myThreadClass thread1;
myThreadClass thread2;

  public void init(){
    thread1=new myThreadClass("Thread 1");
    thread2=new myThreadClass("Thread 2");

    thread1.start();
    thread2.start();
  }

}
```

CODE 29-2

What output would we expect from the applet in the console? Table 29-1 shows the output from three runs of the applet running on a Windows 95 portable (each run is in a separate column).

Thread Thread 1 Count 0	Thread Thread 2 Count 0	Thread Thread 1 Count 0
Thread Thread 1 Count 1	Thread Thread 2 Count 1	Thread Thread 1 Count 1
Thread Thread 2 Count 0	Thread Thread 1 Count 0	Thread Thread 2 Count 0
Thread Thread 2 Count 1	Thread Thread 1 Count 1	Thread Thread 2 Count 1
Thread Thread 1 Count 2	Thread Thread 2 Count 2	Thread Thread 1 Count 2
Thread Thread 1 Count 3	Thread Thread 2 Count 3	Thread Thread 1 Count 3
Thread Thread 2 Count 2	Thread Thread 1 Count 2	Thread Thread 2 Count 2
Thread Thread 2 Count 3	Thread Thread 1 Count 3	Thread Thread 2 Count 3
Thread Thread 1 Count 4	Thread Thread 2 Count 4	Thread Thread 1 Count 4
Thread Thread 1 Count 5	Thread Thread 2 Count 5	Thread Thread 1 Count 5
Thread Thread 1 Count 6	Thread Thread 1 Count 4	Thread Thread 2 Count 4
Thread Thread 1 Count 7	Thread Thread 1 Count 5	Thread Thread 2 Count 5
Thread Thread 2 Count 4	Thread Thread 2 Count 6	Thread Thread 1 Count 6
Thread Thread 2 Count 5	Thread Thread 1 Count 6	Thread Thread 1 Count 7
Thread Thread 1 Count 8	Thread Thread 1 Count 7	Thread Thread 2 Count 6
Thread Thread 1 Count 9	Thread Thread 2 Count 7	Thread Thread 2 Count 7
Thread Thread 2 Count 6	Thread Thread 2 Count 8	Thread Thread 1 Count 8
Thread Thread 2 Count 7	Thread Thread 1 Count 8	Thread Thread 1 Count 9
Thread Thread 2 Count 8	Thread Thread 1 Count 9	Thread Thread 2 Count 8
Thread Thread 2 Count 9	Thread Thread 2 Count 9	Thread Thread 2 Count 9

TABLE 29-1

Notice that the order in which the threads run is different each time the applet is started. The examples were run one after the other, with no difference in the other applications that were running on the machine. Once threads are running they are independent of each other, and run almost as if the machine has more than one processor. The operating system "segments" the amount of time each thread has available from the total time the processor has available to it. Your applet is not the only process wanting access to the processor: the operating system and other applications on your computer are all "fighting" for access. Consequently, you can not guarantee that any thread will run before any other thread in the applet.

Also, be aware that it is possible for one thread to "run away" with almost all the processor time that is available. This could happen if the thread is determined to run a very tight loop of mathematics, with no access to the operating system through system calls. Most modern systems will make sure that such processor hogs behave more or less in a friendly manner, but it is always good manners to make your threads give up the processor intentionally every now and then. You can achieve this by using the "yield" method of the "thread" class. The yield method "suspends" the thread and will schedule other threads your program has created to run in the near future. Notice that you do not actually have control over the order of thread execution; it is entirely up to the operating system and the Java virtual machine. If we modify the previous thread class code so that it can yield to other threads as shown in Code 29-3, we can see some dramatic effects on the order of execution:

```
class myThreadClass extends Thread{
  String myName;
    int i;
  boolean myYield;
  myThreadClass(String name, boolean yieldable){
    super();
    myName=name;
    myYield=yieldable;
  }

  public void run(){
    for ( i=0; i<1000;i++){
      if (i % 100 ==0)
        System.out.println("Thread " +myName+" Count "+i);
      if (myYield==true)
        this.yield();
    }

  }
}
```

CODE 29-3

This example increases the loop size, but only outputs the result every 100 iterations. If we create two instances of the class so that neither will yield (myYield set to false) then we obtain the result shown in Table 29-2 in the left-hand column. However, if we make thread 1 yield, then we get the result shown in the right-hand column.

```
Thread Thread 1 Count 0          Thread Thread 1 Count 0
Thread Thread 1 Count 1          Thread Thread 2 Count 0
Thread Thread 2 Count 0          Thread Thread 2 Count 100
Thread Thread 2 Count 1          Thread Thread 2 Count 200
Thread Thread 1 Count 2          Thread Thread 2 Count 300
Thread Thread 1 Count 3          Thread Thread 2 Count 400
Thread Thread 2 Count 2          Thread Thread 2 Count 500
Thread Thread 2 Count 3          Thread Thread 2 Count 600
Thread Thread 1 Count 4          Thread Thread 2 Count 700
Thread Thread 1 Count 5          Thread Thread 2 Count 800
Thread Thread 2 Count 4          Thread Thread 2 Count 900
Thread Thread 2 Count 5          Thread Thread 1 Count 100
Thread Thread 1 Count 6          Thread Thread 1 Count 200
Thread Thread 1 Count 7          Thread Thread 1 Count 300
Thread Thread 2 Count 6          Thread Thread 1 Count 400
Thread Thread 2 Count 7          Thread Thread 1 Count 500
Thread Thread 1 Count 8          Thread Thread 1 Count 600
Thread Thread 1 Count 9          Thread Thread 1 Count 700
Thread Thread 2 Count 8          Thread Thread 1 Count 800
Thread Thread 2 Count 9          Thread Thread 1 Count 900
```

TABLE 29-2

Because thread 1 is prepared to yield, thread 2 can "grab" more of the processor time and can finish before thread 1 has had time to start. Apart from the yield method, we can tell a thread to sleep for a specified period of time. We encountered the "sleep" method way back in Part A when we used it to time animation loops. The sleep method simply tells a thread to yield for the present and schedule itself to start at a later time. However, because of the nature of the scheduling process we can not guarantee that our thread will wake up at exactly the specified time.

The sleep method of the thread class we have been using up to now takes a single argument giving the number of milliseconds that the thread will sleep for. We have always surrounded a call to the sleep method with a try-catch clause, because the sleep method can throw an "InterruptedException". This exception occurs when our thread has been interrupted by some other thread. Normally this interrupt will be generated by another thread in your program, but it could be generated by the operating system. There is a second sleep method that allows finer control over the amount of time that the thread sleeps. This method takes as its arguments a long type variable giving the number of milliseconds to sleep for, followed by an integer that gives the number of nanoseconds (there are 1,000,000 nanoseconds in a millisecond) that should be added to the first argument. Remember that this method will only be of use if the operating system you are working with is real-time – i.e., if it can guarantee that the times specified in your applet can be honoured.

The first example below shows the sleep method we have been using in the past; the second shows the finer-control sleep method.

```
try{                                         try{
  sleep(1000);                                 sleep(SleepTime,FineTime);
}catch( InterruptedException Et){            }catch( InterruptedException Et){
  System.out.println("Thread                   System.out.println("Thread
"+myName+" has been interrupted" );          "+myName+" has been interrupted" );
  }                                            }
```

As we have seen, the sleep method needs to catch the interrupted exception. A thread can be interrupted by the "interrupt()" method of the thread class. The applet and thread class in Code 29-4 show the interrupt method in action. The applet has two buttons that can send an interrupt to each of the threads. The thread class uses the "interrupted()" method to determine if this thread has been interrupted. Unfortunately, it appears that once a thread has been interrupted there is no way to clear the "interrupted" method; it will always report that this thread has been interrupted. (Interrupts appear to be only partially implemented in current versions of Java. Check your version to see if this program behaves correctly.)

```
import java.awt.*;

public class InterruptTest extends java.applet.Applet{
mySleepClass thread1;
mySleepClass thread2;
Button Int1=new Button("Interrupt Thread 1");
Button Int2=new Button("Interrupt Thread 2");
  public void init(){
    thread1=new mySleepClass("Thread 1",10000);
```

```
    thread2=new mySleepClass("Thread 2",10000);
    thread1.start();
    thread2.start();
    add(Int1);
    add(Int2);
  }

public boolean action(Event evt, Object arg){
  if (evt.target instanceof Button){
    if (arg.equals ("Interrupt Thread 1")){
      System.out.println("Interrupt 1 pressed");
      thread1.interrupt();
      return true;
    }
    if (arg.equals ("Interrupt Thread 2")){
      System.out.println("Interrupt 1 pressed");
      thread2.interrupt();
      return true;
    }
  }
  return false;
  }
}

class mySleepClass extends Thread{
  String myName;
  int i;
  int SleepTime;

  mySleepClass(String name, int SleepTime){
    super();
    myName=name;
    this.SleepTime=SleepTime;
  }

  public void run(){
    for ( i=0; i<10;i++){
      System.out.println("Thread " +myName+" Count "+i+" Sleep "+SleepTime);
      try{
        sleep(SleepTime);
      }catch( InterruptedException Et){
        System.out.println("Thread "+myName+" has been interupted");
      }
      if (this.interrupted()==true)
        System.out.println("I was interrupted");
      if (this.interrupted()==false)
        System.out.println("I was not interrupted");

    }

  }
}
```

CODE 29-4

Pausing and restarting threads

As we have seen, we can tell a thread to sleep for a period of time or to yield to other processes, but what if want a thread to stop temporarily and be restarted at some later date by another thread? We can use the "suspend()" and "resume()" methods of the thread class to do this. The class shown in Code 29-5 will suspend another thread (the reference is passed to it in the constructor) whilst it completes its loop. After the loop is finished, it will resume the thread it had suspended.

```
class myThreadClass extends Thread{
  String myName;
    int i;
  Thread another;
  myThreadClass(String name, Thread other){
    super();
    myName=name;
    another=other;
  }

  public void run(){
    if (another !=null)
      another.suspend();
    for (i=0; i<1000;i++){
      if (i % 100 ==0)
        System.out.println("Thread " +myName+" Count "+i);
    }
    if (another !=null)
      another.resume();
    }
}
```

CODE 29-5

We do however have a problem with thread suspension. Suppose thread 1 suspends thread 2 then sleeps. Thread 2 is supposed to wake up thread 1, but of course it will not because it is suspended! This situation is called deadlock: two threads (or more) are held permanently in suspension because they are awaiting a wake up call that never comes. The situation is worse because sometimes these deadlocks can be very hard to spot in a complicated program. What is more, there is another way that deadlocks can occur: synchronisation.

Synchronisation is a way to allow a thread to lock a resource (method or variable) until the thread has finished with it. Let us consider, for example, Code 29-6. The parent applet holds an array that two threads can modify. A third thread will sleep for a period and then print out the values in the current array. The idea is that at any one time the values in the array should be either 1 or 0 according to which thread altered the array last. However, when we run the applet we find that the array can contain a mixture of ones and zeros. This is because "myArray" is in no way protected and both threads have complete access. We have arranged the code so that each thread "overlaps" in time, so that they can both access the array at the same time.

```
public class ShouldSynchronise extends java.applet.Applet{
ChangeClass thread1;
ChangeClass thread2;
PrintClass thread3;
int myArray[]=new int[10];

  public void init(){
    thread1=new ChangeClass(this,0,200);
    thread2=new ChangeClass(this,1,190);
    thread1.start();
    thread2.start();
    thread3.start();
  }
}
class ChangeClass extends Thread{
ShouldSynchronise myParent;
int Value;
long SleepTime;

  ChangeClass(ShouldSynchronise myParent, int Value,long SleepTime){
    this.myParent=myParent;
    this.Value=Value;
    this.SleepTime=SleepTime;
  }
  public void run(){
    while (true){
      try{
        sleep(SleepTime);
      }catch( InterruptedException Et){
        System.out.println("Thread has been interupted");
      }
      for (int i=0;i<10;i++){
        try{
```

```
        sleep(40);
      }catch( InterruptedException Et){
        System.out.println("Thread has been interupted");
      }
      myParent.myArray[i]=Value;
    }
   }
 }
}
class PrintClass extends Thread{
ShouldSynchronise myParent;
  PrintClass(ShouldSynchronise myParent){
    this.myParent=myParent;
  }
  public void run(){
    while (true){
      try{
        sleep(1000);
      }catch( InterruptedException Et){
        System.out.println("Thread has been interupted");
      }
      for (int i=0;i<10;i++)
        System.out.println("Value "+i+" = "+myParent.myArray[i]);
    }
  }
}
```

CODE 29-6

```
public void run(){
  while (true){
    try{
      sleep(SleepTime);
    }catch( InterruptedException Et){
      System.out.println("Thread has
been interupted");
    }
      synchronized(myParent.myArray){
        for (int i=0;i<10;i++){
          try{
            sleep(40);
          }catch( InterruptedException
Et){
            System.out.println("Thread
has been interupted");
          }
          myParent.myArray[i]=Value;
        }
      }
    }
```

```
public void run(){
  while (true){
    try{
      sleep(1000);
    }catch( InterruptedException
Et){
        System.out.println("Thread
has been interupted");
      }

synchronized(myParent.myArray){
        for (int i=0;i<10;i++)
          System.out.println("Value
"+i+" = "+myParent.myArray[i]);
      }
    }
  }
```

TABLE 29-3

We really need to be able to protect the array so that only one thread can access it at any one time. We can use the "synchronized" statement to protect the array. The code in the left-hand column of Table 29-3 shows how to alter the run method of the "ChangeClass" so that the array is synchronised. The right-hand column shows the synchronised version of the run method for the PrintClass.

The "synchronized" keyword prevents any access to the array variable by another thread whilst a thread is executing the code within the synchronised block of code. Our example has been rather contrived, but you could imagine that the array might hold important data that must be consistent at any point in time.

We may want to protect an entire method so that only one instance of that method can be running at any one time. We can make an entire method synchronised by placing the "synchronized" keyword before the name of the method. If we want to make a synchronised method for our example, we will need to create an update method in the applet. This method will change the value of all the elements of the array. We can not place the update method in the "ChangeClass" object because a synchronised method is only synchronised for that instance of the object. If the "Update" method were placed in the "ChangeClass", we would have two instances of the class (one for each thread) which would not be synchronised. By placing it in the applet, we have only one instance, and so only one synchronised method. Code 29-7 shows the applet with the synchronised "Update()" method. A call to the update method is made in the run method of the "ChangeClass" in the usual way.

```
public class DoesSynchronise2 extends java.applet.Applet{
ChangeClass thread1;
ChangeClass thread2;
PrintClass thread3;
int myArray[]=new int[10];

  public void init(){
```

```
    thread1=new ChangeClass(this,0,200,"Thread 1");
    thread2=new ChangeClass(this,1,190,"Thread 2");
    thread3=new PrintClass(this);
    thread1.start();
    thread2.start();
    thread3.start();
  }

synchronized void  Update(String myName, int Value){
  System.out.println("Update "+myName);
  for (int i=0;i<10;i++){
    for (int j=0;j <100000;j++)
    myArray[i]=Value;
    System.out.println("Update "+myName +"   "+i);
  }
 }
}
```

CODE 29-7

Notice that we have replaced the sleep statement with a "for" loop to provide the delay to generate a noticeable effect in the sample program. In your code you would never use this crude technique. One problem still arises with our example: the "PrintClass" is still synchronised on the array and will still fire up whenever its sleep statement finishes. We would really like our output to appear whenever the update method has finished changing the array. We could make a call to a method in the applet to print the array values, but we are exploring threads here. Java provides us with a pair of methods to achieve the effect we want: a "wait()" statement in a thread will cause the thread to pause until another thread issues a "notify()" to that thread. Code 29-8 shows the use of a "wait"/"notify" pair.

```
import java.awt.*;

public class DoesNotifyApp extends java.applet.Applet implements Runnable{
Thread thread1;
Thread thread2;
Thread thread3;

int myArray[]=new int[10];
  public void init(){
    thread1=new Thread(this,"Thread 1");
    thread2=new  Thread(this,"Thread 2");
    thread3=new  Thread(this,"Thread 3");
```

```
        }
    public void start(){
      thread1.start();
      thread2.start();
      thread3.start();
    }
    public void run(){
      if (Thread.currentThread()==thread1){
        while (true){
          synchronized(myArray){
            for (int i=0;i<10;i++){
              myArray[i]=0;
              System.out.println("Update 1  "+i);
            }
          }

          DoNotify();
          try{
            Thread.sleep(1900);
          }catch(InterruptedException ignored){
            System.out.println("Can't Sleep");
            return;
          }
        }
      }
      if (Thread.currentThread()==thread2){
        while (true){
        synchronized(myArray){
          for (int i=0;i<10;i++){
            myArray[i]=1;
            System.out.println("Update  2 "+i);
          }
        }
        DoNotify();
        try{
          Thread.sleep(2100);
        }catch(InterruptedException ignored){
          System.out.println("Can't Sleep");
          return;
        }
      }
      }
      if (Thread.currentThread()==thread3){
        while (true){
          DoWait();
          for (int i=0;i<10;i++)
            System.out.println("Value "+i+" = "+myArray[i]);
        }
      }
    }

    synchronized private void DoNotify(){
      notify();
    }
```

```
synchronized private void DoWait(){
  System.out.println("Well I'm waiting ");
  try{
    wait();
  }catch( Exception Et){
    System.out.println("Thread has been interrupted");
  }
 }
}
```

CODE 29-8

The code in the example is shown as a single class in order to simplify ownership matters. Three threads are started in the usual manner for a class implementing the "Runnable" interface. The run method of our class uses the "currentThread" method to determine the actions for each thread. Threads 1 and 2 update the array and then issue a "notify", thread 3 waits for the notify and prints the values of the array when it arrives. Notice that both the "wait" and the "notify" are encapsulated in their own synchronised methods. There are a number of other methods of interest concerning the "wait"/"notify" pair:

1. The call to "notify" in Code 29-8 can be replaced by a call to "notifyAll()". NotifyAll will tell all threads that are waiting to wake up.

2. The wait statement method has two relatives that allow your thread to wait for a specified amount of time for a "notify". If this time elapses, the wait will act as if a "notify" has arrived. The first wait will wait for a specified number of milliseconds, whilst the other waits for a specified number of milliseconds combined with a number nanoseconds. See the sleep statements for details of the arguments.

3. All the "notify" and "wait" methods are not part of the thread class but of the "object" class.

Thread groups and rescheduling threads

We have seen in this chapter how to create our own threads and control them through the use of "sleep", "wait" and "notify". However, it was mentioned right back in Part A that there are other threads running, apart from our own. These threads are part of the system, and control such things as the applet's repaint. If we wanted to list these threads, we might try an approach similar to that shown in Code 29-9. This applet gets the current thread and then attempts to list all the other threads that are running using the "enumerate" method of the threads class.

```
public class WhatsRunning extends java.applet.Applet implements Runnable {

public void init(){
  int Number;
  Thread Details[];
  Thread Current;
  Current=Thread.currentThread();
  Details = new Thread[Current.activeCount()];
  Number=Current.enumerate(Details);
  for (int i=0;i<Number;i++){
    System.out.println(""+Details[i]);
  }
 }
 }
```

CODE 29-9

Unfortunately, this program does not give the output we desired; it lists only one thread, the applet. There are other threads running, but we can not see them. This is because Java implements a method of grouping threads together. The "enumerate" method only shows the threads that are in the same group as the thread in the argument passed to it. The other threads must be in other groups. We can group our threads together by creating our own program group and creating the threads in the same group. The small sample code below shows the creation of a thread group and three threads in that group. (Of course, these threads will not actually do anything. For real work you will create your own class that extends the Thread class and uses the super method to create the thread in the thread group.)

```
ThreadGroup myGroup= new ThreadGroup("My Group");
thread1=new Thread(myGroup,"name1 ");
thread2=new Thread(myGroup,"name2 ");
thread2=new Thread(myGroup,"name3 ");
```

Once we have created a thread group, we can control all the threads in the group at once. We can use the control methods we have already learned about ("suspend", "resume" etc.) to control the execution of our threads.

The threads we have created up until now all have the same importance – that is, each thread has the same amount of processor time allocated to it by the operating system. But what if we have a thread that we really want to take precedence over other threads? In Java we can set the priority of threads using the "setPriority" method. Normally this method would take as its argument one of three constant values:

```
MAX_PRIORITY      The maximum priority that a Thread can have.
MIN_PRIORITY      The minimum priority that a Thread can have.
NORM_PRIORITY     The default priority that is assigned to a Thread.
```

Of course, these priorities are actually integer values. The maximum priority is 10, the minimum is 1 and the normal is 5. You can if you choose set the priority to any value between the maximum and the minimum. If you try to set a priority outside of this range, you will generate an "IllegalArgumentException". Code 29-10 shows the example thread program from the start of this chapter, with three threads set to each of the standard priorities.

```
public class PriorityTest extends java.applet.Applet{
myThreadClass thread1;
myThreadClass thread2;
myThreadClass thread3;
  public void init(){
    thread1=new myThreadClass("Thread 1");
    thread2=new myThreadClass("Thread 2");
    thread3=new myThreadClass("Thread 3");
```

```
    thread1.setPriority(Thread.MIN_PRIORITY);
    thread2.setPriority(Thread.NORM_PRIORITY);
    thread3.setPriority(Thread.MAX_PRIORITY);
    thread1.start();
    thread2.start();
    thread3.start();
  }

}
```

CODE 29-10

Notice in this example that we do not try to catch the illegal argument exception because we are using the standard priority constants. One last point: you can retrieve the current priority of a thread with "getPriority", which will return an integer between the minimum and maximum priority. Of course, the "setPriority" method can be applied to thread groups as well, to change the priority of all the threads in the group.

CHAPTER 30

Applications, File-handling and Data Structures

Throughout this book we have been writing applets to reside on web pages. However, it is possible to write Java programs that do not need a web page to reside upon. These Java programs are known as applications, and are more like the classic program that we have all become familiar with. They are still compiled to ".class" files just like applets, but need an interpreter to read them. Not surprisingly, this interpreter is called "Java". (However, when Java is built into the operating system as several manufacturers have promised, you will just have to click on a .class file to start it running.)

The example program below shows a skeleton application:

```
public class MainTest{
  public static void  main(String args[]){
    for (int i=0; i<args.length;i++){
      System.out.println(args[i]);
    }
  }
}
```

Note

1: The definition of the class does not extend java.applet.Applet
2: We have replaced the init() method with a main() method
3: The main method must be defined as public static
4: The main method must take a string array as its parameter

The application is compiled in the normal way, using the javac command (or the javac application on the Apple). As usual, a ".class" file is created after the compilation but in order to run the program you must use the Java command from the command line. If the above application is compiled, it can be run by typing:

```
java MainTest
```

You will not see any output from this example with that command, as the main method is expecting some command-line arguments from the command-line interpreter when it is executed. If you type the following –

```
java MainTest This is a test
```

– you will see output similar to that below in the command window:

```
E:\>java MainTest This is a Test
This
is
a
Test

E:\>
```

The main method is taking each of the words on the command line and using that as an element in the string array. These arguments are similar to the parameters passed to an applet, and can be used in the same way to alter the way the application works. Notice that the first argument is number zero. 'C' programmers should note that the practice of the first argument being the name of the program has been dropped in Java.

We noted above that the main method needs to be defined as static. This means that there is essentially only one instance of the class when the program is executed. Actually, this makes a lot of sense: it does not seem sensible to have more than one main method. Of course, because the class is static it can only operate on static variables. In order to use non-static variables and methods you will need to generate a new instance of the class using the new operator. Code 30-1 shows how it's done. Notice that, because the arguments are only valid within the main method, we take a copy of any valid arguments and transfer them to a static variable for later use. It is probably best to use your main class only as a processor for command-line arguments and use other classes to process these arguments and carry out the main work of the applet.

```
public class Code301 {
  static String StaticArg1Copy;
  String Arg1Copy;
  public static void  main(String args[]){
    if (args.length >=1){
      StaticArg1Copy=args[0];
    }
    Code301 MainInstance= new Code301();

  }
  Code301(){
    Arg1Copy=StaticArg1Copy;
    System.out.println("Variable is "+Arg1Copy);
  }
}
```

CODE 30-1

Although the application does not reside on a web page, it is still portable. The ".class" files can be distributed to any platform that supports the Java compiler and can be used without any changes. If we want to use graphics in our application, we will need to create a frame to display the output. Code 30-2 shows a typical application with a frame. The frame has only one AWT component, a text area. Notice that we use the first argument passed to the program for the name of the frame. If no arguments are passed to the program, a default name is used.

```
import java.awt.*;
public class FrameTest{
  public static void  main(String args[]){
    myFrame Window;
    if (args.length ==1)
      Window= new myFrame(args[0]);
    else
```

```
    Window= new myFrame("Sample application");
    Window.show();
    Window.resize(Window.preferredSize());
  }
}

class myFrame extends Frame {
  private Dimension myDimension;
  private TextArea myTextArea= new TextArea("",25,80);

  myFrame(String title){
    super(title);
    setLayout(new GridLayout(1,1));
    this.add(myTextArea);
    myDimension = new Dimension(200,200);
  }

  public boolean handleEvent(Event ev) {
    if (ev.id==Event.WINDOW_DESTROY) {
      this.dispose();
      System.exit(0);
      return true;
    }
    return super.handleEvent(ev);
  }

  public Dimension minimumSize(){
    return myDimension;
  }

  public  Dimension preferredSize(){
    return myDimension;
  }
}
```

CODE 30-2

The frame in Code 30-2 will not die properly unless the System.exit(0) command is included in the "handleEvent()" method when a Window destroy event occurs. The numeric argument of the exit is passed back to the operating system. You can use it to return error codes to the OS if the program terminates abnormally. Apart from this, the frame appears exactly the same as if it were used within an applet. Suppose you wanted to convert an applet into an application. Code 30-3 shows how to do this. The main method creates a new instance of the example class and then creates a frame for the applet. The applet's init method is called "main" and the applet is added to the frame. Finally, the frame is shown in the usual manner.

```java
import java.awt.*;
public class Example extends java.applet.Applet {
  public static void main(String args[]){
    Example App = new Example();
    myFrame appFrame = new myFrame("Example",App);
    App.init();
    appFrame.add("Center",App);
    appFrame.resize(200,200);
    appFrame.show();
  }

  public void init(){
  }

  public void destroy(){
    System.exit(0);
    super.destroy();
  }
}

class myFrame extends Frame {
  Example app;
  Dimension myDimension;
  myFrame(String title,Example app){
    super(title);
    this.app=app;
    myDimension= new Dimension(200,200);
  }

  public boolean handleEvent(Event ev) {
    if (ev.id==Event.WINDOW_DESTROY) {
      app.stop();
      app.destroy();
      this.dispose();
      return true;
    }
    return super.handleEvent(ev);
  }
  public Dimension minimumSize(){
  return myDimension;
  }
  public  Dimension preferredSize(){
    return myDimension;
  }
}
```

CODE 30-3

Although this technique works well in most cases, you should be careful if your applet loads resources over the network: your application may end up on a stand-alone machine and then will not have access to the network resources.

Handling files: the file dialog

Now that we have been introduced to applications we can start to explore some of the things that they can do that applets can not. In particular, the security model of Java gives applications a lot more freedom. It is assumed that if you are running an application on your machine you know what it is going to do – it is not just something that you have come across on a web page. For that reason, applications have more access to the disk on your machine. For instance, applications can look at the directory structure of your disk, and can read and write files. (Having said this, there is talk that later versions of Netscape and Internet Explorer will allow access to the hard disk, but in some secure manner.)

File access is available through the java.io library. This library provides a large number of classes for handling files, reading and writing them to the disk in a variety of formats. Before we look at actual file input and output, we will look at a useful AWT component to make the selection of files easier. This component is called the file dialog. Code 30-4 shows a simple application that creates a frame and attaches a file dialog to that frame. (We haven't shown the code for the frame class; it's much the same as we have seen before!) The file dialog we have created has the name "File Open" (although this may not appear in the title bar) and is a dialog for loading a file (shown in Figure 30-1).

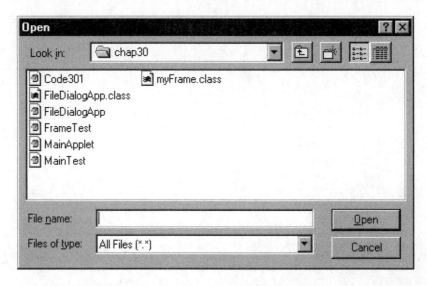

FIGURE 30-1

Once the file dialog is shown, all input from the applet is transferred to the file dialog until the dialog is closed. The application below then uses two methods from the class to retrieve the file name and directory that were selected. If a file is not selected then both arguments will be null.

```
import java.awt.*;
public class FileDialogApp {
  public static void main(String args[]){
    myFrame AppFrame = new myFrame("Testing files");
    AppFrame.show();
    AppFrame.resize(AppFrame.preferredSize());
    FileDialog myFileDialog= new FileDialog(AppFrame,"File
Open",FileDialog.LOAD);
    myFileDialog.show();
    String file = myFileDialog.getFile();
    String directory= myFileDialog.getDirectory();
    System.out.println("In Main "+directory+file);
  }
}
```

CODE 30-4

This previous code demonstrated a file-loading dialog box; if the third argument is changed to "FileDialog.SAVE", then a dialog box similar to that shown in Figure 30-2 is displayed.

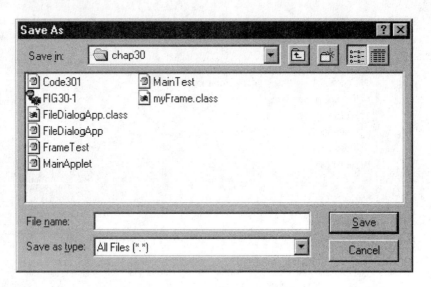

FIGURE 30-2

This dialog works in the same way, with the "getFile" and "getDirectory" methods being used to get the name that was selected. You can set the initial directory with the "setDirectory" method, which takes a string as an argument, or set the initial file with the "setFile" method. Remember, though, that if you are setting the directory you will need to escape any '\' characters by using them twice. The code below creates a file dialog box with the initial directory set to e:\ and the filename set to test.

```
    FileDialog myFileDialog= new FileDialog(AppFrame,"File Open 123
",FileDialog.SAVE);
    myFileDialog.setDirectory("e:\\");
    myFileDialog.setFile("Test");
```

As an alternative, you can of course extend the file dialog to create your own component that will handle the events that the file dialog can receive. The main two events are Event.LOAD_FILE and Event.SAVE_FILE. Be aware, however, that not all versions of Java appear to support these events at present.

Now that we have the names of a directory and a file that the user might want to work with, we can create a File-type object and retrieve details of the file or directory. The details that we can obtain depend on the type of object (directory or file) and whether we want to save or load the file. Table 30-1 shows methods that detail the information you can retrieve from a file or directory, depending on whether you wish to save or load a file. (Note that you can not use the file dialog to retrieve information about a directory. The file dialog will only return when either the OK button or the Cancel button is pressed. If the OK button is pressed and no file is highlighted the dialog box will not return. If the Cancel button is pressed then only the current directory is returned, not the directory the user has highlighted.) In the examples the variable "name" is of File type and has been created from the file and directory names from the file directory as follows:

```
name= new File(directory+file);
```

	Load	Save
Files	**canRead** Returns true if the file is readable `name.canRead()`	**canWrite** Returns true if the file is Writable `name.canWrite()`
	exists Determines if the file exists or not, useful if the file name has not originated from a dialog box `name.exists()`	Useful for checking if the save will overwrite a previous file. If it does exist you should check with the user for confirmation of the overwrite.
	getPath Returns the path to the file from the full path to the file.	
	isFile Determines if the File object is addressing a file. `name.isFile()`	
	lastModified Returns a long integer giving an indication of the time of the last modification. The documentation states that this integer has no real meaning and should only be used to compare the time and date of this file with another file. Useful for finding the most up-to-date file. `+name.lastModified()`	
	length Returns a long integer giving the length of the file. `name.length()`	

	Load	Save
Directories	**getName** Returns the name of the file from a full path. `Name.getName()`	
	getParent Returns the parent directory of this one, or the disk drive if the path is at the top. (Depends on the operating system.) `name.getParent()`	
	isDirectory() Determines if the File object is addressing a directory `name.isDirectory()`	
	lastModified Same as for files	

	list (may not work on versions of Java before 1.1)
	Returns a string array giving the names of all the files in the directory. Can be used with a file filter to list only those files which match the filter.
	`String list[] =name.list();`
	`for (int i=0;i< list.length;i++)`
	`System.out.println("Contains`
	`"+list[i]);`	

		mkdir
		Creates a directory using the file object as a pointer. The method will return a Boolean value indicating the success of the operation. If part of the path does not exist then the operation will fail.
		`File NewDir= new`
		`File("c:\\temp\\xxx");`
		`if (NewDir.mkdir())`
		`System.out.println("Success`
		`in making c:\\temp\\xxx");`

		mkdirs
		Similar to mkdir except that it will make all the directories in the path regardless of their previous existence.
		`NewDir= new`
		`File("c:\\tmp\\xxx");`
		`if (NewDir.mkdirs())`
		`System.out.println("Success`
		`in making c:\\tmp\\xxx");`

TABLE 30-1

The table above mentions using a filename filter to list only files that conform to a set of criteria. To create a filename filter suitable for use in the "list" method, you must create a class that implements the "FilenameFilter" interface. This class should have a constructor which will set up the rules for matching files and a method "accept", which will return a Boolean value indicating whether a filename matches the criteria. Be sure that your class handles the case of file names correctly. An example file filter is shown in Code 30-5. This filter looks for files of a certain extension (set by the constructor). Notice that we have converted all filenames to lower-case to make this filter case-independent.

```
class Filter implements  FilenameFilter{
  String myExtension;
  Filter(String extension){
    myExtension=extension;
  }

  public boolean accept(File dir,
      String name){
    String Lower= name.toLowerCase();
    if (Lower.endsWith(myExtension))
      return true;
    return false;
  }
}
```

CODE 30-5

This filter can be used as follows to list only the batch files in a directory:

```
Filter myFilter=new Filter("bat");
String FilteredList[]=name.list(myFilter);
for (int i=0;i< FilteredList.length;i++)
  System.out.println("Filtered by 'bat' "+FilteredList[i]);
```

Handling files: file input and output

Now that we have a way to allow users to select files, we need to explore how to read and write the contents of the files. In general, we will limit ourselves here to text files, as these are the easiest to handle, but the principles established apply to binary files as well. To begin, we will read in a text file and add it to the text area of our frame in Code 30-2. The method shown in Code 30-6 accepts a "File" type (presumably created from a selection from a file dialog). The method creates a file-input stream and then creates an empty byte array the same size as the file by using the "length" method from the "File" class. It is then a simple method of using the read method to fill the byte array with the contents of the file. The text area is then filled with the text using the "setText" method with a new string from the byte array.

```
public int LoadFile(File Name){
  FileInputStream myInput;
  int Return=-1;
  try {
    myInput = new FileInputStream(Name);
  }catch (FileNotFoundException et){
    System.out.println("That file can not be found");
    return(-1);
  }catch (IOException et){
    System.out.println("Can not open that file");
    return(-1);
  }
  int FileSize=(int)Name.length();
  byte Bytes[]=new byte[FileSize];
  try{
    Return = myInput.read(Bytes);
  }catch (Exception et){
    System.out.println("Can not open that file"+et);
  }
  if (Return !=-1)
    AppFrame.myTextArea.setText(new String(Bytes));
  try{
    myInput.close();
  }catch (IOException et){
    System.out.println("Can not close the file"+et);
    return(-2);
  }
  return(0);
}
```

CODE 30-6

Notice that our method makes no checks on the contents of the file; it will fill a text area with nonsense if a binary file (such as an executable) is selected. After the contents of the file have been read, the file is closed using the "close" method of the "FileInputStream". If you don't want to read the entire file at once, you can read it a byte at a time by using the read method without any arguments (the method returns -1 once it has come to the end of the file), or you can read a section of the file only. This method takes a byte array to hold the data, and two integers: the first points to the first byte to be loaded after the previous block, and the second indicates the number of bytes to load. The code sample below reads a complete file ten bytes at a time; we set all the elements of the array to 0 before each read, in case there are not 10 bytes left to read.

```
while (Return >=0){
  for(int i=0;i<10;i++)
    Bytes[i]=0;
  try{
    Return = myInput.read(Bytes,0,10);
  }catch (Exception et){
    System.out.println("Can not readfrom  that file"+et);
    return(-3);
  }
  System.out.println(new  String(Bytes,10));
}
```

Writing data to a file is just as simple: the "FileInputClass" is replaced with a "FileOutputClass", and the read method with a write method. Code 30-7 shows how to write two strings to a file:

```
public int SaveFile(File Name){
  FileOutputStream myOutput;
  int Return=-1;
  try {
    myOutput = new FileOutputStream(Name);
  }catch (FileNotFoundException et){
    System.out.println("That file can not be found");
    return(-1);
  }catch (IOException et){
    System.out.println("Can not open that file");
    return(-1);
  }

  String message1 = new String (" This is a message from the computer\n");
  String message2 = new String (" And this is another\n");

  byte Bytes[]=new byte[message1.length()];
  Bytes=message1.getBytes();
  try{
    myOutput.write(Bytes);
```

```
}catch (Exception et){
  System.out.println("Can not save that file"+et);
}
Bytes=message2.getBytes();
try{
  myOutput.write(Bytes);
}catch (Exception et){
  System.out.println("Can not save that file"+et);
}

try{
  myOutput.close();
}catch (IOException et){
  System.out.println("Can not close the file"+et);
  return(-2);
}
return(0);
}
}
```

CODE 30-7

If necessary, you can skip a number of bytes when reading a file: use the "skip(int)" method to miss out the bytes you are not interested in. However, if you need to do a lot of moving about in a file, reading from different places (and perhaps writing to different places), then you should use the "RandomAccessFile" class. This class has methods that allow you to move the current location for a read or a write to any part of the file. Because you have the freedom to move through a file, you can use the class to add to files that already exist. The class also has useful methods for reading and writing other types of variables apart from bytes and byte arrays. The table below shows methods which use the random access class. The methods use two files: the first is a list of strings of variable length, and the second contains integers pointing to the start of each string and the length of each. The method on the left will add a string to the end of the string file and the necessary integers to the end of integer file. The method on the right will use the information in the integer file to read a string from anywhere in the string file.

```
   public int AddString(File Pointers,
File Strings, String newString){
    RandomAccessFile Pointerfile;
    RandomAccessFile Stringfile;
    try{
      Pointerfile= new
RandomAccessFile(Pointers,"rw");
    }catch (IOException et){
      System.out.println("Can not open
pointer file");
      return(-1);
    }
    try {
      Stringfile= new
RandomAccessFile(Strings,"rw");
    }catch (IOException et){
      System.out.println("Can not open
string file");
      return(-1);
    }
    long StringfileLength;
    try {

StringfileLength=Stringfile.length();
    }catch (Exception et){
      System.out.println("Can not get
string file length");
      return(-1);
    }
    long
StringLength=newString.length();
    try {

Pointerfile.seek(Pointerfile.length());
    }catch (Exception et){
      System.out.println("Can not get
pointer file length");
      return(-1);
    }
    try {

Pointerfile.writeLong(StringfileLength);
    }catch (Exception et){
      System.out.println("Can not get
pointer file length");
      return(-1);
    }
    try {

Pointerfile.writeLong(StringLength);
    }catch (Exception et){
      System.out.println("Can not get
pointer file length");
      return(-1);
    }
```

```
   public String GetString(File
Pointers, File Strings, int
StringNumber){
    RandomAccessFile Pointerfile;
    RandomAccessFile Stringfile;
    try{
      Pointerfile= new
RandomAccessFile(Pointers,"r");
    }catch (IOException et){
      System.out.println("Can not open
pointer file");
      return(null);
    }
    try {
      Stringfile= new
RandomAccessFile(Strings,"r");
    }catch (IOException et){
      System.out.println("Can not open
string file");
      return(null);
    }
    int PtrPosition=(StringNumber-
1)*16;
    try {
      Pointerfile.seek(PtrPosition);
    }catch (Exception et){
      System.out.println("Can seek end
of pointer file");
      return(null);
    }
    long StringStart;
    long StringLength;
    try {

StringStart=Pointerfile.readLong();
    }catch (Exception et){
      System.out.println("Can read
string start");
      return(null);
    }
    try {

StringLength=Pointerfile.readLong();
    }catch (Exception et){
      System.out.println("Can not get
pointer file length");
      return(null);
    }
    System.out.println("Start
"+StringStart+" Length "+StringLength);
    try {
      Stringfile.seek(StringStart);
    }catch (Exception et){
      System.out.println("Can not seek
to end of string file");
```

```
    try {

Stringfile.seek(Stringfile.length());
    }catch (Exception et){
       System.out.println("Can not get
pointer file length");
       return(-1);
    }
    try {

Stringfile.writeBytes(newString);
    }catch (Exception et){
       System.out.println("Can not get
pointer file length");
       return(-1);
    }
    return(0);
  }
```

```
       return(null);
    }
    byte Bytes[]=new
byte[(int)StringLength];
    try {

Stringfile.read(Bytes,0,(int)StringLength);
    }catch (Exception et){
       System.out.println("Can not
read string");
       return(null);
    }
    return(new String(Bytes,0));
  }
```

TABLE 30-2

Notice that nearly all the methods associated with the random file access throw an IO exception, since there is a lot that can go wrong with this type of file access. For instance, you could try and read the wrong type of variable from the file; you could try and move beyond the end of the file or before the start of the file. Although the methods shown above may appear to be complicated, they are simply accessing the correct portions of the file and using the data to move about in the file. The "RandomAccessFile" class has a rich and varied list of associated methods for handling most types of data access – refer to the Java documentation for a complete list.

Data structures

This small section is different from others in this book: the rest of the book deals with features of Java and its class libraries, but this deals with some techniques to use Java efficiently in your programs. All programs can be broken down into two parts – the algorithms of the program, and the data stored and processed. The algorithm determines how the program will operate on the data that is stored whilst the program is running. However, the method we use to store data can effect greatly how efficient our program is. The efficiency of the program can be measured by the amount of space it takes up in the computer's memory, and by the speed with which the data can be accessed. In Part C we developed a small program to catalogue the details of a record collection, storing the data in an array of fixed length. There are three reasons why this is an unsatisfactory method of data storage:

1. The array is limited in the number of records it can store: once our collection gets too big, we will need to rewrite the program with a bigger array size.

2. If we have a small number of records then most of the array will be empty, but the space to store the records will still be allocated in memory. When our class loads it will take up more memory than it really needs.

3. When we want to find the details of a particular record, we need to step through all the records until we find the one we want.

We really need a way to store data so that the exact amount of memory is allocated for our data set and no more. We need a list which can start with one element, and which will increase in size as we add each element. In order to do this we can implement a data structure that is known as a linked list. In this technique, an element of the list holds a "pointer" to the next element in the list. We can traverse the list by moving along the pointers in each element to the next element. Figure 30-3 shows a simple diagram of a linked list.

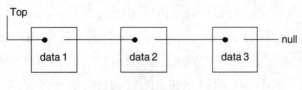

FIGURE 30-3

In Java each element of the list is implemented as a class. The class will have storage space for data, a "pointer" to the next element of the list, a constructor and possibly some methods for manipulating the data in the class. Code 30-8 shows a simple example of a linked list element. The constructor for the class does nothing, but will create an instance of the class. Once the class is constructed we can use the "SetData" method to add data to the class. This simple example only stores a string. But the data could be as complicated as you like. The "NextLink" method creates a new "LinkElement" class and stores it in the class's "Next" variable; this is the "pointer" to the next element of the list. The method returns the "pointer" to whatever invoked the method.

```
public class LinkElement{
  LinkElement Next;
  String Data;

  LinkElement(){
  }

  public void SetData(String newData){
    Data= newData;
  }

  public String GetData(){
    return Data;
  }

  public LinkElement NextLink(){
    Next= new LinkElement();
    return Next;
  }
}
```

CODE 30-8

To use the link elements we must manage two variables. The first variable always points to the first element of the list, while the second points to the current element of the list. When we want to use a linked list with the "ListElement" class we create the first element and make this the top of the list. We store a reference to the first element in a variable; this will allow us to traverse the list by starting at the reference to the first element. The second variable initially points to the first element, but will be updated whenever data is added to the list so that it points to the next element in the list that will contain data. The "NextLink" method is used to keep this variable up-to-date. Let's look at the steps to use this data structure:

1. Create the first element and make the local "next" variable point to this element.
2. Fill in the first element's data.
3. Create the link to the next element and take a local copy.
4. Whenever we want to store new data, store it in the class instance referenced by the current copy of the next pointer.
5. Create a link to the next element and update the local copy.

Code 30-9 shows an applet with a text field and two buttons. When the "add" button is pressed, the current text in the text field is used for the data of the current list element and a new list element is created. When the "show" button is pressed, the contents of the current list are printed to the console.

```
import java.applet.*;
import java.awt.*;

public class TestLink extends java.applet.Applet {
  LinkElement top = new LinkElement();
  LinkElement Next;

  TextField Input=new TextField();
  Button Add =new Button("add");
  Button Show= new Button("show");

  public void init(){
    setLayout(new GridLayout(3,1));
    add(Input);
    add(Add);
    add(Show);
    Next=top;
  }

  public boolean action(Event evt, Object arg){
    if (evt.target instanceof Button){
      if (arg.equals ("add")){
        Next.SetData(Input.getText());
        Next=Next.NextLink();
        return true;
```

```
    }
  if (arg.equals ("show")){
    System.out.println("-----");
    LinkElement Stepper;
    Stepper=top;
    while (Stepper.Next != null){
      System.out.println(Stepper.GetData());
      Stepper=Stepper.Next;
    }
    return true;
  }
}
return false;
}
}
```

CODE 30-9

To display the current text stored in the list, Code 30-9 uses a variable "stepper". This variable is first set equal to the first element of the list and is then set progressively to each element in turn. When all elements have been displayed, the value of the "next" variable of stepper will be equal to "null". Table 30-3 shows the value of all the variables as we step through a list of three elements:

Variable	Top	Stepper	Stepper.next	Data output	
Has the Value	Top	Top	Element 2	Element 1 or top	Before the while loop is executed.
	Top	Element 2	Element 3	Element 2	After the body of the loop has executed once.
	Top	Element 3	Null	Element 3	After the body of the loop has executed twice. This is the last step because when the while test executes again it will evaluate to true.

TABLE 30-3

Now that we have seen a simple linked list, we can look at a more complicated example. Code 30-10 shows a double linked list element. In this structure each element points both to the next element and the previous. The

first and last elements point to themselves. Codes 30-11, 30-12, and 30-13
show how to use the double linked list to add elements, and move backwards
and forwards through the list. The first element is created with a pointer to
null, so that its "Previous" points back to itself.

```
public class DoubleLinkElement{
  DoubleLinkElement Next;
  DoubleLinkElement Previous;
  String Data;

  DoubleLinkElement(DoubleLinkElement Previous){
    Next=this;
    if (Previous!= null)
      this.Previous=Previous;
    else
      this.Previous=this;
  }
  public void SetData(String newData){
    Data= newData;
  }
  public String GetData(){
    return Data;
  }
  public DoubleLinkElement NextDoubleLink(){
    Next= new DoubleLinkElement(this);
    return Next;
  }
}
```

CODE 30-10

```
Next.SetData(Input.getText());
Next=Next.NextDoubleLink();
if (Current==null){
        Current=top;
CurrentText.setText(Current.GetData());
        }
```

CODE 30-11

```
if (Current == null)
        Current=top;
else
    Current=Current.Next;
CurrentText.setText(Current.GetData());
```

CODE 30-12

```
if (Current == null)
    Current=top;
else
    Current=Current.Previous;
 CurrentText.setText(Current.GetData());
```

CODE 30-13

The "Next" variable is initially set to be equal to the first element in the list; the last element in the list always holds blank data. Code 30-11 show us how to add an element to the linked list, but what if we want to remove an element? It is really just a matter of changing the "Next" pointer of the previous element, and the "Previous" pointer of the next element. The code below shows a suitable method for our "DoubleLinkElement" class. Normally the method will change the previous element's "Next" pointer to point to this element's "Next" pointer; the next element's "Previous" pointer will be changed to point to the element that this element's "Previous" pointer points to! There are two special cases, the first and last elements of the list. The first element simply has to make the next element's "Previous" pointer point to itself. Similarly, the last element has to make the "Next" pointer of the last element but one point to itself.

```
public DoubleLinkElement DeleteMe(){
  if (Previous == this){
    Next.Previous=Next;
    return (Next);
  }
  if (Next== this){
    Previous.Next=Previous;
    return(Previous);
  }
  Previous.Next=Next;
  Next.Previous=Previous;
  return (Previous);
}
```

These two examples – the linked list and the double linked list – are only the tip of the iceberg when it comes to data structures. Other examples include "binary trees", "stacks", "queues", "AVL" trees, "B-Trees" and graphs. The subject is just too big to go into in this book, but if you take an interest then you should try a book more dedicated to data structures, such as "Introduction to Data Structures and Algorithms in Java" by Glenn Rowe.

Gaining access to the computer's settings

Because of the gain in freedom that applications enjoy, it is possible to retrieve details about the user and the computer that is being used. The "getProperties" method from the "system" class is used for this purpose. If you know the name of the property that you want, then you can retrieve its value using a "System.getProperty" method call. If you do not know the name, then the name of all properties can be retrieved from the "getProperties" method. For instance, the code below uses the "getProperties" method from the "System" class to retrieve the name and value of all system resources on the local machine. The output of this code is shown on the following page.

```
import java.util.*;

public class PropertiesTest {
  public static void  main(String args[]){
    PropertiesTest myTest=new PropertiesTest();
  }

  PropertiesTest(){
    Properties myProperties;
    String sProperty;
    myProperties=System.getProperties();
      for (Enumeration
        e= myProperties.propertyNames()   ;
        e.hasMoreElements() ;) {
      sProperty=(e.nextElement()).toString()
      System.out.println(sProperty+" Value   "+
      System.getProperty(sProperty));
    }
  }
}
```

```
user.language Value   en
java.home Value   d:\apps\java\bin\..
awt.toolkit Value   sun.awt.windows.WToolkit
file.encoding.pkg Value   sun.io
java.version Value   JDK1.1P
file.separator Value   \
line.separator Value

user.region Value   GB
file.encoding Value   8859_1
java.vendor Value   Sun Microsystems Inc.
user.timezone Value   GMT
user.name Value   ACOBLEY
os.arch Value   x86
os.name Value   Windows NT
java.vendor.url Value   http://www.sun.com/
user.dir Value   E:\InetPub\ftproot\AndyC\working\App2
java.class.path Value   d:\apps\java;;d:\apps\java\bin\..
\classes;d:\apps\java\bin\..\lib\classes.zip
java.class.version Value   45.3
os.version Value   4.0
path.separator Value   ;
user.home Value   C:\
```

Appendix A: Microsoft's Visual J++

■ ■

As this book was being written, Microsoft released early versions of their Integrated Development Environment. Although this appendix is not intended to be a full explanation of the environment, it was felt that at least a brief overview would be helpful. If you are really serious about Java development then an Integrated Development Environment (IDE) is an absolute must. The environment will take care of keeping your projects up to date. It will also allow you to use graphical editors to design your interface. Typically the IDE will allow you to view your project in a graphical manner, enabling you to navigate around as simply as you would the file manager.

We will show some of the major features of the current version of J++; these should change drastically between the first version and the current release of the tool. The current version of J++ is to be made available for download from Microsoft's web site (www.microsoft.com), but may still not be available by the time this comes to press. Check the web site and current magazines for up-to-date news.

The J++ tools form part of Microsoft's Developer Studio. Open it by double-clicking on the Developer Studio icon. If you have more than one development tool, you will need to select the J++ tool. Once the environment has been started, you will be presented with an environment similar to that shown in Figure A-1.

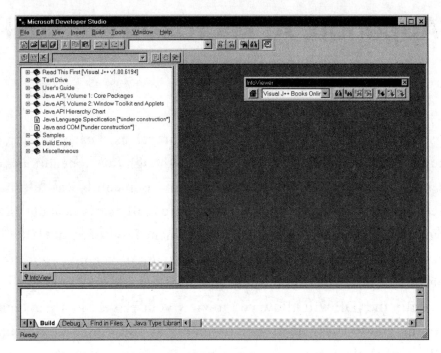

FIGURE A-1

At this point you have the choice of creating a new project or opening an existing one. The applet wizard takes you through a number of questions and then generates the skeleton Java applet classes and the associated HTML file.

To create a new project, select the "New" option from the "File" menu, and enter a name for the new file. You now have a choice between creating a new Java workspace and using the applet wizard. If you choose the applet wizard, you will be presented with a dialog box similar to that in Figure A-2. This allows you to choose between an applet and an application (which can be an applet as well). At this point you can choose the name of the applet. This can be quite different from the project name. It is also at this point that you can choose to include comments in the skeleton. It is a good idea to let the applet wizard generate the comments, at least for the first couple of times you use it. Select the "Next" option to move on to the next dialog box.

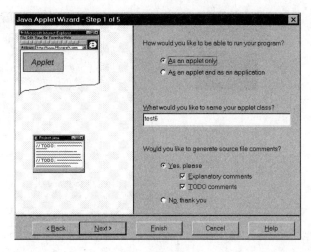

FIGURE A-2

Figure A-3 shows the next dialog box in the sequence. This dialog controls the size of the applet in the sample HTML code. You can choose not to generate any HTML if you want to.

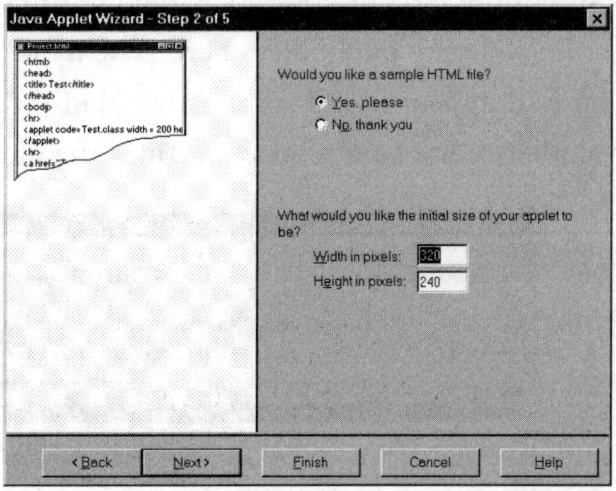

FIGURE A-3

The next dialog box (Figure A-4) controls the threading of the applet. You can choose between a threaded applet and a non-threaded one. This dialog also allows you to add support for images (the skeleton will contain

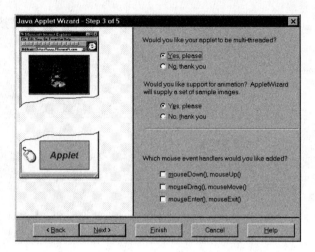

FIGURE A-4

the code needed to wait for any images to load). Finally, this dialog allows you to add skeleton mouse-handling methods. You can choose to add mouse-click support, mouse-movement support and mouse-focus support.

Figure A-5 shows the next dialog box, which defines the parameters your applet will handle. Add any parameters here. The name field sets the name of the variable that will appear in the source code and the applet tag. The next field (called Member in the beta release) defines the name of the variable in

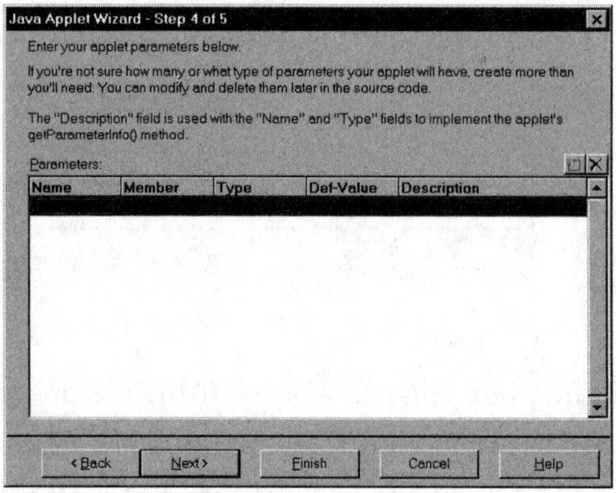

FIGURE A-5

the source code. The next field defines the type of the variable. The source code that is generated will convert from the usual string type to the type defined in this field. The following field is used to define an initial value for the variable. You can enter any comments you want to appear in the source code in the last field.

The final dialog box (Figure A-6) is used to enter any information you want to include in the "getAppletInfo()" method. Before generating the code, the wizard displays the parameters it is going to use to create the skeleton for you.

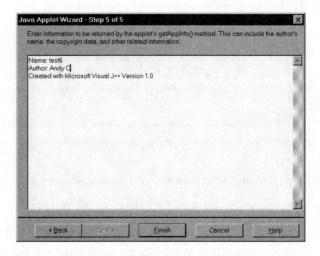

FIGURE A-6

You are now ready to edit the code using the editor provided by the IDE. Before you go any further, you should familiarise yourself with the code generated by the wizard. You should be able to see sections that correspond to the selections you made in the applet wizard. The editor (shown in Figure A-7) contains all the normal functions of a good text editor. You can move through the file using the cursor keys and scroll bars. You can search for text strings or do replacement operations. As is common with modern editors, any keywords in the source code are highlighted using colour in the editor window.

```
test7.java                                      _ □ ✕
    public void init()
    {
        // PARAMETER SUPPORT
        //      The following code retrieves the value of
        // specified with the <PARAM> tag and stores it i
        // variable.
        //------------------------------------------------
        String param;

        // Temp: Parameter description
        //------------------------------------------------
        param = getParameter(PARAM_Temp);
        if (param != null)
            m_Temp = param;

        // int_temp: Parameter description
        //------------------------------------------------
        param = getParameter(PARAM_int_temp);
        if (param != null)
            m_int_temp = Integer.parseInt(param);

        // If you use a ResourceWizard-generated "control
        // arrange controls in your applet, you may want
        // CreateControls() method from within this methoc
        // call to resize() before adding the call to Crea
        // CreateControls() does its own resizing.
        //------------------------------------------------
        resize(320, 240);
```

FIGURE A-7

To the left of the editor window, a display shows the classes in your project; you can click on a class to bring up an editor for that class. A simple arrangement is shown in Figure A-8. If you click on the junction point where the class joins the parent line, the diagram expands to show the methods and variables for that class (Figure A-9). This display will allow you to negotiate your way around your projects, no matter how large your project gets.

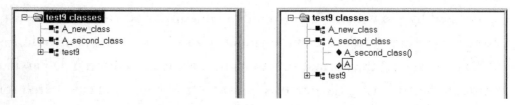

FIGURE A-8   FIGURE A-9

J++ allows you to take the construction of your projects further. It includes a comprehensive Graphical User Interface designer. This allows you to pick and place components for the AWT and then generate skeleton code for the components. It also includes a bitmap editor, a cursor editor, an icon editor, a menu editor and a version editor. From the New menu, select "Resource Template" (shown in Figure A-10), which will bring up a GUI manager window. Within this window you are shown a folder which will contain the GUI resources for your project.

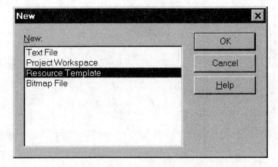

FIGURE A-10

To insert a GUI object from the menu, choose "Insert" followed by "Resource". You will be presented with a window similar to that in Figure A-11, which will allow you to choose the type of object you want to edit.

FIGURE A-11

The bitmap, icon and cursor editors are all very similar (Figures A-12, A-13, A-14), allowing you to edit the objects at pixel-level. All the tools have the usual drawing facilities. These include straight lines, freehand tools, circles and rectangles. They also have flood-fill capabilities and options for colour manipulation. If you are familiar with any drawing package then you should feel very comfortable using these tools.

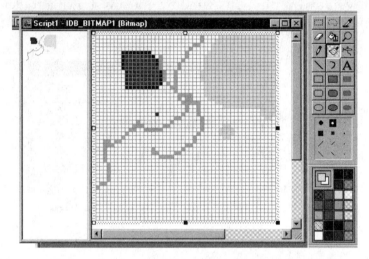

FIGURE A-12

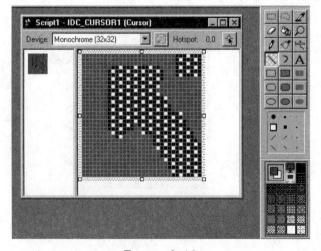

FIGURE A-13

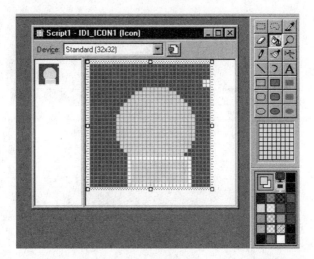

FIGURE A-14

The GUI interface designer works differently to traditional design tools such as Microsoft's own C++. You design your interface and then let J++ generate Java code from this design. When you choose to design a dialog, you are presented with a default dialog with "OK" and "Cancel" buttons. You can rename these by clicking on them with the right-hand mouse button and choosing "Properties". Change the "Caption" option to rename the button. You can delete a button by using the right-hand button and choosing the "Cut" option. Above your dialog design you will see various buttons which you may use to add other GUI components. Figure A-15 shows the box with these items and the dialog box with the default buttons.

You can add components from the button box by clicking on an item and then using the left mouse button to place the item in the dialog box. Items you have added to your dialog box can be moved about or resized, and even deleted altogether. Laying out dialog boxes using this tool is a real pleasure and is certainly a lot better than trying to use the standard layout managers

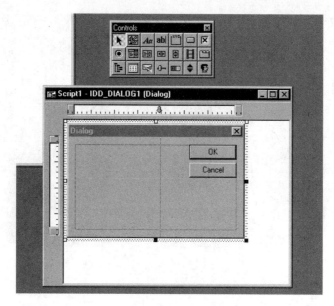

FIGURE A-15

the toolkit provides. Once you are happy with the dialog design you can save
it as a resource and use this to generate the Java code into your applet.

Apart from the editing tools, J++ also includes powerful debugging tools.
These allow you to single-step though an applet, or to set break points in the
code so that execution will stop at that point. You can set watch points on
variables so that you can see how they change during the execution of the
applet. These debugging facilities really make a difference to Java
development, allowing you to quickly track down even the most obscure
errors. No professional software engineer would be without these tools.

J++ also includes a comprehensive Help system, allowing you to find
details of classes and methods from the Java library quickly and easily.
Figure A-16 shows an example of the kind of help you can expect from the
J++ package.

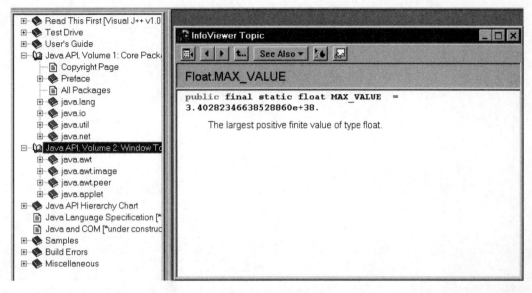

FIGURE A-16

With all these facilities it pays to invest in an integrated development environment, either Microsoft's J++ or one of the others created by the many other software houses developing these packages.

Appendix B: Java 1.1

▪▪

In 1997, Sun released Java version 1.1. This development kit contained a number of major and minor changes and improvements to the Java language and class library. Despite that, Sun maintain that support for Java programs written under Java 1.01 and 1.02 will continue for some time. Some of the changes are completely transparent; for instance, the AWT has been completely rewritten. Some of the changes are minor improvements with additional classes and Java keywords. Some changes affect some aspects of existing class libraries and will change the way you write your applets. There are of course some major additions adding to the functionality of Java – the major additions to this release are "Remote Method Invocation" and "JDBC". Java Database Connectivity (JDBC) allows a Java program to access database servers through SQL or ODBC. JDBC is a large and complicated subject, too big to cover here (besides, a number of third-party solutions are starting to appear which will make the task of connecting an applet to a database considerably easier than it is using native Java).

Beyond these additions, Sun have rewritten various aspects of the Java virtual machine to achieve performance gains. This means that applets and applications running under Java 1.1 should run faster. To see these improvements with applets you will need to be using a browser that supports the new virtual machine. Sun have also made some improvements that allow Java applets to run more smoothly on Apple machines.

This appendix will run through some of the new features that have been introduced in Java 1.1, although because of space restrictions only the major amendments will be dealt with. For instance, Java 1.1 begins to introduce the concept of data transfer (drag and drop) and a Clipboard. Unfortunately, these facilities are not completely implemented yet and may well change drastically before the next version.

Jars

Whilst using applets, you may have noticed that they can be rather slow to start. This is often caused by the applet having to load more than one class, and indeed images and sounds, using many different calls to the http server. With Java 1.1 Sun have introduced the idea of "Java Archive files" or jars. This file format is based on the zip format that has become popular around the world for compressing and archiving executable files along with their documentation. To use these jar files you first create your archive using the "jar" command and then change the applet tag on the web page to point to the archive. To create a jar archive of all classes with the associated .gif and .au files, use the following command:

```
jar cvf lib.jar *.class *.gif *.au
```

The options (cvf) tell the Jar command to create a new archive called "lib.jar" from all class files, all .gif files and all .au files. If you specify a directory in the list of files then all files from that directory will be added to the archive. You can view a list of files in an archive by changing the command options to "tvf". The meaning of each option is shown in the following table.

Option	Option Meaning
c	Create a new archive from the files specified
v	Report which files are being added to the archive
t	List the files in the archive
f	The next argument is the name of the archive to create or list files from.

To use the jar file in an applet tag, add a "param" definition as shown below.

```
<param name=archives value="animator.jar">
```

Alternatively, you can use the "archives" tag in the actual applet definition as follows:

```
<Applet code="hawk.class"
  width="600"
  height="400"
  archives="hawk.jar"
  >
</Applet>
```

Although using these jars does speed up access, remember that it forces all resources to be loaded at the same time. If your applet loads resources at different times, using jars may actually slow down the process. It is wise to experiment, or provide multiple pages, one with the jar files and one without.

Security and signed applets

If you are at all worried that your applets could be tampered with to produce unwanted effects, or you want to assure your users that applets you provide can be trusted, then Java 1.1 comes to your aid. Java 1.1 adds a new tool, "javakey", which allows you to sign your jar files with a digital signature that assures your users that the files have indeed come from you and have not been tampered with. The javakey tool maintains a database on your computer about you and any of your colleges. This database uses secure cryptographic techniques to ensure that the database is not tampered with. Using these techniques it is possible for you to certify jar files produced by others in your organisation. Java also provides classes and methods to access these security techniques should you want to add this security to your own applications and methods. Applets that have been signed and approved are allowed greater access to the computer's resources.

Before you start to issue certificates and sign jars you must initialise the javakey database with the names of your organisation and individuals who are trusted to sign applets. You can add an organisation using the -c option of the command, and an individual with the -cs (create signer) command.

```
Javakey -c MyFirm true
Javakey -cs Andy true
```

This creates an identity for "myFirm" in the database and adds an indivdual "Andy" who is trusted to sign applets. If we replace the "true" argument to javakey with "false", we identify this individual as not trusted. Before applets can be signed, the individual needs a pair of security keys. One of these keys is public and can be sent to any individual your signer trusts. The second key is private and should never be disclosed if you want to keep security tight. The Java security model allows a large number of key-encoding methods, but not all are implemented at present. For now we will use the Digital Signature Algorithm (DSA). The DSA algorithm can implement keys of differing lengths (the longer the key the more secure, but also the more time-consuming to decode). To create a pair of keys for our signer Andy, we use the -gk (generate key) option:

```
javakey -gk Andy DSA 512
```

This creates a pair of keys using the Digital Signature Option with a key length of 512 bits. Now that we have generated the keys for our signer, we must associate at least one certificate with that individual. This certificate gives important information about the signer of the jar file. Typically it will give information about the organisation that is signing the jar, and a period of time that the certificate is valid for. To generate a certificate we create a text file with the information about the certificate. This file may contain the following statements:

name	The database name of the individual
real.name	The real name of the individual
org.unit	The suborganisation the individual works for. This is typically a branch of a larger firm
org	The main organisation the indivual works for
serial	The serial number of this certificate. Each individual should keep their own list of serial numbers.
country	The country the organisation is based in
start.date	The date that the certificate becomes valid
end.date	The date that the certificate becomes invalid
out.file	The name of a file to copy the contents of the certificate (optional)

For example:

```
issuer.name=Andy

subject.name=Andy
subject.real.name=Andy C
subject.org.unit=Microcentre
subject.org=University of Dundee
subject.country=UK

start.date=29 Jan 1997
end.date=31 Dec 1997
serial.number=1

out.file=cert.cer
```

In this name the issuer and the subject are the same entity in the certificate file. If they are different then both individuals must appear in the database with the appropriate keys.

The certificate is added to the javakey database by using the -gc (generate certificate) command. If the details of the certificate are to be held in a file called CertFile then the certificate is added by:

```
javakey -gc CertFile
```

Now that we have a certificate, we can sign our applets. We must provide a control file to determine the signer and the certificate to use. This file is of course a text file with four fields:

signer	The name of the signer from the javakey database to use
cert	A valid certificate number from the individual's list of certificates
chain	Currently the chain field is not supported; always set this to zero
signature.file	A file name to store copies of the signature block.

For example:

```
signer=Andy
cert=1
chain=0
signature.file=AndySig
```

We can sign a jar file using the -gs directive (generate signature). If we have a jar file called "myJar.jar" and a directive file called SigFile, we can make a signed jar file with the command:

```
javakey -gs SigFile myJar.jar
```

This will generate a file "myJar.jar.sig". You should rename this signed jar file for use in your applet tag.

The Java Development Kit provides a set of classes and methods to access signature files and generate keys, which you can use if you wish. You should refer to the documentation for more details.

Some changes to Java and additional class wrappers

With the introduction of Java 1.1 the language now allows you to net class definitions within other class definitions. This means that a class can be local to another class and have no visibility outside of the class that defines it. Take the example below:

```
class OuterClass{
  class InnerClass{
    InnerClass(){
      System.out.println("Creating Inner class");
    }
  }
  OuterClass(){
    System.out.println("Creating Outer class");
    InnerClass myInner=new InnerClass();
  }
}
```

The "OuterClass" defines a new class "InnerClass". This class is local to the outer class and can only be used by the outer class. An instance of the InnerClass is created in the OuterClass constructor, but if any other class were to attempt this, a compiler error would be generated. Additionally, three new wrapper classes have been added: the "Byte", "Short" and "Void" classes. The Byte and Short classes will help in passing and returning these variable types to methods. In addition there is a whole new type of variable for "big" numbers, which come in two types, decimals and integers. This class of variable can hold a number of practically unlimited precision. This means that for financial or scientific calculations the accuracy is no longer fixed. The big number classes come with a large set of methods to handle calculations and comparisons. This appendix can only skim over these briefly; refer to the documentation for the complete details of big numbers.

Generally, "BigIntegers" are constructed from Strings and Byte arrays whilst "BigDecimals" are constructed from "BigIntegers", Doubles and Strings. The example below shows the construction of two big numbers of different types and some maths operations upon them.

```
import java.math.*;
public class BignumTest {
  public static void main(String args[]){
    BignumTest myTest=new BignumTest();
  }

  BignumTest(){
    BigDecimal myBignum= new BigDecimal((double)(22.0/7.0));
    System.out.println("Big  number"+myBignum.toString());

    BigInteger myInt= new BigInteger("22");
    System.out.println("Big Integer "+myInt);
    BigInteger myIntPow= myInt.pow(20);
    System.out.println("Big Integer power "+myIntPow);
  }

}
```

Be warned, though: although you can create variables with very high precision, the computing overheads will rise very rapidly as the number of digits increases.

The network class library also contains a number of extensions, not least of which is a new set of exceptions which allow you to handle errors more accurately. These new exceptions are listed below:

BindException	When trying to bind to a local port, the port is already in use and can not be used.
ConnectException	The connection has been refused by a remote server. It may be that no server is listening on that port.
NoRouteToHostException	The attempt to connect to a remote port did not succeed because the remote server could not be reached.

Accessing resource files

Our applets and applications often make use of resources stored on the local machine or a remote machine attached to the network. Typically these resources will be files containing graphics or a sound, or they may be files of data you want to use. Java 1.0 accessed resources through a URL; typically applets will use the getCodeBase() method to retrieve resources over the net. Java 1.1 provides a mechanism for locating resources in a location-independent manner. That means that whether the resource is stored on a local machine or on a server accessed through a URL, or even in a jar file, a single type of method can be used to retrieve the resource. Two actual methods are provided by Java. The first returns an "InputStream" to the resource, whilst the second provides a string representation of the URL to the resource. The code below shows how an applet ("PropertiesApplet") can use the "getResourceAsStream" method to open a file "InnerTest.java" and read its contents.

```
InputStream  Name=PropertiesApplet.class.getResourceAsStream("InnerTest.java");
  try {
    Length=Name.available();
  }catch(Exception et){
    System.out.println("Caught "+et+" "+Name);
}

  byte Buffer[]= new byte[Length];
  try {
    Name.read(Buffer,0,Length);
  }catch(Exception et){
    System.out.println("Caught "+et);
  }
```

Alternatively, the applet can retrieve the URL of the file by using the "getResource" method as shown below:

```
URL  Urlname=PropertiesApplet.class.getResource("InnerTest.java");
```

The URL can of course be converted to a string by using the "toString()" method of the URL class.

Changes to the AWT

The introduction to this appendix mentioned that the AWT had been radically overhauled to improve both the coding of Java programs and the speed at which applications and applets will execute. This has been achieved both by rewriting the AWT in the case of Windows 32 platforms, and by adding new functionality. One major change to the AWT is the new way that it handles events. Although this change alters the way you should write your programs from now on, you do not have to rewrite your old programs if you don't want to. Previously, if you wanted to handle events, you would subclass one of the AWT components and override either the action method or the handleEvent method. One effect of this was to link the application code with the user-interface code, lowering the code readability and hence its ease of maintenance. The new way to handle events is called the "Delegation Event Model".

In this model any object in your Java program is able to handle events from any source. This allows the event-handling to be grouped into a single class or to be distributed amongst classes. An object that wishes to handle an event must implement an Event Listener. The distributed model encourages the programmer to split the user interface from the main body of the program. Typically there will be two main classes for your applet or application; one will handle the appearance of the program, whilst the other will do the work. For now, let us call these two classes the GUI (Graphical User Interface) class and the application class (although of course this might be an applet). The GUI class will typically add AWT components to the applet or add event listeners to the appropriate components. These event listeners are classes that implement an appropriate event interface.

Before we look into these event interfaces, let's look at a simple example. In Part B we presented a simple button applet that allowed toppings to be added to an imaginary pizza. Let's look at this again. First, let's look at the application interface; we want to be able to add and delete named toppings from our pizza. The application class will have at least two methods, an add method and a delete method. Each of these methods will accept a string to indicate which topping will be added or deleted. Our example here will not show the code for handling the construction of the pizza – that is entirely up to the application designer. We will design our interface to have buttons to add and delete a small range of toppings. When a button is pressed it should call a method in the application to either add or delete a toping. We therefore want to create two event classes, one to add toppings and one to delete toppings.

```
class AddCommand implements ActionListener{
  MakePizza App;
  String Topping;
  public AddCommand(MakePizza App,String Topping){
    this.App=App;
    this.Topping=Topping;
  }
  public void actionPerformed(ActionEvent e){
    App.add(Topping);
  }
}

class DeleteCommand implements ActionListener{
  MakePizza App;
  String Topping;
  public DeleteCommand(MakePizza App,String Topping){
    this.App=App;
    this.Topping=Topping;
  }
  public void actionPerformed(ActionEvent e){
    App.delete(Topping);
  }
}
```

Both of these classes implement the "ActionListener" interface and define the "actionPerformed" method of the interface. Note that in order to implement the interface you need to import the java.awt.event class library. The constructors of these two classes accept references to the application instance and also the type of topping to handle. We can now show the code for the GUI class:

```
class HandleInterface{
  Button Cheese=new Button("Add Cheese");
  Button Tomato=new Button("Add Tomato");
  Button Garlic=new Button("Add Garlic");
  Button Chilli=new Button("Add Chilli");
  Button DCheese=new Button("Delete Cheese");
  Button DTomato=new Button("Delete Tomato");
  Button DGarlic=new Button("Delete Garlic");
  Button DChilli=new Button("Delete Chilli");
  TextArea CurrentPizza=new TextArea();

  HandleInterface(NewInterface applet,MakePizza App){
    applet.add(Cheese);
    Cheese.addActionListener(new  AddCommand(App,"Cheese"));
    applet.add (DCheese);
    DCheese.addActionListener(new  DeleteCommand(App,"Cheese"));
    applet.add(Tomato);
    Tomato.addActionListener(new  AddCommand(App,"Tomato"));
    applet.add(DTomato);
    DTomato.addActionListener(new  DeleteCommand(App,"Tomato"));
    applet.add(Garlic);
    Garlic.addActionListener(new  AddCommand(App,"Garlic"));
    applet.add(DGarlic);
    DGarlic.addActionListener(new  DeleteCommand(App,"Garlic"));
    applet.add(Chilli);
    Chilli.addActionListener(new  AddCommand(App,"Chilli"));
    applet.add(DChilli);
    DChilli.addActionListener(new  DeleteCommand(App,"Chilli"));
    applet.add(CurrentPizza);
  }
}
```

This class creates a set of buttons and then adds an action listener to each button. The instance of the action listener contains all the information it needs to be able to carry out the action – i.e., a reference to the application and the name of the topping it will handle. When a button is pressed, the action listener associated with that button receives an event and calls the appropriate method in the application.

The AWT defines two different levels of event listeners: low-level listeners which accept events that can be described as physical, and semantic listeners which describe a type of action. These event listeners are described in the following table.

Low-level interfaces	Description	Methods to implement
MouseListener	Receives high-level mouse events.	mouseClicked(MouseEvent) mouseEntered(MouseEvent) mouseExited(MouseEvent) mousePressed(MouseEvent) mouseReleased(MouseEvent)
MouseMotionListener	A lower-level mouse listener, receives events when the mouse is moved.	mouseDragged(MouseEvent) mouseMoved(MouseEvent)
KeyListener	Receives events when keys are pressed and released.	keyPressed(KeyEvent) keyReleased(KeyEvent) keyTyped(KeyEvent)
WindowListener	Receives events when a window's status is changed.	windowClosed(WindowEvent) windowClosing(WindowEvent) windowDeactivated(WindowEvent) windowDeiconified(WindowEvent) windowIconified(WindowEvent) windowOpened(WindowEvent)
FocusListener	Receives events that determine whether the component has the keyboard focus.	focusGained(FocusEvent) focusLost(FocusEvent)
ComponentListener	Receives events that occur when a component changes its visibility on the screen. Generally you should not implement this interface unless you want to be notified of these events.	componentHidden(ComponentEvent) componentMoved(ComponentEvent) componentResized(ComponentEvent) componentShown(ComponentEvent)
High-level interfaces		
ActionListener	Receives events when the user generates an action. Typically an action is an event with no data, i.e. a button has been pressed	actionPerformed(ActionEvent)
ItemListener	Receives events when an item changes state. The item can either be on or off.	itemStateChanged(ItemEvent)
AdjustmentListener	The Adjustment event may contain data about the component that has been adjusted. E.g., a scroll bar will generate this event when the user moves it.	adjustmentValueChanged (AdjustmentEvent)
TextListener	The text in a text box has changed in some way	textValueChanged(TextEvent)

As you can see from the table above, each of the listener interfaces has an event class associated with it. These event classes will typically contain useful information about the event. In fact, in the case of adjustment events, without accessing the event you can not retrieve the user's intent. The table below shows some of the more useful event classes and methods to retrieve the information which the instance of that class will contain.

Event	Methods	Comments
ActionEvent	getActionCommand	Returns a string giving the name of the action that caused this event. E.g., in menus this will be the name of the menu item.
ItemEvent	getStateChange	Gets the new state of the component. One of ItemEvent.SELECTED or ItemEvent.DESELECTED
AdjustmentEvent	getAdjustmentType	Returns the type of adjustment the user performed. One of: AdjustmentEvent .UNIT_INCREMENT AdjustmentEvent .UNIT_DECREMENT AdjustmentEvent .BLOCK_INCREMENT AdjustmentEvent .BLOCK_DECREMENT AdjustmentEvent .TRACK
	getValue	Returns an integer with the new value of the component.
MouseEvent	getX and getY	Returns the X and Y locations of the mouse pointer.
KeyEvent	getKeyChar()	Returns a character representing this key press.
	getKeyCode()	Returns an integer representing this key press.

Each of the AWT interface objects can listen for one or more types of events depending on the functionality of the component. For instance, it would not make sense for a button to expect to receive an adjustment-type event. The following table lists the AWT components and the events they can listen for.

Component	ComponentListener FocusListener KeyListener MouseListener MouseMotionListener
Container	ContainerListener
Dialog	WindowListener
Frame	WindowListener
Button	ActionListener
Choice	ItemListener
Checkbox	ItemListener
CheckboxMenuItem	ItemListener
List	ItemListener ActionListener
MenuItem	ActionListener
Scrollbar	AdjustmentListener
TextArea	TextListener
TextField	ActionListener TextListener

Extending AWT components

In Part C we saw how to extend AWT components to increase their functionality. Using the event delegation model reduces dramatically the need to extend AWT components. You should only extend components if you need to extend their appearance or functionality of components – for instance, if you need a canvas class with a picture painted upon it. If you do need to subclass an AWT component then there are two levels of event-handling methods you can override. The first handles all events for the class, whilst the second class mirrors the type of events that the component can handle. So all AWT components offer the "processEvent(AWTEvent)" method, while, for example, the button component offers the "processActionEvent(ActionEvent)" method. You can override these methods in your extended component provided the overriding method calls the superclasses event-processing method somewhere in the processing method.

Your extended components will only receive events if they register themselves via a call to "enableEvent". This takes a list of events that have been combined with a bitwise. For instance, if you have extended the list's class then you would register it for item and action events with a call to enable events in the constructor of the class like this:

```
enableEvents(AWTEvent.ACTION_EVENT_MASK | AWTEvent.ITEM_EVENT_MASK);
```

Pop-up menus and the ScrollPane container

With the arrival of Windows 95 and Windows NT 4 (which uses the Windows 95 interface) a new type of user component was added to the Microsoft interface. This is known as the pop-up menu, and is similar to the pull-down menu except that it does not have to be attached to anything. Although other operating systems have had this component for some time, Java was without it until the release of 1.1. The popupmenu class can be constructed in the same manner as the menu classes, and menu items are added to it in the same way. The major issue with the class is the type of trigger event that displays the component. On Windows NT and Windows 95 pop-up menus appear when the right-hand mouse button (on a right-handed mouse) is clicked and released. On the other hand, a Dec alpha running OSF Unix and X-windows will pop up a menu when the left-hand mouse button is pressed. Our program must be able to handle the different trigger events.

The code below shows an applet that creates a pop-up menu and adds a number of menu items. Each menu item has an instance of a handler class added as an action listener. The applet also adds a mouse listener to itself to look for trigger events. Notice also that we have added almost empty methods to carry out the actions selected by the user from the menu.

```
import java.awt.*;
import java.awt.event.*;

public class TestPopup extends java.applet.Applet{

PopupMenu myPopup= new PopupMenu();
MenuItem OpenItem= new MenuItem("Open");
MenuItem ExploreItem= new MenuItem("Explore");
MenuItem FindItem= new MenuItem("Find");
MenuItem SharingItem= new MenuItem("Sharing");
MenuItem CutItem= new MenuItem("Cut");
MenuItem CopyItem= new MenuItem("Copy");

  public void init(){
    myPopup.add(OpenItem);

    myPopup.add(ExploreItem);
    myPopup.add(FindItem);
    myPopup.addSeparator();
    myPopup.add(SharingItem);
    myPopup.addSeparator();
    myPopup.add(CutItem);
    myPopup.add(CopyItem);

    OpenItem.addActionListener(new HandleMenu(this));
    ExploreItem.addActionListener(new HandleMenu(this));
    FindItem.addActionListener(new HandleMenu(this));
    SharingItem.addActionListener(new HandleMenu(this));
    CutItem.addActionListener(new HandleMenu(this));
    CopyItem.addActionListener(new HandleMenu(this));
    add(myPopup);
    this.addMouseListener(new HandleMouse(myPopup));

  }
  void Open(){System.out.println("Open");}
  void Explore(){System.out.println("Explore");}
  void Find(){System.out.println("Find");}
  void Sharing(){System.out.println("Sharing");}
  void Cut(){System.out.println("Cut");}
  void Copy(){System.out.println("Copy");}

}
```

Each menu item added an action listener to wait for the selection of that item. All this listener needs to do is select the appropriate method in the applet.

```
class HandleMenu implements ActionListener{
TestPopup App;
  HandleMenu(TestPopup App){
  this.App=App;
  }

  public void actionPerformed(ActionEvent e){
    String Command=e.getActionCommand();
    if (Command.equals("Open"))
      App.Open();
    if (Command.equals("Explore"))
      App.Explore();
    if (Command.equals("Find"))
      App.Find();
    if (Command.equals("Sharing"))
      App.Sharing();
    if (Command.equals("Cut"))
      App.Cut();
    if (Command.equals("Copy"))
      App.Copy();
  }
}
```

We can now look at the class that handles the mouse event. We are interested in two types of mouse events here, the mouseClicked event and the mouseReleased event. We could create a class that implements the "MouseListener" interface but that would mean we would have to provide methods for the other mouse events, which we are not interested in. Instead we use an adapter class provided by the AWT, which provides empty methods for the mouse action events, and overrides the events we are interested in:

```
class HandleMouse extends MouseAdapter{
PopupMenu menu;
  HandleMouse(PopupMenu menu){
    this.menu=menu;
  }
  public void mouseClicked(MouseEvent e){
    if (e.isPopupTrigger()){
      menu.show(e.getComponent(),e.getX(),e.getY());
    }
  }
  public void mouseReleased(MouseEvent e){
    if (e.isPopupTrigger()){
      menu.show(e.getComponent(),e.getX(),e.getY());
    }
  }
}
```

This class waits for the mouseClicked and the mouseReleased events and checks to see if these are the popup triggers. When a trigger is received, the methods show the menu at the current location of the mouse.

As we saw in Part B, under Java 1.0 using scroll bars could be a difficult chore. There was no high-level support for the component; the programmer had to handle all the adjustments to the scrollbars by himself. With Java 1.1 a new class is introduced that simplifies scroll bars immensely. The "ScrollPane" class can automatically add scroll bars to any component that it contains. When creating the "ScrollPane", three options are available:

ScrollPane.SCROLLBARS_ALWAYS	Always add scroll bars
ScrollPane.SCROLLBARS_AS_NEEDED	Only add scroll bars if they are needed
ScrollPane.SCROLLBARS_NEVER	Never add scroll bars; let the program implement them

Creating and using a scroll pane couldn't be easier – you simply create the pane and then add a component to view in that pane. The example below creates the pane and adds an extended canvas (myCanvas) capable of drawing images upon itself.

```
import java.awt.*;
import java.net.*;
public class ScrollTest extends java.applet.Applet{
Image myImage;
ScrollPane Pane;
MediaTracker myTracker;
  public void init(){
    URL Urlname=ScrollTest.class.getResource("andy.gif");
    myImage=getImage(Urlname);
    myTracker=new MediaTracker(this);
    myTracker.addImage(myImage,0);
    try {
       myTracker.waitForID(0);
    } catch(Exception et){
      System.out.println("Some error tracking image"+et);
      return;
    }
```

```
        Pane = new ScrollPane(ScrollPane.SCROLLBARS_AS_NEEDED);
        Pane.add(new myCanvas(myImage));
        Pane.resize(110,110);
        add(Pane);
        resize(150,150);
    }
}
```

Desktop colours, printing and animation images

With the previous release of Java there was no way for an applet to appear
in the user's preferred desktop colours. Java 1.1 remedies this with a
collection of system-colour classes that mirror the user's desktop. These
colours are defined in the package java.awt.SystemColor. These system
colours are a subclass of the color class and can be used wherever a color
class is used. The sample code below shows an applet that mimics the look
of other applications on the desktop.

```
import java.awt.*;
public class DesktopApp extends java.applet.Applet{
  public void init(){
    setBackground(SystemColor.desktop);
    setForeground(SystemColor.textText);
    myButton Ok = new myButton("OK");
      add(Ok);
  }
  public void paint(Graphics g){
    g.drawString("This is text",10,10);
  }
}

class myButton extends Button{
  myButton(String text){
    super(text);
    setBackground(SystemColor.control);
    setForeground(SystemColor.controlText);
  }
}
```

There are a large number of colours defined in the System colour class –
refer to the documentation for a complete list. Should you need to know the
RGB equivalent of a system colour, the class has a "getRGB" method that
returns an integer representation of the three colours. These colours are
packed into the integer in the usual manner.

Another of the shortcomings of Java 1.0 was that printing from applications and applets was extremely difficult. Java 1.1 adds a new printing API that should make it easier, although applets will still need to be run in a secure manner to allow printing. The code below shows a very simple action listener that will print the contents of a frame when it receives an action event. This class could be added to the action listener of a button using the addActionListener method.

```
class PrintCommand implements ActionListener{
Frame frame;
  PrintCommand(Frame frame){
    this.frame=frame;
  }

  public void actionPerformed(ActionEvent e){
     PrintJob pjob = frame.getToolkit().getPrintJob(frame,"Printing Test",
(Properties)null);
       if (pjob != null) {

      Graphics PrintGraphics = pjob.getGraphics();
      if (PrintGraphics != null) {
        frame.printAll(PrintGraphics);
        PrintGraphics.dispose(); // This will make the page actually flush
to the printer.
      }
      pjob.end();
    }
  }
}
```

When the class is called, it takes care of handling the dialogue with the user concerning the page layout – i.e., the page size and orientation. It is up to your application to take care of the pagination of the printout. Two methods from the "printjob" class will help in this task, "getPageDimension" and "getPageResolution". If you do not want to print the entire frame (the "printAll" method in the above code does this) then you can use the "print(Graphics)" method from the container class to print just the components you want.

Previous versions of Java have included a memory image source class to build images from an array of integers. Each element of the array represents a colour for a pixel in the final image. Previously, if you wanted to create an animation from these pixels, you had to create a new instance of the memory image class for each frame. Java 1.1 allows a single instance of the memory source to control the final image, with changes in the pixel array being mirrored on the image. The start of the applet shown below uses an integer array to create a "MemoryImageSource" that is then used to create a screen image.

```
import java.awt.*;
import java.awt.image.*;

public class Animate extends java.applet.Applet implements Runnable{

Thread myThread;
MemoryImageSource myImageSource;
Image myImage;
int pixels[];

public void init(){
  pixels = new int[255 *255];
  myImageSource=new  MemoryImageSource(255,255,pixels,0,255);
  myImageSource.setAnimated(true);
  myImage=createImage(myImageSource);
  setBackground(Color.black);
  resize(300,300);
}
```

The image we have created will be 255 by 255 pixels large (the first two arguments of the "MemoryImageSource" constructor); usually the final argument of the constructor is the same as the width of the image. The "setAnimated" method of the class flags this instance as capable of being changed and these changes should be propagated to any images based on this image source. The "setAnimated" flag needs to be set before any images are created from the source, or else the changes will not be propagated properly. Now that we have created the image source, we will need a run method which updates it and calls a repaint() to draw the new image:

```java
public void run(){
int x=0;
int y=0;
double theta=0;
int RedInt[] = new int[10];
Color Red= Color.red;
  if (Thread.currentThread() == myThread){
  for (int i=0;i<10;i++){
    RedInt[i]=Red.getRGB();
    Red=Red.darker();
  }
  while(true){
    try{
      Thread.sleep(10);
    }catch (Exception ignored){
      return;
    }
    theta=theta+Math.PI/20;
    double delta;
    for (int StreakCount=0; StreakCount <10;StreakCount++){
      delta=StreakCount*Math.PI/20;
      x=(int)(120*Math.sin(theta-delta)+128);
      y=(int)(120*Math.cos(theta-delta)+128);

      for (int i=0;i<5;i++){
        for (int j=0;j<5;j++){

          pixels[(y+j)*255+(x+i)]=RedInt[StreakCount];
        }
      }
      myImageSource.newPixels(x,y,5,5);
    }
    repaint();
    }
  }
}
```

This run method manipulates pixels to create a red square moving in a circle with a trail of squares behind in ever diminishing shades of red. Importantly, note that the changes in the pixels' values are not included in the memory image source until the "newPixels" method of the class is called. This method allows all or a subset of pixels to be updated; in this case only the block of 25 pixels that have changed are updated.

Remote Method Invocation

With the release of Java 1.1, Sun have introduced a technique known as Remote Method Invocation (RMI). This allows a Java applet to invoke a method in a class that is running on the server and not on the applet's browser. Typically, the server that served the applet will also be running a Java application that has made its methods available to Java applets. These remote applets can ask the server application to run one of these methods and return a result back to the applet. Figure B-1 shows the relationship between the server, the application and the applet. It is important to remember that when we call a method remotely, the method is not executed on the machine that is running the applet but on the machine that is running the server.

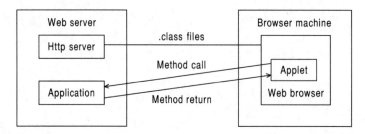

FIGURE B-1

Remote Method Invocation is a very powerful technique that allows applets to interact safely with the server in a way that would be considered a security risk using any other method. By remotely invoking a method, the applet has access to the hardware and data on the server. Suppose a robot arm were attached to the server: by providing methods in the server implementation class, remote applets could control the arm. Furthermore, if the server has a device attached that collects data (such as meteorological data or radiation levels), an applet can use the remote server to gain access to the data. Applets can thus collect and display data in near real-time. You could also use remote invocation to gain access to a server with a particularly powerful processor (or group of processors) with custom methods capable of doing some complex calculations. You could write applets to gain access to these methods, meaning that you would not need to implement the calculation yourself.

To use RMI, two matched programs need to be developed. A server application will be written which will make available some of its methods for remote invocation; a Client (or application) applet will be written that will be able to connect to the server application and use its methods. Notice that this is not a breach of security since the applet can only call methods in the server that have been explicitly registered for remote invocation. The server machine will also run a program from the JDK called "rmiregistry" which is responsible for serving the RMI objects.

First, let's look at creating the application that will run on the server and advertise its methods for remote invocation. Our example is a cryptographic server that will contain two methods. The first takes a string to encode and a key to use to encode it, and returns a key and the coded string. The second method takes a key and a string, and returns the decoded string. We must create a .Java file that contains definitions for the methods that are going to be available for remote invocation. In fact, we create an interface where the definitions simply list the arguments and the return types for the methods, complete with any exceptions that may be thrown. The methods must throw the java.rmi.RemoteException error. The sample code below would be stored in a directory called "Cryptoserver", with a file name of "Crypto". Notice that we are creating a package for the classes, also called "Cryptoserver".

```
package CryptoServer;
public interface Crypto extends java.rmi.Remote {
  String Encode(String Encoder, String ToEncode) throws
java.rmi.RemoteException;
  String Decode(String Decoder, String ToDecode) throws
java.rmi.RemoteException;
 }
```

In the same package (and hence the same directory) we must also create the application file:

```
package CryptoServer;
import java.rmi.*;
import java.rmi.server.UnicastRemoteObject;
public class CryptoImpl
     extends UnicastRemoteObject
     implements Crypto
{
  private String name;
  public CryptoImpl(String s) throws java.rmi.RemoteException {
     super();
     name = s;
  }

  public static void main(String args[])
  {
     // Create and install the security manager
     System.setSecurityManager(new  RMISecurityManager());

     try {
       CryptoImpl obj = new CryptoImpl("Cryptograph");
       Naming.rebind("Cryptograph", obj);
       System.out.println("Registered and started the Cryptograph server");

     } catch (Exception e) {
       System.out.println("Failed to start the Crypto server");
     }
  }

  public String Encode(String Encoder, String ToEncode) throws
RemoteException {
     return ( "Encoded "+ToEncode +"with"+Encoder);
  }
  public String Decode(String Decoder, String ToDecode) throws
RemoteException {
     return "Decoder";
  }
}
```

The constructor of this class calls the super class, in this case UnicastRemoteObject. Our RMI object is extending this class which uses the default transport mechanisms for RMI objects. Our main method for the class sets a security manager and then creates an instance of the RMI object and registers it using a rebind method, in this case giving it the name "Cryptograph". The security manager ensures that the class behaves in a responsible manner; without it your class will be limited in its operation. The instance of the object must be bound to the registry running on the same host as the application. You can not bind to a registry on another host, as this could have security implications. In our application above, the encode and decode methods do NOT work as intended – they simply return strings to show that they have been called. (Your RMI methods can return integers, floating-point numbers and strings – including string buffers – without any extra work from you. If you want to return instances of classes then you will need to look at the object serialisation interface, which we do not deal with.)

The application must now be compiled, and the generated classes placed in a location accessible from the web server. In the command shown below, the classes are compiled from the directory above the package directory, and the compiler is instructed to place the resultant class files in a different directory (..\..\..\web\classes).

```
javac -d ..\..\..\web\classes CryptoServer\*.java
```

Once compiled, some stubs need to be created and placed in the same directory as the server class files. A program called "rmic" generates two stub files, Classname_Stub.class and Classname_Skel.class. For our cryptographic server the rmic command will generate CryptoImpl_Stub.class and CryptoImpl_Skel.class. The rmic command uses the class files that the javac command generated. Our javac command placed the .class files in a different directory from the source code. We must run the rmic command from a place relative to the .class files. In this case the rmic command should be run from the classes directory under the web directory. The "-d ." directive tells the rmic command to store the generated files relative to the current directory.

```
rmic -d . CryptoServer.CryptoImpl
```

Alternatively, copy the class files from the web directory to the source directory and from the same directory as the compile line use the command:

```
rmic -d ..\..\..\web\classes CryptoServer.CryptoImpl
```

We are now ready to build an applet to use our RMI application. Normally this applet's source code would be in the same directory as the application's source code. However, you may be writing an applet to talk to an application for which you do not have the source. If this is the case, you will need to obtain a number of files from the original author. You will need the class file of the interface (in this case Crypto.class) along with details of the package structure. You will also need the stub class if the applet is to run on a different machine from the application. Remember, however, if the applet is on a different sever from the application, the security model will need to be relaxed. The code below shows a simple applet to talk to our application server.

```
package CryptoServer;

import java.awt.*;
import java.rmi.*;

public class CryptoApplet extends java.applet.Applet {
  String message = "";
  public void init() {
    try {
      String[] List= Naming.list("//andyc.mcs.dundee.ac.uk");
      for (int i=0; i<List.length;i++)
        System.out.println(List[i]);
      Crypto obj = (Crypto)Naming.lookup("//andyc.mcs.dundee.ac.uk/
Cryptograph");
      message = obj.Encode("encode with this", "Hello");
      System.out.println(message);
    } catch (Exception e) {
      System.out.println("CryptoApplet: an exception occurred:");
      e.printStackTrace();
    }
  }

  public void paint(Graphics g) {
    g.drawString(message, 25, 50);
  }
}
```

This applet does two things in its "init" method. It first uses the "Naming" class to retrieve a list of services running on a remote machine, and then obtains an instance of the remote object using the "lookup" method of the naming class. Once an instance of the remote object has been made (in this case the variable obj), a call is made to the "Encode" method. The applet can be compiled in the usual way:

```
javac CryptoServer\CryptoApplet.java
```

If the applet is to be sourced from the same server as the application, the resultant class files should be placed in the same directory as the application. The "-d" option of the javac compiler is a convenient way to achieve this. If the applet files are on another server, you must mirror the directory structure exactly. An .HTML file is needed for the applet on the same server as the applet's files:

```
<HTML>
<p>
<applet
  code="CryptoServer.CryptoApplet"
  codebase="classes"
  width=500 height=120>
</applet>
</HTML>
```

Before you run the application on the server, you must run the rmiregistry.

Unix-based systems	Windows-based systems
rmiregistry &	start rmiregistry

The application should be started with a complete reference to the code base. On a Windows system use the start utility:

```
start java -Djava.rmi.server.codebase=http://andyc.mcs.dundee.ac.uk/
classes/ CryptoServer/CryptoImpl
```

Finally, the applet can be viewed with the applet viewer:

```
appletviewer http://andyc.mcs.dundee.ac.uk/Crypto.html
```

At the time of writing, the only web browser that can view RMI-based applets is an extended version of Sun's HotJava browser.

Appendix C: Internet Resources for Java Developers

This short appendix will list the more important Internet resources for the Java programmer. Some of these resources are for the more experienced programmer, but most are suitable for the beginner. All of these resources can be vital, not only to get answers to your questions but to bring you a sense of community.

Web sites

JavaSoft: http://www.javasoft.com

The home page of the company developing Java and its associated products. From this site you can find out about all the latest developments in the world of Java. These include new versions, documentation and details of conferences concerning Java. The site is of course very busy and so you might find it a little slow. There is also an ftp site, at ftp://ftp.javasoft.com.

JavaSoft Mirror: http://src.doc.ic.ac.uk/Mirrors/ftp.javasoft.com/

A mirror site of the Javasoft ftp server, located in London. If you are in the UK and need a fast transfer then it is best to start here. You should find all the latest versions of Java and the related documentation.

GameLan: http://www-b.gamelan.com/index.shtml

This is the official directory for Java. You will find thousands of example Java applets listed here, many including the source code. The applets are listed by category: Arts and Entertainment, Business and Finance, Educational, How-to and Help, Multimedia, Network & Communications, Programming in Java, Related Technologies, Tools & Utilities.

The Java Developer: http://www.digitalfocus.com/faq/

This site includes the extremely useful "How Do I" section. A must visit if you are really stuck, especially if you have got that "how do I even begin to do this" feeling.

Java world: http://www.javaworld.com/

An on-line magazine with up-to-date articles on developments in the Java world. The site covers both technical and political aspects of Java. A very good read.

Newsgroups

There are currently eight Java newsgroups. As always with newsgroups, obtaining an answer is a combination of pot luck and picking the right group to ask the question. Some of these groups are extremely busy with a high throughput of questions. The groups are:

java.lang.advocacy	Devoted to discussions around Java compared to other languages.
java.lang.announce	For announcements of new Java products
java.lang.api	Discussion based around the JDK Application Programmers' Interface (API)
java.lang.misc	For anything that doesn't fit into any of the other groups
java.lang.programmer	The main newsgroup for programmers and in particular questions about Java programming
java.lang.security	All aspects of Java security are covered here
java.lang.setup	Trouble with setting up your Java Development Kit? Try here for support
java.lang.tech	The technology behind Java. Discussion of the insides of Java and the Java virtual engine

Mailing lists

http://www.javasoft.com/mail/index.html

Javasoft runs a large number of special-interest mailing lists. These lists tend to have very experienced programmers on them and usually a member of the Java development team. Mostly for the experienced programmer.

Javap-uk

A UK-based mailing list for Java programmers. Usually a very quiet list that sometimes wakes up to a particular subject. A mixed bunch of members, some very experienced but also some total beginners. Send the message "subscribe javap-uk" to mailbase@mailbase.ac.uk to join.

INDEX

Symbols

SERIES TITLES

The Complete Guide series of comprehensive books provide all you need to know for a total solution. Titles available for:

Java	1-874029-48-2	Payroll	1-874029-24-5
Visual Basic 5	1-874029-64-4	Quicken 5 - UK	1-874029-55-5
Visual Basic 4	1-874029-36-9	Quicken 4 - UK	1-874029-38-5
		Sage Sterling/Win	1-874029-34-2

In easy steps series is developed for time-sensitive people who want results fast. It is designed for quick, easy and effortless learning. Titles available for:

Access	1-874029-57-1	PagePlus	1-874029-49-0
CompuServe UK	1-874029-33-4	PowerPoint	1-874029-63-6
CorelDRAW	1-874029-72-5	Publisher	1-874029-56-3
Excel	1-874029-69-5	Quicken UK	1-874029-71-7
FrontPage	1-874029-60-1	Sage Instant Accntg	1-874029-44-X
HTML	1-874029-46-6	Sage Sterling for Win	1-874029-43-1
Internet Explorer	1-874029-58-X	SmartSuite (97)	1-874029-67-9
Internet UK	1-874029-73-3	Upgrading Your PC	1-874029-76-8
Microsoft Money UK	1-874029-61-X	Visual Basic	1-874029-74-1
Microsoft Office 97	1-874029-66-0	Visual J++	1-874029-75-X
Microsoft Works	1-874029-41-5	Windows 95	1-874029-28-8
Netscape Navigator	1-874029-47-4	Word 97	1-874029-68-7
PageMaker	1-874029-35-0	WordPerfect	1-874029-59-8

These books are available from your local bookseller now, or in case of difficulty, contact Computer Step at:

Southfield Road . Southam
Warwickshire CV33 OFB . England

Tel: 01926 817999
Fax: 01926 817005

http://www.computerstep.com